VISION

VISION

A Memoir of Blindness and Justice

DAVID S. TATEL

Little, Brown and Company
New York Boston London

Little, Brown and Company
Hachette Book Group
1290 Avenue of the Americas
New York
NY 10104

littlebrown.com

First Edition: June 2024

Little, Brown and Company is a division of Hachette Book Group, Inc. The Little, Brown name and logo are trademarks of Hachette Book Group, Inc.

The publisher is not responsible for websites (or their content) that are not owned by the publisher.

The Hachette Speakers Bureau provides a wide range of authors for speaking events. To find out more, go to hachettespeakersbureau.com or email hachettespeakers@hbgusa.com.

Little, Brown and Company books may be purchased in bulk for business, educational, or promotional use. For information, please contact your local bookseller or the Hachette Book Group Special Markets Department at special.markets@hbgusa.com.

ISBN 9780316542029

LCCN is available at the Library of Congress

Printing 1, 2024

MRQ

Printed in Canada

For Edie

VISION: *1a.* the act or power of seeing; *2b.* a thought, concept, or object formed by the imagination.

—Merriam-Webster Dictionary

Let no one be discouraged by the belief that there is nothing one man or one woman can do against the enormous array of the world's ills, against misery and ignorance, injustice and violence. Few will have the greatness to bend history itself. But each of us can work to change a small portion of events, and in the total of all those acts will be written the history of this generation. It is from numberless diverse acts of courage and belief that human history is shaped. Each time a man stands up for an ideal, or acts to improve the lot of others, or strikes out against injustice, he sends forth a tiny ripple of hope, and crossing each other from a million different centers of energy and daring, those ripples build a current that can sweep down the mightiest walls of oppression and resistance.

—Robert F. Kennedy, June 1966

Contents

Contents

PROLOGUE

A Braided Life

I F YOU PICKED UP THIS BOOK BECAUSE YOU WANT TO LEARN more about the beautiful German shepherd on the cover, you're in luck. Vixen, my guide dog, is even more amazing than she is beautiful. I'm eager to tell you all about her. But I hope you won't be too disappointed to learn that this is my memoir, not hers.

I've lived a rich and varied life: as a civil rights lawyer, as a federal judge, as a husband of sixty years, as a father of four, as a grandfather of eight, and now as a great-grandfather. I've spent my professional career in the pursuit of justice, and I could have written a memoir entirely about that pursuit. But unlike most lawyers and judges, I've been blind for over half my life due to a rare, inherited eye disease called retinitis pigmentosa (RP). Throughout my thirty years on the nation's second highest court, the United States Court of Appeals for the District of Columbia Circuit (known as the "D.C. Circuit"), I could neither read a word of the thousands of legal briefs submitted to my court nor see the faces of the hundreds of lawyers who argued before me. A blind judge sounds like a cliché, I know—like the statue of Lady Justice wearing a blindfold and holding her scales. But it's no cliché to me.

I can't see, but I can listen closely. I didn't need to see the lawyers to hear their arguments, and I absorbed all the written material by having it read to me or, later, by using digital audio devices. For decades I fooled myself into thinking that my blindness was irrelevant to my work and my worth. Only now, in my eighties, and in writing this memoir, have I finally come to accept my blindness as an essential part of who I am.

This memoir is about my life in the law and my journey into blindness. It's also about the Supreme Court, and my grave concerns about the state of our judiciary. To give you a sense of how those pieces fit together, I'll tell you a short story about a recent and dramatic case that Vixen helped me navigate. It concerned the first federal execution in seventeen years. This story will give you a glimpse of how I functioned as a blind judge (before I retired), a taste of the appellate process, and a sense of how today's Supreme Court has veered off course.

———※◦※———

The day we heard the case—July 13, 2020—began like any other sunny summer morning in the foothills of the Blue Ridge Mountains. Vixen and I headed down our long dirt driveway for our first job of the day: fetching the daily newspapers. My wife Edie and I spend most of our time here in rural Virginia, which is just over an hour from D.C. but a world away in temperament. The novel coronavirus was running rampant, so the D.C. Circuit, like most federal courts, was operating remotely. Although the internet out here isn't what we're used to in the city, it works well enough to Zoom with my colleagues and law clerks. We even heard oral arguments online, with no one in Zoomland knowing that beneath my black robe I wore shorts and sneakers.

That July morning, Vixen guided me down the driveway to get the *Washington Post* and the *New York Times,* which had been tossed somewhere in the vicinity of the mailbox. "Vixen, find it" is all I had to say. She let me know when she located the papers by pointing her nose at them. In return, she got one of Edie's specially baked dog treats. I scooped the papers into my old McGovern-Shriver shoulder bag and said, "Vixen, forward. Let's head home." She turned around, picked up the pace, and guided me back up our driveway to have breakfast with Edie and read the papers. That day the headlines were about the Trump administration's response to the pandemic and whether the delayed baseball season would finally get underway.

After breakfast I went upstairs to my desk to begin what I thought would be a normal workday. My court doesn't schedule arguments in the summer, and that recess allowed us judges to finish writing our opinions and get started on the cases we'd be hearing in the fall. So I had work to do, but none of it was urgent. I'm an enthusiastic patron of email, and I wanted to catch up with our four kids and the latest legal gossip, including about the Supreme Court's recent decisions involving President Trump's financial records.

But everything changed at 10:30 a.m. when I received an email from court staff reporting that a district court judge had just blocked the first of several executions scheduled by the Trump administration. The government had planned to execute a convicted murderer, Daniel Lewis Lee, by lethal injection that very afternoon at the federal death chamber in Terre Haute, Indiana. But the district court had temporarily halted the execution, and our staff anticipated that the Justice Department would quickly ask us to reverse the district court and let the execution proceed. Until that morning I knew nothing about Daniel Lewis Lee or his legal claims. But now — on that otherwise ordinary day — a human life was hanging in the balance, and we had to act quickly.

Let me be clear: I oppose the death penalty. I think capital punishment is often applied arbitrarily and discriminatorily. Were I a member of Congress, I'd vote to abolish it. But I wasn't a member of Congress. I was a judge. I took an oath to apply the law faithfully, and that includes the federal death penalty. So the question I would have to answer was not whether I agreed with the government's decision to execute Lee. It was whether Lee's execution would violate the Constitution. To answer *that* question, I needed to understand the details of Lee's case and the nature of his claims.

Lee had been convicted of robbing, torturing, and murdering a firearms dealer, his wife, and their eight-year-old daughter, whose bodies were found in a bayou with plastic bags over their heads. The murders were heinous. No one disputed that Lee had committed them. Nor was there any question that he would eventually be executed. The only legal issue in the case was how Lee would die. The government planned to use a drug called pentobarbital. Lee argued that the drug would cause "extreme pain and needless suffering" and thus violate his Eighth Amendment right to be free from "cruel and unusual punishment." His case turned on a single unresolved question: Might a massive dose of pentobarbital cause Lee's lungs to fill with fluid, make him feel like he was drowning, and inflict extreme and unnecessary pain? If not, the government was entitled to execute him as planned. If so, the government would have to find another method. Until that factual question was answered, the execution couldn't proceed.

The district judge had found that Lee's allegations about the effects of pentobarbital were plausible, so ordered the government to hold off on the execution. A brief delay, the district court reasoned, would give it time to hear from experts, look at the evidence, and determine whether the government's proposed method of execution was "very likely" to cause the pain and suffering Lee claimed.

At 11:52 a.m. the Justice Department informed my court that, as anticipated, the government wanted us to immediately reverse the order blocking Lee's execution so it could move ahead as planned. Now it was up to our three-judge panel—two other D.C. Circuit judges and me—to review the district court's ruling and decide whether Lee would live or die that very day.

Ordinarily, the appellate process takes many months, if not longer. Lawyers need time to do legal research, write briefs, and argue the case. Judges need time to do their own research, deliberate with each other, and write an opinion that explains their reasoning. Emergency requests, as in Lee's case, are not the norm. Courts can rule quickly when strictly necessary, but they lose the benefit of the extended deliberation undertaken in most cases. Death penalty cases, in particular, can be grotesquely rushed. Speed is what you want when you're trying to catch a flight. You don't want undue haste in judging, and you definitely don't want it with a life on the line. Nevertheless, respecting the government's request for speed, we ordered Lee's lawyers to respond by 5:15 p.m. and the government to reply by 7 p.m.

While we waited for Lee's brief to arrive, I decided to take a walk to clear my mind. Vixen and I go for afternoon walks together almost every day. She's always on my left and always in the lead. Until Vixen, I'd never appreciated the many pleasures of walking a dog, not least of which are the serendipitous conversations with other folks we encounter. We talk about the weather and last night's ball game, but mainly we talk about our dogs. Everyone wants to know about Vixen. "How was she trained?" "How did you get her?" "Can she really guide you across busy streets?" "What's her name, and did you name her?" In the coming pages, I'll answer all those questions for you, just like I answer them for passersby. But I'll tell you now that the answer to the last question is no. Vixen was in the "V" litter, so she and all her siblings were given names starting with "V." (We once met her brother Viper, a ninety-pound long-haired giant beloved by his owner.) People also want to tell me their aunt is blind, to ask how they can get a dog like Vixen, or to find out how they can become a puppy raiser. In these rural parts of Virginia, I might very well be discussing the ins and outs of German shepherds with a full-fledged MAGA supporter without realizing it, since I can't see the red hat. Dogs bring people together.

For nearly forty years, I couldn't take these country walks by myself, even with my white mobility cane, so I treasure the independence and solitude Vixen's given me. Sometimes I plug in my earphones and listen to a book, but mostly I just walk, savoring the breeze and the birdsong and the ripples of the Thornton River. Vixen makes these walks possible. She stops only when there's danger or if she sniffs a deer or fox or another irresistible scent—or when she has to pee. That's what her wet nose on my hand means.

On that day, our walk was shorter than usual. But it did the job. I returned home refreshed and ready to reengage. When the briefs arrived, my law clerk read them aloud to me over Zoom, going as fast as possible and stopping only for sips of tea to save her voice. We both knew we had no time to waste. Even Vixen knew something important was happening. As I read the government's arguments about why it should be allowed to execute Lee using pentobarbital, and Lee's arguments about why the district court had been right to delay the execution for fuller consideration of his claim about pentobarbital's effects, Vixen kept pushing her nose under my elbow. She didn't need another walk. She wasn't hungry. She simply sensed my tension, and this was her way of offering some comfort.

Two hours and hundreds of pages later, I concluded that there was nothing unlawful about the district court's order delaying Lee's execution. The law guarantees due process for everybody—murderers, presidents, and everyone in between. Lee's lawyers had raised a serious claim that demanded a thorough evaluation of medical and scientific evidence, and only the district court could conduct that evaluation. Appeals courts don't normally answer factual questions: They don't hold trials, they don't hear witnesses, and they don't weigh competing evidence. Their job is just to apply the law to the facts as the district court finds them. Here, the district court had reasonably determined it needed more time to weigh the evidence and evaluate the effects of pentobarbital. I had no choice but to uphold its order delaying Lee's execution. My two colleagues, Judges Thomas Griffith and Patricia Millett, agreed.

If you've become accustomed to viewing judges as politicians in robes, you might think it relevant that Judge Griffith was appointed by a Republican president (George W. Bush) and Judge Millett by a Democrat (Barack Obama). But they're judges, not politicians, and both saw what I (appointed by Democrat Bill Clinton) saw: a serious constitutional claim, a thoughtful district court order, and no legal basis to overturn it. Regardless of our personal views about the death penalty, the neutral legal principles we'd sworn an oath to uphold required that we pause Lee's execution so his claim could be given the consideration it deserved. To be clear: If those principles had required us to allow the execution to proceed, we wouldn't have hesitated to say so. Indeed, a few weeks later I signed off on another Trump-ordered execution, and a prisoner was put to death hours after we turned down his appeal.

My law clerk and I began drafting an opinion, she on her desktop, me on my black Braille computer. The size of a keyboard, it has six rectangular Braille buttons and connects to an earphone that allows me to hear the words as I type them. As soon as we had a draft, I sent it to Judges Griffith and Millett for their input. We were exchanging edits and refining the draft when, at 9:51 that evening, we received word from the Supreme Court that the justices were growing impatient. The Court, we were told, "would really like us to act tonight"—and, if possible, "within an hour." That kind of pressure was highly unusual, but, recognizing the Supreme Court's higher authority, we did our best to comply. At 11:24 p.m., we released our opinion rejecting the government's request to proceed with the execution. The case, we explained, involved "novel and difficult constitutional questions" that required "further factual and legal development." We then scheduled all remaining briefing to occur within the next ten days, far faster than usual.

Fewer than three hours later, around 2 a.m., the Supreme Court voted 5–4 to reverse us. The Court's order was unsigned, but the names of those who approved Lee's immediate execution were obvious because all four justices who objected signed their names to a dissent. The five in the majority were the Court's purported conservatives: Chief Justice John Roberts and Justices Clarence Thomas, Samuel Alito, Neil Gorsuch, and Brett Kavanaugh. All had been appointed by Republican presidents. The four who thought Lee merited a hearing? All appointed by Democrats.

The Supreme Court's opinion was nothing short of astonishing. For starters, it made sure to emphasize that Lee had murdered a child, even though nobody representing Lee had suggested that he deserved sympathy or that he'd been wrongfully convicted. With respect to the sole issue actually before the Court—the propriety of the district court's order delaying the execution to give it time to consider conflicting expert testimony about the possible inhumane effects of pentobarbital—the Court said very little. It acknowledged the evidentiary dispute, yet it refused to give the district court the time it needed to assess that evidence and resolve Lee's legal claim. And it never even mentioned the ruling by my court. Instead, the Supreme Court invoked a need for urgency—"expeditiously" was the word it used—so that "the question of capital punishment" can remain with "the people and their representatives, not the courts, to resolve." But no one was questioning the validity of capital punishment. And anyone who thinks limiting briefing to ten days isn't acting "expeditiously" has never spent much time in the US court system. Anyway, isn't ensuring that the government doesn't execute a person in violation of the Constitution precisely the role of the courts?

Fewer than six hours later, at 8:07 a.m., the government executed Daniel Lewis Lee. He died never having been given the opportunity to prove his claim, a claim that two lower federal courts believed worthy of careful consideration and that the Supreme Court itself acknowledged raised an unresolved factual issue. That isn't how our legal system is supposed to work, especially when a human life is at stake.

———◈———

This book chronicles my journey from a curious student to a passionate civil rights lawyer to the seasoned federal judge you saw at work on the Lee case. It also chronicles another, more private journey, from shame about my deteriorating vision, to denial about the effects of my blindness, and ultimately to acceptance and equanimity. This memoir is the coda to both of those journeys. And yes, it's also about a love story and a marriage made challenging at times by my blindness. Without Edie, my partner in life and in love, my story—let alone this memoir—would not have been possible.

The decision to write this book—and to name it *Vision*, of all things—has not been an easy one. For most of my life, I was embarrassed by my disability and would have recoiled even from the use of that word in connection with me. In my early years, I tried to hide my declining sight. On the ball field, in the classroom, as a young lawyer in a large firm, and in the Carter administration, I had a repertoire of strategies to conceal how little I could actually see. And I was pretty good at it. Edie, when she was my girlfriend in law school, knew that I had an eye disease and that my vision might deteriorate. But few others knew until I started to use a white cane. Even once I became completely blind and could no longer hide it, I still avoided the subject as much as I could. I know that President Clinton nominated me to the D.C. Circuit in part because my blindness made me a "first." I was thrilled to be on the bench, but I had zero interest in being known as "the blind judge." Even now, my blindness is something I've never much talked about with anybody other than Edie and my children. To my great regret, it took me until I was seventy-seven to get a guide dog.

I'll try to explain the evolution of my thinking as I've navigated the challenges of losing my sight and living with blindness. There have been many, ranging from the simple (learning to listen to audiobooks), to the difficult (learning to use the cane), to the sublime (entrusting my life to a dog). The deeper lessons of my journey—tackling life-altering change, dealing with uncertainty, surviving fear—are universal. And the most profound lesson is one I've learned only very slowly: Don't deny your challenges, embrace them.

Please understand me, though: I'd rather not be blind. For all that I've learned about personal growth, trust, the ineffable love of family, and the abiding devotion of a wondrously skilled German shepherd, I'd rather be able to see. I'd like to see my grandchildren's faces. I'd like to play tennis and to wander on my own through a bookstore. I'd like to see cumulus clouds on a crisp afternoon, the Milky Way on a moonless night, and Edie's beautiful white hair. Being blind is hard, every day. It tests me. It tests Edie. It tests our marriage and our family. I love Edie's daily touches, many of which happen because she's simply helping me move around safely when Vixen's off duty. I'd still rather not be blind. But I am.

At long last, though, I'm comfortable with that part of me. As much as I'd like to be just like anyone else, the reality is that I most assuredly am not. And as much as I'd like my blindness to be irrelevant to my story, it most assuredly is not. My blindness affects how I function, how I relate to people, and how I view the world. In most ways that's okay—maybe even more than okay. There's just one exception. When it came to my service as a federal judge, I always strove to ensure that my blindness never affected my rulings. I know that the presence of a blind judge on a federal appeals court was inspirational to people both with and without disabilities. But when sitting on the bench, I was a judge first. My decisions flowed from the law and the facts, and I did my best to make sure that nothing else, including my blindness, got in the way. I was not a blind judge, you see. I was a judge who happened to be blind. To me, that's not just a semantic difference.

The two threads of this memoir have inverse trajectories. When I was coming of age, I was inspired by the role that lawyers and courts were playing in enforcing the guarantees of our great Constitution. But I was unwilling and unable to deal with my declining vision. Now, a half century later, I've made peace with my blindness. But I'm concerned about the Supreme Court's apparent disregard for the principles of judicial restraint that distinguish the unelected judiciary from the two elected branches of government—and about what that might mean for our planet and our democracy. Braided together, those two threads are my story.

CHAPTER 1

My Childhood

E ARLY ON, I COULD SEE.
I grew up in the 1950s in idyllic Silver Spring, Maryland, a suburb just outside of Washington, D.C. We lived in a little three-bedroom house on Eton Road among lots of government scientists, lots of kids, and lots of stay-at-home moms. Family social life revolved around school, my father's science lab, the neighborhood pool, and the Jewish Community Center. Our family had dinner together every night, the four of us — my father Howard, my mother Molly, my younger sister Judy, and I — crowded together around the table, talking about my dad's work, my mom's activities, what Judy and I had done in school, and, of course, politics. My mother was a Democratic precinct captain, and my parents voted twice for Adlai Stevenson — the moderate Democrat whose intellectual approach to politics was exactly my parents' cup of tea. Ike was president. JFK and LBJ

were senators. McCarthyism was rampaging the country. At school, duck-and-cover drills made me worry enough about the Cold War that I felt safer when we traveled far away from the bull's-eye that was D.C.

When I wasn't worrying about nukes, Washington felt like a quiet, sleepy place. The whole city seemed like a large suburb. We spent most of our time in our neighborhood, but went downtown to visit the pre-panda National Zoo, see the iconic monuments, ride the paddle boats on the Tidal Basin, and watch the giant locomotives come and go at Union Station. The long, gray two-story Quonset huts built during World War II still stood on the National Mall. In Rock Creek Park, the beautiful, wooded area that cuts through D.C. along the meandering and aptly named Rock Creek, there were still places where the road ran straight through the water. My father loved to drive through those fords with the doors on his blue Studebaker open so Judy and I could see the waves the wheels made. Of course, there were no seat belts then.

Silver Spring itself didn't have much going on, but we made our own fun. My buddies and I loved riding the green, orange, and white D.C. trolleys that swayed mightily around turns. At the Maryland turnaround at Georgia and Alaska, we'd hop on the trolley down to Griffith Stadium or up to Glen Echo's amusement park and Crystal Pool. Hot Shoppes was my idea of drive-through gourmet. Through a speaker, we ordered triple-decker Mighty Mo burgers and Orange Freeze milkshakes that carhops delivered to a tray attached to the car door. It was an idyllic place for those of us lucky enough to live there.

But not everyone was so lucky. As I better understood later, racial covenants (restrictions in deeds that prohibit sale to certain racial groups) and steering (real estate agents directing Black customers away from white neighborhoods and into Black neighborhoods) kept suburbs like Silver Spring virtually all white. My schools were also pretty much all white, even after *Brown v. Board of Education* was decided in 1954. The Crystal Pool we enjoyed so much was segregated. (The owner eventually closed that beautiful pool rather than admit Black swimmers.) And I still remember the "Whites Only" signs posted in restaurants and shops in Virginia. About my only exposure to Black people was when my friends and I went to the downtown Silver Spring bowling alley, where the "pin boys" were Black. When we finished a game, we'd roll a dime down the alley as a tip. I don't recall ever having a conversation with a pin boy. Looking back, I'm guessing those pin boys were actually pin men.

Most of the dads in our neighborhood had come to Washington to aid the war effort. My father had, too. He was part of the team of scientists that invented the proximity fuse, a radio-controlled sensor in the nose of an artillery shell that could trigger a detonation without hitting a target. Along with radar, the proximity fuse played a major role in the Allied victory in Europe. I still have one of the fuses on my dresser. It looks like an oversized bullet, 10 inches long and surprisingly heavy. I'm fairly certain it's disarmed.

All those chemists, physicists, and engineers had hobbies that filled our neighborhood with model rockets and remote-controlled airplanes. Weekends on Eton Road were like a giant science fair. We kids wandered from house to house to check out the latest offerings. The father of one of my friends built a computer so large it occupied the entire first floor of their house. We were awed by all of its lights and switches. A ham radio built by another friend's father let us talk to people all over the world.

Like my father, I loved science—particularly astronomy. But overall, I didn't care much for school, which seemed boring compared to ham radios. I was an average student, excelling only in science, math, and print shop. Science fairs were always the high point. One year, with my dad's help, I built a working Wilson cloud chamber, which allowed us to see misty trails of ions, atomic particles otherwise invisible to the naked eye. I won first place in the physics category but lost the grand prize to a kid who'd built a replica of the human eye (his father was an ophthalmologist). My high school, Montgomery Blair, had a shooting range in the basement, which was not uncommon in the 1950s. The US Army supplied the rifles, ammo, and targets, and the NRA sponsored our school's shooting team. I took my turn firing at a target. Throughout my high school years, I made extra pocket money by washing dishes in the cafeteria, which got me a free lunch plus fifty cents a day.

Even though my schools were public, we began each day reciting the Lord's Prayer together, and then one of us would be chosen to read from the New Testament. At the end of the day, I went off to Hebrew school, where I was supposed to learn enough Hebrew to survive my bar mitzvah. The religious incongruity didn't seem to bother my parents, and it certainly didn't bother me. Nor did any of us complain when "under God" was added to the Pledge of Allegiance in 1954. I went through with the bar mitzvah, but mostly for my parents' sake. To my mother, a boy's bar mitzvah was an essential part of growing up. My father, raised in a secular Jewish family, was fine with my completing that rite of passage as long as he didn't have to help with the studying or carpooling. Of course, he did come on the big day.

My extracurricular life focused on band (I played clarinet, poorly), chaperoned dances, and anything with a ball. I loved football, basketball, and tennis — and I was totally obsessed with baseball. I played pickup ball with friends in the neighborhood and devoured the sports pages of the *Washington Post* and *Evening*

Star. My true love was the hapless Washington Senators. I went to as many games as I could and listened to the rest on the radio. I even saw history made at the ballpark on April 17, 1953. Mickey Mantle of the loathsome New York Yankees hit his mammoth 565-foot homer off the National Bohemian beer sign in center field. I booed. I was aware even then that the Senators had a serious shortcoming: They were one of the last major league teams to sign a Black player. "I will not sign a Negro for the Washington club merely to satisfy subversive persons," the owner, Clark Griffith, said in a 1952 interview. And of course, Griffith Stadium itself was segregated, with Black people confined to the bleachers.

Baseball was responsible for my longest grounding. In tenth grade, I skipped Spanish to watch the 1956 World Series on TV at a friend's house. I gleefully told my mother the grounding was worth it because I got to see Don Larsen's perfect game. She added a second week to my sentence.

———⋄•⋄———

My mother was raised in a large Orthodox Jewish family, the second of seven Abramowitz children from Lakewood, New Jersey. Her Lithuanian parents had arrived at Ellis Island on the last westbound voyage of the *Lusitania*. Mom had one older brother, Bill, who loomed large in my life. When Bill was at MIT earning his degree in chemistry, he had a roommate he wanted my mom to meet. That roommate's name was Howard Tatel. They married in 1939 and drove across the country in a Model A Ford to Stanford, where my father got his PhD in physics. After Uncle Bill's brief career as a matchmaker, he started a plastics company. Among his many inventions was a thick white adhesive. We had mason jars of it around our house and called it Uncle Bill's glue. When Bill sold his company to Borden, Uncle Bill's glue got a new name: Elmer's glue. Later, Bill started another company, this one specializing in plastic pipe. With that company, he helped introduce America to the Hula-Hoop.

Mom, like many women back then, never attended college. But she went to secretarial school, which later came in handy. Over the years, she also launched assorted side ventures, including selling World Book encyclopedias throughout the neighborhood and running a network of penny gumball machines around town. I expect her gumball business would have been more profitable if Judy and I hadn't liked to break into the big boxes of Bazooka bubble gum she kept in our basement. Mom worked her whole life and ran her own visa business well into her eighties. I guess it's fair to say that early retirement doesn't run in the family.

My dad's great-grandfather owned a shoe factory in St. Petersburg, Russia. Family lore is that he made shoes for the czar. Dad's grandfather had a dry goods store, S. Tatel & Sons, in Brooklyn. And my dad's father owned a women's clothing store in Quincy, Massachusetts. But my father never wanted to be a merchant. He was always going to be a scientist. As a kid he built a six-inch reflecting telescope, made a seismograph to detect earthquakes (though mostly just recorded the rumble of passing buses), and modified a toaster so that even years later it ejected bread with such force that we had to catch it on a plate before it hit the floor.

After World War II, Dad became a staff physicist at the Carnegie Institution for Science, one of the nation's premier science laboratories. He was studying the earth's crust well before anyone knew about plate tectonics. On many Saturdays he took me with him to the lab. I always had an assignment. Sometimes he'd give me an elaborate piece of equipment to take apart. Other times he'd ask one of the engineers in the workshop to put me to use. That big room full of lathes, drill presses, and saws was a playground for a kid interested in science. The lab even had a cyclotron. I don't know if I ever did anything useful, but I sure had fun.

At home, Dad was a relentless, imaginative tinkerer. He made a record player for Judy, a go-cart for me, and an air-conditioning system for our house. Our most prized possession was a model wooden sloop we made using Uncle Bill's glue and sailed across the Reflecting Pool at the Lincoln Memorial. My father could make mischief with his tinkering. Before we moved to Silver Spring, we lived in a tiny apartment on Tuckerman Street in D.C. where a nasty neighbor delighted in blaring Father Coughlin's fascist, anti-Semitic radio broadcasts. Sure enough, Dad figured out how to short out her electricity at the appointed hour.

Because Dad loved technology, we were one of the first on the block to get a TV, a huge walnut-colored thing that occupied an entire corner of our small living room. It had just two knobs, one for on/off and volume, and the other to cycle through the four available channels—yes, only four. During the one hour a day we were allowed to watch, Judy and I wore the headsets he rigged to the set so we didn't bother him while he was working. When Sid Caesar's *Your Show of Shows* was on, our parents let us stay up to watch with them.

My earliest memories—visual memories—include my dad sitting in his big striped upholstered chair in the living room, wearing wire-rimmed glasses, wielding his mechanical pencil and slide rule. He'd fill notepads with precise drawings, complex diagrams, and long, long formulas. He seemed to know just about everything about just about everything. At the beach, we learned why seawater is salty. During a thunderstorm, we learned all about lightning. On an airplane, we learned how the wings lift the plane. When driving in the country, we learned why the Appalachian Mountains are short and rounded and the Rockies tall and sharp. I'm exactly the same way with my own children and grandchildren. I'm not quite the science encyclopedia my dad was, but I take their questions seriously and answer as many as I can. What the grandkids really want to know about, though, are my court cases. They ask for the details, then try to argue both sides. It's great fun.

In time, my father became a pioneer in radio astronomy, a field that strove to understand the universe through radio waves emitted by stars, galaxies, and all other celestial objects. He and his colleagues set up a radio telescope on the Carnegie campus. It was a German radar antenna that had been captured during World War II. Dad also designed the first eighty-five-foot radio telescope at the Green Bank Observatory in West Virginia. Named in his honor, the Tatel Telescope discovered the black hole at the center of the Milky Way. It was also used in 1960 by astronomer Frank Drake in the very first search for extraterrestrial intelligence. (I'm no expert, but it just can't be that we're alone.) You can buy a T-shirt at Green Bank's visitor center that commemorates the "Howard E. Tatel Radio Telescope (85-1)," as it is officially known. The original model he built with copper wires and one of Mom's plastic cereal bowls sits on our bookshelf to this day.

My father made lots of other amazing discoveries along the way. In 1955, Carnegie astronomers detected some radio waves with their telescopes, but they couldn't figure out where they were coming from. My dad solved the riddle. The radio waves, he realized, were coming from Jupiter. The *New York Times* reported on the discovery the very next day: "Sounds on Jupiter...400,000,000 MILES AWAY...Are Detected by Carnegie Men." In the wake of that discovery, one astronomer asked my dad, "Howard, how do you bring all these things together? How do you see connections the rest of us miss?" "We live on a surface," he replied. "I'm interested in anything that's *off* it!"

In fairness, he was interested in the things that were on it, too. While my father was trained as a scientist, he was a true polymath or at least a multipotentialite, which is the kind of word he'd use at dinner just so Judy and I would have to look up what it meant. My grandson, Cameron, once asked me what impact my father had on me. "He made me interested in everything," I told him. What greater gift is there than that? My mother often said—with 90 percent admiration and 10 percent exasperation—"You're just like your father." That always gave me great comfort.

CHAPTER 2

Diagnosis

It seems fitting that I first began to suspect that something was wrong with my eyes while gazing at the stars. Throughout my childhood, we spent many clear nights in our backyard looking at the moon, stars, and planets through the six-inch telescope that Dad had built in his teens and then reconstructed for us. He delighted in showing us the moons of Jupiter that Galileo had discovered. I loved those evenings. But as my early years ticked by, it became harder and harder to see those moons. By the time I was eight or nine years old, when my father would point the telescope and tell me, "Take a look, David," I'd sometimes have to ask him what he was talking about. "I can't see anything, Dad," I'd say. My father never pressed, but I know he realized that something was wrong. A few years ago, I came across a letter he wrote to an ophthalmologist around that time describing my symptoms and hypothesizing about possible causes.

Ever the scientist, his guesses about retinal dysfunction were on the mark, even if at the time no one knew much about retinitis pigmentosa.

Still, things weren't too difficult for me at first—at least in the daylight. I did fine with my *Washington Post* paper route. And reading was okay. Spotting fly balls at Griffith Stadium wasn't easy, though to my great disappointment none ever came my way. It was after the sun went down that things got harder. Seeing those moons of Jupiter, catching fireflies, and making it home from a friend's house after dark all presented challenges. At Camp Ramblewood, when we played capture the flag at night, I captured no flags. Trick-or-treating was no treat. And going to the movies with friends was tricky. I could get to my seat just fine when the lights were on. But if I went for popcorn after the lights dimmed, I had to count the seats sideways, then the rows up and down, to have any chance of making it back to the right spot.

Somehow I feared my friends' judgments about my declining vision more than the decline itself. Like most kids, I just wanted to be "normal," and I thought my friends would think less of me if they knew what was going on. So I began building a repertoire of cover-up strategies. Instead of saying to my friends, "I can't see the ball," I made up excuses like, "Can't believe I missed that one." (As if being a lousy ballplayer were better than being a poorly sighted one.) Instead of telling my friends at the movies, "I have trouble seeing in the dark; could someone else get the popcorn?" I did the search-and-find maneuver. (As if struggling through the theater were less strange than just asking for help.) In his fine book *The Beauty of Dusk*, Frank Bruni, a *New York Times* columnist, writing about his sudden loss of sight in one eye, describes a friend who concealed his vision loss through "an exhausting charade that required a layer of energy on top of all the other layers." I sure knew how to play that tiring game. Not until I was nearly forty years old—when I finally succumbed and started using a white cane—did my subterfuges end.

———

My declining vision became impossible to ignore by the time I was twelve. One spring afternoon when I was playing with friends at Oak View Elementary, a ball hit me smack in the face. I never saw it coming. That was 1954, and none of the ophthalmologists I visited over the next few years had any idea what was wrong with my eyes. "Have him eat lots of carrots," they advised. I did, but it didn't help. One particularly clueless eye doctor urged my mother to teach me basket weaving so I'd be able to earn a living if I ever became completely blind. Wisely, she decided instead to bring me to the National Institutes of Health for more testing.

There, in early 1958, when I was a junior in high school and about to turn sixteen, I was finally diagnosed with retinitis pigmentosa (RP), an affliction of the retina, which is in the back of the eye. Most ophthalmologists had never heard of RP. That's why I went undiagnosed for so long. The NIH doctor who finally discovered what was wrong with me was Eliot Berson. I've never forgotten his name. What he told me that day rewrote my life.

Before he diagnosed me, I endured a full day of eye tests, some really uncomfortable. The worst was an electroretinogram that required me to wear a huge, miserable contact lens with wires connecting it to a machine. Every blink hurt. The tests and all the waiting in between took hours. Late in the afternoon, Dr. Berson called my mother in and spoke to her privately while I sat in the waiting room. Their conversation seemed to take forever.

Dr. Berson then invited me to join my mom in his office. After explaining how the retina works, he told me that I had a disease called retinitis pigmentosa, that it was very rare, and that they didn't know a whole lot about it. What they did know, he told me, is that people with RP usually lose vision gradually, that my vision would plateau from time to time, and that some people lose their vision entirely. I don't remember whether he ever used the word "blind." He said that at that time the only treatment was to take large doses of vitamin A. I came away with the impression that total blindness was only a remote possibility. I don't know whether that was Dr. Berson's doing or mine. Did I actually hear everything he said? Or did I just hear what I wanted to hear? What fifteen-year-old wants to hear that he's going to go blind?

I know much more about RP now than Dr. Berson did back in 1958. RP is caused by a genetic mutation, and scientists were only just starting to understand genes at the time of my diagnosis. In fact, it was only five years earlier that scientists discovered that DNA consisted of two strands of genes winding around each other like a rope, creating a double helix. Every human has about twenty-two thousand genes, and every single gene contains a code represented by some combination of just four letters: "A," "C," "G," and "T." That code determines everything about our bodies. Are we tall or short? What color eyes do we have? What color hair? How long are our toes? But sometimes there are misspellings — mutations — that can cause diseases like cancer, Down syndrome, and RP. In the case of RP, the mutated gene doesn't produce the proteins essential to the health and function of the eyes' rods and cones, the photoreceptors that make vision possible. At least eighty different genes, when mutated, can cause RP, and RP affects different people differently depending on which exact mutation they have. Some can't see well at night, some have limited central vision, and some, like me, eventually lose their sight altogether. Thanks to a $2,400 genetic test, I learned my exact mutation: Within the RPGR gene, which is just one of those eighty different genes, lurks a "G" that should have been an "A."

It's as if there were just one misspelled word in this entire book. That's all it took to rob me of my eyesight.

My form of RP is called X-linked retinitis pigmentosa because my mutated gene is on my X chromosome. Since we males get our single X chromosome from our mothers, my mutation was most likely inherited from my mom. Less likely is that my RP resulted from a fluke-of-nature mutation that started with me. That's possible because we know of no one in my mother's entire family who had night blindness or any other RP symptoms. But because neither my mother nor any of her relatives ever had a genetic test, we'll never know for sure whether my RP is inherited or spontaneous.

Of course, we heard none of that from Dr. Berson that day. My mother may have understood more about my prognosis than I did, that some degree of blindness was inevitable and that total blindness was a possibility. I'll never know. She rarely talked to me about my vision, though she insisted that I keep up with my doses of vitamin A and that I return to NIH every year for monitoring. I hated those visits, especially the peripheral vision test. I had to stare into a dark box and respond when I could see the little white moving dot. Yes, yes, yes, no, yes. Each year, there were fewer yeses and more nos. It was as if my sight were vanishing before my eyes.

Why didn't Mom talk about my diagnosis? I think she wanted to protect me and to help me lead as normal a life as possible. But I also think she didn't know what to say. And perhaps she was in denial, too. Here she was, thirty-nine years old, with a twelve-year-old daughter and a fifteen-year-old son she suddenly learns may go blind, possibly because of her genes. At the time, was I hoping she would talk to me more about my condition? Definitely not. We were both much happier pretending there was nothing wrong.

Although my mother may have modeled unhealthy repression by not talking with me about blindness, she also modeled strength and optimism by expecting me to live a normal life. She didn't even object to me getting a driver's license when I turned sixteen a few months after my diagnosis. I could still read the eye chart, which was all I had to do at the DMV. No one asked if I had an eye disease, and I certainly didn't volunteer that information. There was no test for peripheral or night vision, which I would have flunked. Yes, Mom worried about my driving, but I think she was proud of me, too. I drove her two-toned Chevy, with its whitewall tires and tail fins (a car I assume still lives somewhere in Havana). I was pretty good at driving during the day, turning my head side to side to compensate for my narrowing vision. I'm sorry to report that I even drove at night, guided by headlights and taillights. I shouldn't have been driving at all, so I'm lucky I didn't hurt myself or anyone else.

———

And where was my dad in all of this, you might wonder? Perhaps you're already imagining him hard at work in his laboratory, turning his attention from telescopes to retinas — racing toward a cure. I wish that were the answer. The truth is that retinitis pigmentosa wasn't the only reason my junior year in high school was the worst year of my life.

But it sure didn't begin badly. In the early fall of 1957, six months before my diagnosis, my dad invited me to join him and eight of his colleagues on a ten-week scientific expedition to the Peruvian Altiplano, the largest high plateau in the world outside Tibet. The adventure of a lifetime *and* more than two months off school! (My parents had managed to convince my reluctant principal that the trip would be educational. Judy was promised the next trip.) I couldn't believe my luck. My dad and I were together almost the entire time, sharing hotel rooms except when Mom visited for a week and I was exiled to a room with a very nice, and very smelly, engineer.

We had come to the Andes with one goal: to measure the thickness of the earth's crust. For years, my dad and his colleagues had traveled up and down the western spine of North and South America in the same pursuit. I had gone with them to the Colorado Rockies when I was in the third grade, my first time on an airplane. But this was a much bigger trip. Sixty-seven countries had declared 1957 the International Geophysical Year, and the Carnegie expedition was doing its part. We were based in Arequipa. The city sits almost eight thousand feet above sea level, at the foot of the towering cone of El Misti Volcano.

My father's team had a daily routine, and I was part of it. We'd have breakfast at dawn, review our maps, and head out into the mountains in rumbling "carryall" trucks. The men—yes, the scientists were all men—would fan out across the Altiplano and set up seismic stations, ready to measure the shock waves created by blasting at the Chuquicamata copper mines six hundred miles away in Chile. I manned my own station, which included a seismograph, chronometer, pen recorder, and two-way radio—all in a beautiful blond wooden box with a compartment for my lunch of empañadas. After my dad dropped me off, he drove away and I was on my own, except for the occasional herder passing by with his bleating llamas. It was cold, and very, very windy. My job was to position the seismograph, which was about the size of a coffee can, on bedrock and cover it with a plastic dome to protect it from the wind. Then I'd connect it to a pen recorder, wind the chronometer, turn on the two-way radio, and wait for the blasting at Chuquicamata to begin. Once the clock struck twelve, the blasting would start, and a few minutes later, when the shock waves arrived, the needle on my device would begin jumping. Occasionally, it would pick up the footsteps of wandering llamas—which tickled me to no end, even though it told us nothing at all about the thickness of the earth's crust.

One morning, after I had set up my equipment, I noticed a couple of kids herding their llamas and kicking a soccer ball around. They waved me over, and I joined their game. I couldn't speak their language, and they couldn't speak mine, but we had a great time together, running full tilt at sixteen thousand feet elevation but hardly even breathless. We were kids. I knew I'd need to begin recording at noon, so at 11:30, using a combination of hand signals and smiles, I asked them to move along. Otherwise, my seismograph would record only the pounding of their llamas' feet and the rumble of their soccer game. Somehow they understood. By the time I got back to my equipment, they were far off in the distance. My data that day was excellent. I've always wondered what happened to those boys, who were so like me but whose lives seemed so very different. Do they still live on the Altiplano? Do they also have grandchildren? Do they remember the junior scientist they played soccer with a half century ago? Did one of them ever become a judge?

At the end of each day, my dad would pick me up, and we'd make the long drive back to Arequipa. Over dinner, the whole team would compare their data, mine included. I felt so grown up, and so important, to be part of my dad's scientific team. I liked hearing the guys talk about other stuff, too. At times they even seemed to forget they had a kid along. On October 4, we were astonished to read in the local newspaper that the Soviets had launched Sputnik. Within an hour, we'd rigged up a radio and sat around the table listening to the *beep beep beep*s from space. Out on the Altiplano in the days that followed, I kept looking up and wondering where Sputnik was at that very moment.

Fifty years later, Edie and I returned to Arequipa and visited the hotel where we had stayed. Even though I could no longer see El Misti, I could "see" that towering snowcapped cone perfectly in my mind's eye. I asked the desk clerk whether anyone at the hotel might have been there in 1957. "Only him," he said, gesturing out back at the four-hundred-pound Galapagos tortoise basking in the sunshine. I remembered him well. As a teenager, I'd fed leftover lettuce to that amazing creature every night.

I often look back on Peru as my earliest exposure to rigorous analysis and principled, collaborative decision-making. Beginning with a hypothesis, the scientists collected and examined data, debated possibilities, and listened to each other's views. Using different tools, judges do the same thing.

Our trip had a tragic ending. As we made our way from Peru to Chile, my dad began having unbearable headaches. He thought they were due to the altitude. I worried that his chronic allergies were making them worse. Neither of us thought they were anything more serious. But in our hotel in Antofagasta, on our last night together before I returned home to resume high school, I found him lying in bed with an ice pack over his head.

When he got back to D.C. a week after I did, he was diagnosed with a brain tumor. He never made it out of surgery. I was at school when my dad's closest friend and the leader of our Peru expedition, Dr. Merle Tuve, pulled me out of class and drove me to the hospital. That's where I learned that my father had died. One moment my dad and I were having the time of our lives; the next moment, he was dead. A peerless scientist, a treasured colleague, a loving husband, my father—all gone at just forty-three.

It's hard to imagine what my life would have been like if my dad had lived. What new discoveries he might have made. Whether I might have ended up a scientist like him. How he might have helped me as my vision declined. How life would have been for our family. How much he would have loved Edie and all his grandchildren and great-grandchildren. And how much happier my mother's life would have been with him by her side. Mom lived to be ninety-six, but never remarried. Maybe she knew she'd never find what she had in her twenty wonderful years with my father.

Several months after my dad died, Dr. Tuve sent me a letter and $1,060 for my expeditionary expenses. "You obtained as many good and reliable readings as any of us," he wrote. "All of us would sign you on for another trip with complete confidence." And my father, he added, had particularly "admired" my performance. His words meant so much to me.

I haven't seen my dad in sixty-seven years, but I can still picture his face. Our short time together molded my entire life. The chronometer that I used with him in the Andes long sat in my chambers. I have it to this day. I can no longer see it, but I can still hear it ticking.

CHAPTER 3

Then Came the Sixties

A FTER I GRADUATED FROM HIGH SCHOOL IN 1959, I HEADED off to Ann Arbor to attend college at the University of Michigan. I wanted to become a scientist, just like my dad. The school ran in our family. My father had taught physics there for a year, which explained the two bicycles with ANN ARBOR license plates in our basement. And Michigan was relatively affordable for my cash-strapped mother, who had two kids to send to college. To help pay for my room and board, I worked part-time shelving books in the undergraduate library and washing dishes in a sorority kitchen. I didn't mind the work—plus, I figured both jobs would be a good way to meet girls.

No such luck. Even so, Michigan turned out to be a perfect antidote for the heartbreak of the previous two years. While I had been a middling high school student, I thrived in college. I started as an engineering major, with minors in math and physics.

(Perhaps the slide rule hanging from my belt explained my dating problem.) But as the semesters clicked by, my interests blossomed. A great liberal arts university is supposed to do that. My friends were taking courses in history and political science, and their books—Mill's *On Liberty*, de Tocqueville's *Democracy in America*, and Joseph Heller's *Catch-22*—sounded much more interesting than mine on differential calculus. And so much was changing out there in the real world. The Supreme Court's desegregation ruling in *Brown v. Board of Education* was only a few years old, and the South was clinging tight to the past. Rosa Parks had galvanized the Montgomery bus boycott. President Eisenhower had sent federal troops to Little Rock to desegregate Central High. We devoured the latest updates on the Freedom Rides, lunch counter sit-ins, and voter registration drives.

Ann Arbor was an epicenter of student activism, and the campus crackled with speeches and demonstrations. Every day I read the *Michigan Daily*. Its editor, Tom Hayden, later cowrote the Port Huron Statement, a manifesto of the student activist movement. I also started reading the *New York Times* religiously. Columnists like James Reston, Tom Wicker, and Anthony Lewis gave me new insights about the world. I was energized by big ideas and excited about the possibilities of the future.

The 1960 presidential race beckoned as well. During my sophomore year, Senator John F. Kennedy, in what wound up being a crucial appearance, visited the Michigan Union three weeks before Election Day. He spoke late at night, well past girls' curfew. (Yes, girls had curfews, boys didn't.) My guy friends and I were right there when he told the adoring crowd that he was a graduate of the "Michigan of the East—Harvard," and promised that, if elected, he'd create a new public service program for young people. A few weeks later, he gave it a name: the Peace Corps.

After JFK took office, he pioneered another initiative that gave thousands of college students summer jobs in the government. Inspired by Kennedy's ideas, I got one of those jobs in both 1962 and 1963. At the beginning of each summer, the president greeted all of us summer interns on the South Lawn of the White House and spoke about the value of public service: "Let every man and woman who works in any area of our national government, in any branch, at any level, be able to say with pride and with honor in future years, 'I served the United States government in the hour of our national need.'" Most of us were already primed for this message, focused as we were on what was going on in the South. It felt like our whole lives were ahead of us. We couldn't wait to make a difference.

During both summers, I worked at the Labor Department's Bureau of Labor Statistics (BLS), the office that issues the monthly unemployment numbers that still make headlines today. I was classified as a "GS-5 Economist," a lofty title, I thought. In fact, I was the lowest ranking person in the office, assigned a little bit of research and a whole lot of Xeroxing. Every Tuesday, summer interns were given tokens to ride the bus to Uline Arena, where the Beatles would later give their first US concert, and where, each week, a different member of the Kennedy cabinet addressed our group. Their speeches were different, but the message was always the same: Public service is a noble undertaking.

I believed those words, and I saw them in action all around me. The career civil servants who supervised us and explained their work seemed so dedicated to the agency's mission. To them, the unemployment data they collected weren't just a bunch of numbers. Those numbers represented real people—people with families, people on their own, people who needed jobs and were doing their best to get by. Those civil servants told us that the problems those people faced were too large for any one person — or even any one government office — to solve alone. But playing their small part in the bigger mission, the BLS folks were putting into practice what the president was telling the country, that government could work, and work for the good of all.

During my second summer, I felt like I won the lottery when a college friend arranged for four of us to meet Ted Sorensen, one of JFK's closest advisors, at the White House. Two of us sat on the couch and two on the floor as Sorensen spoke. There was a knock on the door. It swung open, and in walked the president of the United States. After Sorensen introduced us, the president asked about the work we were doing that summer. We could barely reply. He shook hands with each of us. None of us washed ours for the next two weeks. He was assassinated just four months later.

That same summer, at the end of the March on Washington, I heard Dr. Martin Luther King Jr. deliver his famous "I Have a Dream" speech at the Lincoln Memorial. Sitting with a friend at the edge of the Reflecting Pool, our tired feet in the water, I was deeply inspired. Just a few months earlier, King had published his timeless "Letter from the Birmingham Jail." His words moved me then, and they move me still. At our Passover Seders, I quote passages from King's letter and remind my family that the Passover story is a universal one that speaks to the history of Black people just as it does to the history of the Jews. "Injustice anywhere," as Dr. King put it so perfectly, "is a threat to justice everywhere." At the Lincoln Memorial that day, equally powerful was the last speaker of the afternoon, John Lewis, who declared, "'One man, one vote' is our cry!" Fewer than two years later, Lewis and other civil rights demonstrators would be brutally beaten in Selma, Alabama, inspiring Congress to finally pass the Voting Rights Act of 1965. I was twenty-one years old. How tragic that in 2013, the Supreme Court of the United States, reversing an opinion I wrote for the D.C. Circuit, would declare part of that majestic statute unconstitutional.

Sadly, many politicians, pundits, and even some judges view the sixties as the source of today's problems. They blame the activism and counterculture; they condemn SDS, Black Panthers, and Weathermen; and they decry the violence of the antiwar movement. But that contemptuous focus on isolated extremes ignores the important values that emerged in the sixties: equal justice under law, fairness, and the importance of challenging authority. JFK's focus on connecting young people to their country—and to service—is perhaps his greatest legacy. I know it changed my life. And the values I later brought to the bench—treating people equally and protecting individual rights—trace back to that era. Those values are not "liberal." They're American.

How could I go back to calculus after all that? My summers in D.C. had transformed me. I still loved science and mathematics, but I was done with engineering. I switched to political science, which I thought would make me the kind of citizen that JFK had urged us to become. I took courses on intellectual history, public policy, and political philosophy, the kinds of things that I ran from in high school but that now seemed like the only important subjects. All I wanted to do was debate with my friends about the role of government, the meaning of fairness, and the future of our nation. It was a thrilling time. I loved college but couldn't wait to get back to the government and start making a difference.

Then, during the spring semester of my junior year, I took a course called Constitutional Law. My term paper was about the constitutionality of the nineteenth-century Comstock Act, which forbade sending obscene materials through the postal system. (Who could have guessed then that fifty years later, a federal judge in Texas would use the Comstock Act, forgotten for decades, as the basis for invalidating the FDA's approval of an abortion pill?) Taking that course was like lifting a veil that had been obscuring the gears that made the government move—and the restraints that kept it on the rails. The law, I realized, made the whole thing tick. So I looked for other classes about the law, and started devouring books about important legal issues of the day. I read about courageous Southern judges like Frank Johnson, John Minor Wisdom, and Richard Rives, who rose above their segregated roots and bigoted communities, enforced the Constitution and the civil rights laws, and helped America become "a more perfect union." I also read about lawyers who used the courts to defend the rights of society's most vulnerable people. I wanted to do that, too. Now determined to go to law school, I dreamed of working in the Civil Rights Division of the Justice Department, the office charged with enforcing our nation's civil rights laws.

Before Michigan I hadn't even considered becoming a lawyer. And frankly, a career in the law was a far cry from what my family had expected of Howard Tatel's son. (I think everyone assumed I'd have invented the "Tatel Telescope.2" by now.) But looking back on it, what at that time seemed like a completely new interest really did begin at home with our nightly debates about politics, culture, and the news of the day. We had watched the 1956 political conventions together, and I vividly remember going with my dad to a march at the White House protesting the executions of Julius and Ethel Rosenberg. So perhaps I should have seen it coming. Anyway, my mom didn't mind that I left science. On the contrary, she beamed with pride at the focused young man I was becoming. I'm sure my dad would have, too.

Even as I moved away from science, I didn't leave it behind entirely. My fondness for all things science, one of the many gifts that I inherited from my dad, has never faded. My divergent interests would later come together in my two decades on the National Academy of Sciences' Committee on Science, Technology, and Law. Composed of scientists, judges, and lawyers from across the country, the committee studies and reports on issues at the intersection of law and science in areas like forensic evidence, genetic therapies, and artificial intelligence. For seven years, I cochaired the committee with Nobel laureate David Baltimore. This was not merely a side project. I'm proud of the important work the committee accomplished during my tenure and believe that work made me a better judge. Environmental, pharmaceutical, and even criminal cases often rely on complex scientific records. And as you'll hear more about later, good judging looks much more like good science than you might think.

The year after I graduated from college, I enrolled at the University of Chicago Law School. A combination of scholarships, loans, and a part-time job in the university's legal office paid the way. Chicago had a track record of producing professors, and academia seemed like a good backup plan in case the Justice Department didn't work out. Like most elite law schools in the 1960s, Chicago had only a handful of women and was virtually all white. I'm happy to report that the law school looks very different today, even though the Supreme Court has now made it harder for schools to enroll a diverse class.

Law school was even better than I'd hoped. I admired my professors, giants like Harry Kalven, Walter Blum, Soia Mentschikoff and Malcolm Sharp. The basics of lawyering—how to read and interpret statutes and court opinions, how to ask questions, how to reason from one fact pattern to another—agreed with me. Law felt like science, but with words, or like political science, but with rules. Throughout my years on the D.C. Circuit, I often found myself thinking and writing in ways I learned long ago in Chicago.

It was when my classes touched on current events and issues involving civil rights that I felt most engaged. We studied Supreme Court decisions that desegregated schools, struck down racial covenants, and required counsel for poor defendants. My Constitutional Law professor, Philip Kurland, taught us that the role of the courts is to "protect the individual against the Leviathan of government and to protect minorities against oppression by majorities." The Supreme Court that I studied was using its awesome power to do just that. Even better, the Court wrote opinions explaining *why*. My professors taught me how to parse those opinions, to separate good legal reasoning from bad. Indeed, their teaching never stopped. Decades later, when I was on the D.C. Circuit, one of my favorite professors, Bernard Meltzer, occasionally wrote to me commenting on my opinions, and twice even explained why he thought his former student had gotten it wrong.

At that time in my life, I could still mostly see the statutes and opinions I was reading. In the law library, I sought out the tables with the brightest lighting. I took notes with a thick black pen. Blackboards were a challenge. When I couldn't make out a professor's writing, I'd ask to borrow a classmate's notes—not that I ever revealed why I was asking. I was having more and more difficulty getting around at night, especially on the then-unlit Midway. Streets with noisy traffic and bright streetlights were my best routes. I could still play touch football as long as the ball contrasted with a bright sky and didn't get lost in front of a big leafy tree.

The decade I chose the law was also the last in which I functioned on my own. The future would bring readers, white canes, and ultimately, Vixen.

CHAPTER 4

Thanks, Mr. Jensen!

M Y CHICAGO DAYS WERE LIFE-CHANGING IN MORE WAYS than one. In the spring of 1965 I met Edie. She'd been in the class behind me at Michigan. I knew who she was, though we'd never met. I'd glimpsed her one night in the coffee shop of the undergraduate library, where I spent much of my time studying or shelving books. "That's Edie Bassichis," my friend said. "She's the president of AEPhi." AEPhi was the Jewish sorority with all of the cool women. Like many of my friends, I'd always wanted a date with an AEPhi. But I never actually managed it, and not for lack of trying. I had friends there, but no girlfriends. My twenty-year-old self wouldn't have believed that I'd end up marrying one.

In Chicago, Edie was living on the North Side, while I lived near the law school on the South Side. We were set up by a mutual friend from Michigan. Our first date — a blind date — was at

Jimmy's, my favorite Hyde Park bar. It was a seedy joint, which we called "bohemian." On the night of our date, they were having their first, and probably last, poetry reading. Perfect, I thought. Edie was a teacher and getting her masters in English at Northwestern, so I figured she'd be impressed. I tried to play it cool, to give the impression that I did this sort of thing all the time. The room was dark, with a spotlight fixed on an earnest young poet reading his own creations along with Keats and Yeats. I nodded along with Edie when the poems were good and laughed with her at the poet's lame literary jokes. But I'm not sure I really heard a word. I couldn't stop watching her. Afterward, we strolled along Lake Michigan, talked into the late hours, and kissed. "Sparks sparked," as Edie describes it. "And they still do."

Until we sat down to write this memoir, I didn't know that she was dating two other guys at the time, "Ralph" and "Teddy." Apparently, she called both the very next day, explained how much she liked them, and then bade them farewell.

At first I kept up the same ruse with Edie as I did with everyone else. But as we grew closer, I soon began to worry about when and how I'd tell her that something was wrong with my eyes. I'd thought long and hard about what to say and when to say it, so I remember the conversation well. One sunny afternoon as we walked hand in hand around the 55th Street Point, the peninsula jutting out into Lake Michigan, we wandered over to one of the big cement benches, sat down, and listened to the waves. "I need to tell you something," I began, and described what I had learned—or, at least, what I had chosen to hear—from Dr. Berson seven years earlier. Now it was Edie's turn to decide what she wanted to hear. Looking back on it, Edie thinks I told her that although my vision would dim over time, and that blindness was theoretically possible, it was all uncertain and "a long way off."

Edie was the very first person in whom I confided. I remember the huge feeling of relief that washed over me when she told me it was all okay with her. Of course, neither of us knew what we were getting into. Remember, Edie didn't meet a blind man. She met a man who looked and lived like a sighted person, who read thick law books, rode a bike, and shopped for groceries. How, at the start of a blossoming relationship, was she supposed to process the news that someday my life might be very different?

With that elephant off my chest, we got back to the all-consuming business of falling in love. We began spending almost every day together, and I couldn't wait to introduce her to my mom. When the semester ended, we hopped on the Capitol Limited train to Washington. It sounded so romantic. It wasn't. The train was cramped and thick with cigarette smoke, so for most of the night we sat in the roomier, but still smoky, bar car and watched Peter Sellers in *Dr. Strangelove* on a drop-down screen. When we finally got off at the B&O station in Silver Spring, we smelled like ashtrays.

My mother adored Edie. A nice Jewish girl and a teacher to boot! I proposed the very next day. She said yes. Edie's parents approved—a nice Jewish boy and a lawyer to boot!—but nonetheless counseled her, "You shouldn't think you need to be in a hurry." Edie said it took her five years to decipher that they were offering help in case she was pregnant. She wasn't. Edie had told her parents what she knew about my vision: that I had an eye disease, sometimes had trouble seeing in the dark, and that it might get worse. They weren't worried because we weren't worried. The future seemed so bright.

As I write this memoir, neither Edie nor I remembers avoiding the truth. Edie accepted what I told her about my RP because she trusted me. We both believed that blindness was unlikely. Still, if Google had existed back then, she'd have searched for "retinitis pigmentosa" the first chance she had. If she had known then how likely it was that I'd lose my sight entirely, would our budding love still have prevailed? Would Edie's parents still have approved of our marriage? It's one thing to have compassion for a person with a disability, but quite another to accept that their own daughter's husband might become blind.

Barely four months after that fateful blind date, we got married in Cleveland, where Edie had grown up. I was twenty-three. She was twenty-two. We wonder what our reactions would have been if one of our own kids had announced they were marrying — at twenty-two — someone they'd known for just four months! Would we have been as calm and supportive as our parents had been? Sidley, Austin, Burgess, & Smith, a venerable Chicago law firm where I was working that summer, played a supporting role in our marriage. The firm gave me a week off for the ceremony and honeymoon. When I went to the travel agent to pick up our plane tickets, however, I discovered I'd booked only one — and I didn't have enough cash for a second. Oops! Credit cards were ten years in the future. Luckily, Sidley's office manager, an affable fellow named Jensen, kindly arranged for a loan from the firm. Thanks, Mr. Jensen!

After our honeymoon in Bermuda, where we swam in the first warm ocean water either of us had ever known and rode motorbikes all over the island, we moved into a third-floor walk-up apartment in Chicago's South Shore neighborhood for $105 a month. Not coincidentally, Edie's parents' generous wedding gift was a monthly check for $105, which meant we could get by on Edie's teaching salary while I finished law school. With help from friends, I painted the walls, but not very well. Beneath the white paint forever lurked the artwork we had doodled on the old walls, with the "What, Me Worry?" face of Alfred E. Neuman smiling through the second coat of paint. Our big weekly splurge was Vala's ice cream, which billed itself as "the world's most expensive," serving "32 obscenely delicious flavors." The pints came in a psychedelic pink and purple paper bag so sturdy that one bag carried my lunch for the entire year.

My third year of law school was easy. By then I'd mastered the art of taking law school exams, had already secured an offer to return to Sidley after graduation, and was soaking up what I knew would be my last year of school. Edie, though, worked hard. Every weekday, she'd be up at the crack of dawn, head to Harlan High School at 95th and South Michigan Avenue, teach six different English classes, and return home to make dinner, eat with me, and refine her lesson plans for the next day. Sometimes after dinner she said she'd take a quick nap, but that usually meant she'd be out cold until morning. I did the dishes, as Edie's and my dads had always done when we were kids.

Life was good. We were young and optimistic and in love. We talked about the trips we hoped to take, the careers we hoped to have, and the family we hoped to build. We spoke of my vision only rarely. We didn't know when, or even if, any further decline might be coming. And even if we'd known that blindness was in our future, why dwell on it?

My diagnosis actually came in handy when, in 1966, I heard from my draft board that I'd have to show up downtown for a 6 a.m. physical. When I arrived, I couldn't avoid noticing that most of the men in their skivvies and socks were Black or Hispanic, presumably without the wealth and connections to avoid the draft and the chance to go to Vietnam. The guy ahead of me in line asked for a second sheet of paper to list his criminal history. One of the first commands we heard was, "All doctor letters in this box." I had a letter. NIH, on their official stationery, had written: "To Whom It May Concern: Mr. David Tatel is legally blind as a result of Retinitis Pigmentosa." I had received that letter five years earlier but kept it in a briefcase that I rarely used. It was the only document in there. Maybe I thought that by keeping the letter hidden, it didn't really exist. I showed it to no one until I dropped it into that box. But I still had to go through with the physical. At the very last station, three military ophthalmologists examined me with excitement. None of them had ever seen a case of RP. They "oohed" and "aahed" as they examined my deteriorating retinas.

Edie and I both felt immense relief a month later when my new draft card declaring me 4F—exempt—arrived in the mail. The 4F card was a reality check. It confirmed the obvious, and its presence in my wallet alongside my Maryland driver's license highlighted how much my life had already changed. I'd stopped driving a few years earlier, other than occasionally shoehorning Edie's blue '57 Chevy into a tight parking space. But when I put that 4F card in my wallet, it really hit me. I'd never drive again.

And I never did. Our four children would never see me drive anywhere—not to the grocery store, not to nursery school, not to the Y, not on vacation. In our family, only Edie would drive. Our kids thought nothing of it. When they saw a friend's father behind the wheel, they each had the same reaction: "I didn't know that dads could drive!" They were also surprised when they found out that nobody else's family listened to "talking books"—early audiobooks—together. When you're a kid, you often don't see the ways in which your family is different from other families. To our kids, having a blind father was normal. Our daughter Emily remembers friends asking her, "What's it like to grow up with a blind dad?" Her answer: "It was no different than growing up with a dad who wasn't blind. I always felt heard and safe and respected and loved and *seen*." I'm so glad she felt that way.

But fatherhood was still a long way off. I was about to graduate from law school and ready to start making a difference in the world. My summer at Sidley had made me think I might enjoy practicing law at a big firm. The partners were smart, interesting, and engaged in their communities. While the firm did lots of work for big companies, it also supported pro bono activities, including on racial justice issues. (*Pro bono publico* is Latin for "You don't get paid.") Of course, the lifestyle, which the firm made sure we summer associates got to see, was also seductive. We ate at fancy restaurants. We went to swanky country clubs. We were paid well. And most importantly, we went to lots of ball games at Wrigley Field. So Sidley's offer to return after law school was very tempting.

But with my student years coming to a close, I realized I still had the academic itch. As fate would have it, my criminal law professor, Frank Allen, had just become dean at Michigan's law school. When he asked if I wanted to spend a year as a teaching fellow, it seemed like the stars had aligned. Edie and I had loved Ann Arbor in our separate undergraduate lives there, so we were excited about returning, this time together. Sidley thought the whole thing a lark, but they wished me well anyway. Edie got a job in Ypsilanti, a nearby town, teaching eighth- and ninth-grade English, eighth-grade Spanish, and seventh-grade girls' gym.

Again, Edie's job proved far more demanding than mine. I taught Legal Research and Writing just once a week. I liked my students, most of whom were as excited as I was about the possibilities of the law. Teaching definitely made me a better writer. (If you want to master something, teach it—so the old saying goes.) I also played a small role in the law school's first-ever affirmative action program. Each teaching fellow was assigned to tutor one of the four Black students in the first-year class. I think I got more from that program than my student, who later became a judge himself. Today's Supreme Court would have declared that program unconstitutional by a vote of 6–3.

During my second semester, a law professor invited me to teach a class on the section of the Internal Revenue Code that exempts charities, foundations, colleges, and other nonprofit organizations from federal income taxes. My first problem? Although I'd taken tax law at Chicago, I knew next to nothing about the exemption. Cramming, I got up to speed quickly. My second problem was more daunting: The class was huge, and I needed a seating chart legible enough for me to call on the students. I solved the problem by creating a chart in heavy black marker on a huge sheet of paper that I folded up for transport and then unfurled on the lectern. I was more worried about hiding my limited vision than the fact that I'd learned most of what I knew about the nonprofit exemption only a few days before my students. I think I got away with both ruses. If anyone suspected I had a vision problem, I never heard a peep about it.

Between classes, I spent my time in my first-ever office, high in the corner tower of the law library. To get there, I climbed up a straight, very steep staircase. Windows on three sides gave me a fine view of Dominick's across the street, a bustling bar and restaurant open only during the school year. (A Dominick's employee and his brother later started a billion-dollar pizza chain you'll have heard of, and which still goes by a very similar name.) My job was to keep an eye on the crowd. When things let up, the other teaching fellows and I headed over for coffee or beer, depending on the time of day.

That year I took up a new sport, bottle pool, a hybrid game we played at the Michigan Union, where JFK had spoken seven years before. As described by the *New York Times*, the game combined "elements of billiards, straight pool and chess," but was "basically a form of ritualized warfare with cue sticks." Because of the contrast between the dark felt table and the white balls, I could see all the action. Playing that challenging game with good friends nearly every day was great fun.

Such was my experience in academia: morning coffee in the faculty lounge, meetings with students, lunch, the occasional class, another coffee break, a game of bottle pool, and evenings with Edie. It was a good year, but my itch to teach had been scratched. My undergraduate summers in D.C. had stuck with me, and I wanted to be on the front lines of the Civil Rights Movement. First, though, I needed some experience. I was a lawyer, but I'd never practiced law. Apparently, good grammar and a passing knowledge of nonprofit tax exemptions takes one only so far.

So, in the summer of 1967, we returned to Chicago and I rejoined Sidley. Edie taught tenth-grade English at the University of Chicago Laboratory High School, the job she credits with professionalizing her as a teacher. We immersed ourselves in Hyde Park and the great city of Chicago—this time, with an extra bit of pocket money because we were both working real jobs. We spent our evenings and weekends riding our bikes along the lake; catching plays at Court Theater, comedy at Second City, and music at the Chicago Symphony; visiting museums; and, of course, cheering for the Cubs at Wrigley Field. We feasted on sauerbraten at Berghoff's, Black Russians at the roof bar of Outer Drive East, and, yes, more Vala's ice cream. The world was our oyster.

CHAPTER 5

"Where Are All the Lawyers?"

B ACK AT SIDLEY I WAS FINALLY WORKING AS HARD AS EDIE. I started with traditional litigation work, primarily with Howard Trienens, a partner who specialized in railroad and antitrust issues. The firm was deeply involved in the early stages of AT&T's antitrust troubles, and that's where I initially spent most of my time. The University of Chicago taught me the law; Trienens taught me how to practice law. Advice to young lawyers: After law school, find a superb lawyer to work for, in any specialty, and dig in. In a year or two you'll start to know what it is that you're doing.

At the beginning, even the simplest tasks seemed hard. During my first appearance in court, I had to argue a routine motion for an extension of time. That kind of motion is usually granted as a matter of routine. But the judge turned out to be Julius Hoffman, who later notoriously presided over the federal trial of the Chicago Seven. After giving me a hard time about who I was, what I was doing, and why I was bothering him with such a piddly request, he denied my motion. When I reported back to the lawyer who had sent me on that fool's errand, I expected a scolding. Instead, he commiserated, "That SOB never grants extensions."

After that bumpy start, I slowly began to gain confidence and feel like a real lawyer. As much as I enjoyed it, though, I still had my sights set on civil rights—and that work soon began to consume me.

It started when the firm asked if I'd be interested in getting involved with a major school desegregation case in the Illinois Supreme Court. At the very moment they asked, I was slogging through the economic details of a railroad merger and cataloging hundreds of freight car movements. So of course, my answer was a resounding yes. School desegregation was exactly the kind of issue I'd hoped to work on as a lawyer, and I couldn't believe I was getting a chance to start so soon. I'd be writing an amicus, or "friend of the court," brief on behalf of the Chicago Urban League, one of Sidley's pro bono clients. Amicus briefs are filed not by the parties to a case, but rather by individuals or organizations who have some relevant expertise or experience and want to share their views with the court. The Chicago Urban League had plenty to say about school desegregation, and my job was to help them say it. Right place, right time.

The case, called *Tometz v. Board of Education of Waukegan City School District,* involved a challenge to an Illinois law that required school districts to readjust their boundaries in order to promote racial balance. The Chicago Urban League wanted to defend the law. Eager to get started, I immediately visited Tometz's lawyer,

Al Polikoff, a partner at another major Chicago law firm. Al's office was filled with hundreds of volumes on securities law, which was how he spent most of his time. But here he was, working pro bono on a major civil rights case. "Wow!" I thought. "Here's another lawyer I want to be like when I grow up." With Polikoff's help, I crafted an amicus brief arguing that "America's greatest domestic problem" was racial discrimination. Describing the many educational benefits of integrated education, the brief concluded, "It would indeed be ironic if American statesmen, after decades of using racial categories for purposes of separation, could not now use those same categories to cure the sores caused by that separation." We won, and as a result, the Waukegan schools in suburban Chicago became more integrated.

It was a very different time. If that case had come before today's US Supreme Court, we would undoubtedly have lost. Indeed, in 2007, the Court ruled that school districts cannot take any account of race, even to promote integration. "The way to stop discrimination on the basis of race," Chief Justice Roberts opined on behalf of a sharply divided Court, "is to stop discriminating on the basis of race." So much for healing the festering sores of segregation.

Tometz was my first taste of school desegregation litigation, which would go on to occupy much of my pre-judicial career. It was also my first real opportunity to see successful big-firm lawyers using their prodigious talents and skills to litigate important civil rights issues. Lawyers like Trienens and Polikoff were private citizens in the public square.

———

The year 1968 was tumultuous for America: civil rights struggles; Vietnam War protests; LBJ's decision not to seek reelection; the assassinations of Martin Luther King Jr. and Robert Kennedy and the urban riots that followed; the divisive Democratic National Convention in Chicago; the Black Power salute by John Carlos and Tommie Smith at the Mexico City Olympics; the election of Richard Nixon. The country was in chaos.

It was a big year for Edie and me as well. During the riots following Dr. King's assassination, we were at the University of Chicago Hospital greeting our brand-new baby, Rebecca. Looking out the hospital window, we could see smoke billowing just blocks away. What a bittersweet way to begin our lives as parents. But as Edie says, "Once we had our baby in our arms, we both felt our hearts grow." We knew we'd be okay, and that we'd both do whatever we could to make the world a better place for our daughter.

When we decided to have children, did we worry about their vision? Truthfully, we didn't. We understood that any pregnancy had risks. At the time, we knew next to nothing about whether or how RP might be passed down to our children. Were we in denial? Did our excitement about becoming parents color our thinking? Maybe. We now know a lot more about RP, including that our three daughters, who inherited one of their X chromosomes from me, are carriers and that their children are at some risk as well. But they're not afraid. When we discovered the nature of my mutation and learned what it meant for them, they all shrugged. For our family, blindness has been a challenge we've managed pretty well.

Still, through those final years of the sixties my vision continued to deteriorate. I did my best to make sure no one at work caught on. And I dove headfirst into the new world of civil rights work that was opening up before me. After the riots, Sidley loaned me to the Chicago Riot Study Committee, a panel appointed by Mayor Richard J. Daley to explore the causes of the urban unrest. Right place, right time yet again.

Along with another young lawyer borrowed from a different law firm, I spent the summer exploring schools on Chicago's South and West sides, interviewing teachers, administrators, parents, and students. We learned that at some schools students had vandalized buildings, broken windows, and set off fire alarms. Many had torched and looted local businesses. At other schools, though, students had stayed composed and focused, somehow avoiding the violence and strife that plagued schools just down the block. Most of the fortunate schools, we found, had one thing in common: They were led by teachers and administrators who inspired their students to express their anger constructively in assemblies and classrooms, rather than destructively out in the streets. The difference, in other words, was leadership. Some of that leadership, we learned, came from Chicago's street gangs. While some gangs sparked trouble, a handful played a constructive role, urging calm. Where "the leadership of these gangs and organizations committed their groups to maintaining social peace," our report concluded, "there were few incidents of serious civil disorder."

Even leadership, however, couldn't make up for lack of resources. And the absence of "serious civil disorder" by no means meant the presence of serious educational achievement. Sadly, we concluded, Chicago's public schools, "with a few notable exceptions," are "failing in the ghettos." (I know, not the right way to put it. But that was the language of the 1960s.) Today, Chicago certainly has some successful schools, but unfortunately that fifty-year-old verdict still holds true for many schools serving the city's poorest children. The pervasive, structural challenges we identified back then are much the same as those that led to the 2020 unrest following the murder of George Floyd in Minneapolis.

Edie saw those challenges up close, first as a Chicago Public Schools substitute all over the city while she was still in graduate school, and then as a full-time teacher at Harlan High. She loved her work and was really proud of her students. But she and her students often felt like they were fighting an uphill battle. She didn't expect the indifferent administrators, the crowded classrooms, the boring and outdated textbooks, and the low expectations set by many of her fellow teachers. She was surprised and delighted midyear when more of her students tested out of "Basic" to "Regular" level sections than any other teachers', even though she was a novice among so many veterans.

The *Tometz* desegregation case, my work for the mayor's riot committee, and Edie's firsthand experiences opened my eyes to the real struggles, and real stakes, of the fight for equal educational opportunity. Although I returned to Sidley when my work on the riot committee concluded, I now knew for sure that I wanted to practice civil rights law full-time. I had learned a lot representing the firm's corporate clients and appreciated the opportunity to do important civil rights work on the side. But "on the side" was no longer good enough for me. I wanted to devote all my energy to people who needed lawyers but couldn't afford them. Let someone else help the railroads.

Since Richard Nixon had just won the presidency—largely on the basis of his cynical, racist "Southern Strategy"—my dream job as a Justice Department civil rights lawyer wasn't going to happen anytime soon. I didn't want to work for the Nixon administration, I wanted to sue it. I soon got the opportunity to do just that when, in May 1969, I took my first full-time civil rights job, as founding director of the Chicago Lawyers' Committee for Civil Rights Under Law.

The Lawyers' Committee traces its roots to the summer of 1963 and the South's increasingly violent response to the Civil Rights Movement — Bull Connor fire-hosing demonstrators in Birmingham, the assassination of civil rights leader Medgar Evers in Jackson, and the arrest of hundreds of civil rights workers and demonstrators, to name just a few. Watching those horrors unfold, Robert Kennedy, then attorney general, asked a simple question: "Where are all the lawyers?" His brother, the president, answered by summoning nearly 250 leaders of the American bar to the White House's East Room. There, according to several people who were in the room, President Kennedy reminded them that lawyers have a special obligation to ensure that civil rights issues are resolved "in the courts, not the streets." And he challenged them to do more to fulfill that obligation. Hundreds of lawyers from across the country heeded the President's call. Traveling south under the banner of the newly organized President's Committee — soon renamed the Lawyers' Committee for Civil Rights Under Law — those dedicated volunteers represented civil rights workers in both federal and state courts, filing suits that challenged police harassment and the suppression of lawful demonstrations.

It worked. Those lawsuits helped to rein in some of the violence that was sweeping the South. But it soon became clear that the need for lawyers was not limited to the South. In 1968, the Kerner Commission on Civil Disorders, which President Johnson had established to explore the causes of the urban riots that started in Los Angeles and spread across the country, warned that our nation was "moving toward two societies, one black, one white — separate and unequal." LBJ called on the Lawyers' Committee to expand its southern efforts to the rest of the country. Thus were born eleven big-city Lawyers' Committees, including one in Chicago. In coordination with law firms, along with the ACLU and other advocacy groups, the Chicago Lawyers'

Committee was formed right in my own backyard to help bring justice to the powerless.

I'd long admired the great lawyers that Robert Kennedy had assembled at the Justice Department, many of whom had risked their lives in the South and become leaders of the Lawyers' Committee nationwide—people like Burke Marshall, John Doar, Nicholas Katzenbach, and Barrett Prettyman Jr. How did a young law firm associate like me get a chance to work with those giants and lead the Chicago Lawyers' Committee? It was mostly thanks to one man: Louis Oberdorfer.

About the same age my father would have been, Lou grew up in Birmingham, Alabama, where he'd seen racial segregation up close. He had quite a résumé. As an assistant attorney general in the Kennedy Justice Department, he had helped to desegregate the University of Mississippi. And he'd been in charge of delivering the food and medicine that Fidel Castro had demanded in exchange for releasing the Bay of Pigs prisoners. His greatest early achievement, though, may have been that East Room gathering of 244 lawyers. Lou wasn't just there to hear JFK's call to legal arms; the whole thing was largely his idea.

While Lou returned to private practice after leaving the Justice Department, he was never far from the Civil Rights Movement. As cochair of the National Lawyers' Committee, Lou was the one who interviewed me for the Chicago job. We hit it off right away. Lou believed in his bones that every lawyer has an obligation to represent the underrepresented—to be a "citizen lawyer" and a "lawyer statesman." And he believed that access to the courts for all, no matter one's race or wealth, was a mainstay of the rule of law. I wanted to be just like him, and I eagerly accepted his offer to lead the Chicago Lawyers' Committee. It was the first time—but not the last—that Lou's professional path would cross mine. Four decades later, when I eulogized Lou after spending years serving with him on the federal bench, I marveled, "That our paths crossed at precisely that moment—when I was seeking a way forward and Lou was searching for comrades in arms—has always seemed like magic. My life, it's no stretch to say, has never been the same. Lou didn't just give me a job. He gave me a mission."

The Chicago Lawyers' Committee worked out of a small office on the sixteenth floor of the old Monadnock Building in Chicago's South Loop. When built in the 1890s, it was the world's largest office building. By the time I showed up in 1969, it had seen better days. Still, the Monadnock fit us well—solid, efficient, and cheap. There were just three of us working full-time at the Chicago Lawyers' Committee: me, a secretary, and a secondhand Xerox machine. My main job was to identify potential civil rights plaintiffs who needed counsel and to match them with lawyers at law firms willing to work pro bono. I did that by coordinating closely with other civil rights groups in the area, like the ACLU and Chicago Legal Aid. And I worked alongside our pro bono volunteers, helping them navigate difficult legal questions and complicated procedural problems. Today, that sort of collaboration between private sector lawyers and legal nonprofits is commonplace. Back then, it was pathbreaking.

Working together, we challenged racially discriminatory actions and policies in housing, education, and employment. We represented a Black police officer fired under dubious circumstances, a white subcontractor terminated because he hired Black laborers, doctors working with the Black Panthers to establish a community health center, and organizations building racially and economically integrated day care centers. With a front-row seat to Chicago's finest lawyers at work, I got a crash course in civil rights law and good lawyering. I've always remembered our first board meeting, held in our shabby conference room. Just three years out of law school and one month free of those piles of railroad merger documents, I found myself chairing a meeting with eight of Chicago's most powerful lawyers. I was beyond intimidated. But to my surprise, they seemed to take me seriously, considering every case I presented and generally deferring to my recommendations. "Well, of course they did," Edie responded when I told her all about it at dinner.

I never informed anyone I worked with about my eyesight. Not the Lawyers' Committee board members, not the public interest groups with whom we collaborated, not our private sector partners. I didn't even tell my secretary. Maybe some of them noticed that I frequently moved my head from side to side as I walked, compensating for my dwindling central vision. Maybe they realized that I sometimes had trouble recognizing people in dark restaurants or that I kept a bright light on whatever I was reading. If they suspected, they never asked questions. I believed I had them all fooled.

So that I'm not fooling you, however, I should be clear about one important aspect of my move from the private sector to the public interest. If you're at all familiar with how the legal market works today, you're probably assuming that I was making some big financial sacrifice by leaving a plush big-city law firm for a nonprofit civil rights organization. I wasn't. The Lawyers' Committee paid about the same as what I earned at Sidley: $7,900 a year. Imagine what we could accomplish if nonprofit work paid the same as big law today. And here's the really interesting point: Edie was earning $8,100 a year as a Chicago Public School teacher. How much better might our schools be today if teachers earned the same or more than young associates at major law firms, which is now over $200,000 a year? What a difference it would make if we paid new teachers even half that amount.

A few months into my tenure at the Lawyers' Committee, in the frosty predawn hours of December 4, 1969, an undercover Chicago police van pulled up in front of 2337 West Monroe Street. Armed with shotguns, fourteen officers were there to execute a search warrant for weapons they claimed the Black Panthers had stockpiled inside. According to Cook County State's Attorney Edward Hanrahan, who had ordered the raid, "a fierce gun battle" ensued. Hanrahan even congratulated the officers for "bravery and restraint in the face of the vicious Black Panther attack." A federal grand jury later found, however, that only a single shot had been fired by anyone inside the building. The police, by contrast, had sprayed nearly one hundred bullets through doors and walls. When the raid ended, two men were dead: Fred Hampton, the twenty-one-year-old charismatic chairman of the Chicago Black Panthers, and his deputy, Mark Clark. The 2021 film and podcast *Judas and the Black Messiah* both tell that story.

It was no isolated incident. The Chicago police of the late 1960s were infamous for the violence they inflicted on some of the communities they were charged with protecting. The Lawyers' Committee decided we had to take a stand. Not one of us supported the militant tactics of the Black Panthers. But as lawyers—officers of the court sworn to uphold the integrity of the judicial system—we easily coalesced around the idea that whether you're Black or white, rich or poor, radical or mainstream, you're entitled to the full protection of the law. When the police disregard the rights of those they are policing and take the law into their own hands, they need to be held to account.

We sent a telegram to John Mitchell, the US attorney general, warning that the Black Panther incident had "exacerbated to a critically dangerous level the already tense relations between the Black community and the police." We called for a federal grand jury investigation. "None of us is accustomed to petitioning government," we wrote. "That we now do is a measure of the depth of our concern." Like the 244 lawyers in the East Room at the Lawyers' Committee's founding, the lawyers who signed that telegram ranged in ideology and political beliefs. But on the primacy of the rule of law, we were unified. Mitchell convened a grand jury the very next week, and it was that grand jury's report that confirmed that the hail of bullets came from the police. For all his misdeeds as attorney general (he later went to prison for his role in the Watergate scandal), Mitchell didn't ignore what respected Chicago lawyers told him about a high-profile police assassination.

To ensure that Hanrahan and his officers were held accountable, we asked the chief judge of the Circuit Court of Cook County to convene a state grand jury to look into the assassinations. I was in the courtroom when one of our board members stood before the chief judge and argued the motion. The crowd was electric; no one expected a Daley judge to act against the Daley police department. But he did. And most of the police officers involved, including Hanrahan himself, were indicted. This still being Chicago, however, they were all ultimately acquitted. But at least some "justice" was done: Two weeks after his acquittal Hanrahan lost his bid for reelection, ending his political career, including as a potential successor to Mayor Daley. Thirteen years after the raid, a federal court finally approved a $1.85 million settlement to Hampton's and Clark's families and to survivors of the raid. The settlement was paid by the city, the county, and the federal government, whose anti-Panther efforts had been led by FBI director J. Edgar Hoover.

The whole episode gave the young Chicago Lawyers' Committee instant visibility, credibility, and self-confidence. We were energized. We knew our efforts had led to the appointment of the federal grand jury and to the subsequent indictments. Our success inspired our members and attracted new law firm partners, which in turn allowed us to take on more cases.

———————

The Chicago Lawyers' Committee received requests for assistance from all over Illinois. Cairo (pronounced CAY-roe), a small city at the confluence of the Mississippi and Ohio Rivers at the southern tip of Illinois, was particularly desperate for our help. It was a complicated place. The southernmost city in a free state, Cairo had been an indispensable stop on the Underground Railroad. Mark Twain made it Huck Finn and Jim's initial destination as they paddled.

But it wasn't always a romantic destination. Charles Dickens, visiting "dismal Cairo" in 1842, called it "a grave uncheered by any gleam of promise." In 1909, Will "Froggy" James, a Black laborer accused of raping and murdering a white woman, was lynched by a frenzied Cairo mob, his head put on a spike for all to see. Photos of the gruesome scene appeared on sepia postcards sold as souvenirs.

Cairo was rigidly segregated, and racial discrimination was rampant. Most Black people lived in Pyramid Court, a shoddy public housing project consisting of rows of two-story apartment blocks. Their children were consigned to underfunded and poorly performing schools. Gangs of white men drove around in their pickup trucks, brandishing their weapons and terrorizing the town's Black residents. If not for the accents, you'd have thought you were in rural Mississippi. Fed up, the Black community began to boycott the pharmacy, gas station, department store, and other local businesses that refused to employ Black people. An all-white group calling themselves the White Hats (referring to the white civil defense helmets they wore) retaliated violently. It was practically public knowledge that they were vigilantes deputized by the county sheriff, who looked the other way as they left rack and ruin in their wake.

In 1970, the White Hats shot up the office of Bob Lansden, the lawyer we partnered with in Cairo. Lansden was lucky. When the shooting happened, he was next door having lunch at the, you guessed it, Mark Twain Restaurant. Lansden and his brother and law partner Dave—both white Princetonians—were fish out of water in Cairo, characters "straight out of a Faulkner novel," observed the *New York Times* in reporting on the incident. The Lawyers' Committee's annual report proudly displayed a picture of the bullet hole in the office's Xerox machine. Unbelievably, the machine still worked. Xerox should've put the photo in an ad.

When he wasn't busy helping the Lawyers' Committee, Lansden represented the local bank. To discourage him from working with us, the White Hats organized a run on the bank and demanded that Lansden be fired. In a coffee shop on Chicago's LaSalle Street, I met with Adlai Stevenson III, Illinois's state treasurer and the son of my parents' favorite presidential candidate, and asked him to deposit state funds into the bank to compensate for the loss caused by the withdrawals. He quickly agreed, and state money began flowing in. We also got several corporations, all clients of Chicago Lawyers' Committee board members, to make deposits. I hadn't ever expected that propping up a bank would be part of my job description at the Lawyers' Committee. But that was what it took to save Lansden's law practice—and our only major resource in Cairo. Shortly after we intervened, the run ended. The bank survived, and Lansden continued both his work for the bank (which kept his lights on) and his civil rights work with us (which the people of Cairo so badly needed), now with new money and lawyers from big Chicago law firms. Little did I know as we were trying to save the Cairo bank that a similar situation was evolving in another small town four hundred miles to the south. A few years later, that town, Port Gibson, Mississippi, would be the setting for the most important case of my pre-judicial career.

I spent just one year at the Chicago Lawyers' Committee. But it was a transformative one. I started the year as a young law firm associate eager to make a difference but with almost no real-world experience. I finished it as a maturing civil rights attorney.

CHAPTER 6

"Too Beautiful to Burn"

I THRIVED AT THE CHICAGO LAWYERS' COMMITTEE, BUT NOW with two young children, Edie and I started to feel the pull of my hometown, Washington, D.C. I also understood that if my work was to have nationwide impact, I needed to go where the federal government was. I needed to be, in the words of Lin-Manuel Miranda, in the room where it happens. If Hubert Humphrey had won the White House in 1968, I would have sought a civil rights position in his administration. He didn't, which is why I got to create the Chicago Lawyers' Committee instead. But just a year later, Sidley offered me a position in its D.C. office. There I could continue my work with Trienens and at the same time handle some Lawyers' Committee cases—and Nixon wouldn't be in office forever.

Edie and I left Chicago in our little blue Renault, a replacement for the red VW Beetle that had disappeared from the street in front of our apartment. (It was the third bug stolen that morning, explained the police officer who took our report. She thought it was probably well on its way to becoming a California dune buggy, but with the back seat filled with a baby seat, portable crib, and diaper bag, we always hoped it found its way to a good family in need.) Since I couldn't drive, my job as we drove through the night was to keep three-year-old Rebecca and baby Stephanie asleep during our rest stops by rocking the car—yes, the whole car—while Edie ran in for coffee. As I said, it was a little car.

D.C.'s Sidley office had only five lawyers. Its best-known partner was J. Edward Day, JFK's Postmaster General and the man who gave us ZIP codes. Nearly every day we all had lunch together at the nearby Statler Hilton, with Day shaking dozens of hands along the way. In Washington, former Cabinet members are celebrities.

I'm sure you won't be surprised to learn that I told neither Day nor any of my other Sidley colleagues about my vision problem. Instead, I continued to perfect my clandestine navigational strategies. At an elevator, I'd let others get on first, then ask, "Could you please hit seven?" At a revolving door, I'd extend my arm just enough to feel the door fins pass by but not far enough to get amputated. When I couldn't find a door or a passageway, I'd wait for others to walk by. Women in high heels going in the direction I wanted to go were the best, as their clicking heels were easy to follow. I trailed many women, but fortunately, no one ever got the wrong idea. When meeting friends at a dark restaurant, I'd chat with the maître d' so that I could follow his voice as he led me to the table. And when I got there, I'd make sure to say "Hello, everyone," so I could hear their responses, identify who was there, and figure out where to sit.

And then there was the challenge of commuting to and from work on the L7, the express bus that ran up and down Connecticut Avenue. In the morning, I had no problem getting on the right bus because it always left from the same spot. On the way home, if it was dark, I could make out the illuminated number in the bus window. But if it was still light, I'd ask someone standing nearby if the arriving bus was the L7. Sometimes I'd even delay leaving the office until it was dark enough for me to see the illuminated sign. Of course, that's not what I told Edie when I arrived home too late for family dinner. When Edie first read this paragraph and heard about the illuminated bus sign, she began to simmer, then to boil. She'd always assumed I missed dinners with the kids because of pressing work obligations. Work was work, and she believed in what I was doing as much as I did. But staying late just to avoid the embarrassment of asking for help? She's right: That was nuts.

Back at Sidley, most of my billable hours were for railroads, AT&T, and other clients with matters before federal regulatory agencies. They wanted to know how to comply with—or, sometimes, challenge—federal regulations. And they often found themselves the targets of federal investigations or lawsuits. We also spent a lot of time ensuring that clients were complying with the new wage-and-price controls imposed by the Nixon administration in 1971. "Socialism!," the clients protested. It was interesting work, and my first real exposure to the kinds of regulatory issues that would later dominate my judicial career.

One lawsuit took me back to my childhood. Sidley's client was Borden Chemical, which made the plastic wrap used to package grocery store meat. Back then, grocers cut the plastic from big rolls by drawing it across a heated wire. "Hot wiring," it was called. Shears would have been the better choice because burning plastic produces toxic fumes that can cause respiratory ailments. Once grocery workers figured that out, they sued Borden. The case was supervised by Sidley's main office in Chicago, but the firm needed someone in D.C. to visit several East Coast Borden facilities, interview engineers, and inspect company documents. That someone was me. What a surprise: A decade earlier the Borden plant in suburban Boston had been one of my Uncle Bill's plastic factories. Looking back, I wish I'd asked if it still made glue.

———◦•◦———

When I wasn't working on billable matters for Sidley, I was working on pro bono cases, including for my old friends at the Lawyers' Committee. After two years, those old friends wanted me back, this time as director of the *National* Lawyers' Committee. It was a promotion and a homecoming all at once.

In that role, I was responsible for raising funds from the big New York foundations like Rockefeller and Ford. I can't say fundraising was my favorite part of the job, but I was committed to the mission, and we needed money to accomplish it. Fortunately, there was much more to the job than fundraising. I thought it was important for lawyers in the national office to work closely with our local committees in places like San Francisco, Boston, Philadelphia, Washington, and my very own Chicago. We took on cases involving a range of issues, including employment, housing, school finance, and health care. I also did on a national scale what I'd done in Chicago: recruit law firms to take on civil rights cases. Most were in the South. Mississippi, a hotbed of racial discrimination, was our primary focus. Lawyers in our Jackson office pursued discrimination suits against the state's virtually all-white highway patrol, the infamous Parchman prison, and other state agencies that discriminated against Black citizens.

The Lawyers' Committee had two other big issues on its agenda: busing and South African apartheid.

Busing was one of the most divisive issues of the time. In 1971 the Supreme Court had ruled that in order to desegregate schools as required by *Brown,* federal courts could order busing.

No sooner than the ink on that opinion was dry, Congress took up legislation to prevent the courts from doing just that. The Lawyers' Committee opposed that bill. For us, the issue was as much about judicial independence as it was about desegregation. When I appeared before the House Judiciary Committee with Lawyers' Committee cochair Lloyd Cutler (who would later play an important role in my nomination to the D.C. Circuit), we sat right next to Attorney General Richard Kleindienst. Cutler and I had recently met with Kleindienst, who explained to us why the Nixon administration was supporting the anti-busing bill and urged us not to get involved. Fortunately, the bill never passed. Kleindienst later pleaded guilty to failing to testify "accurately and fully" about a corporate contribution to Nixon's campaign. How many civil rights organizations can boast dealings with not one, but two corrupt Nixon attorneys general?

The Lawyers' Committee Southern Africa Project was an effort to apply the lessons we'd learned fighting Jim Crow in the US to fighting apartheid in South Africa. Despite its unconscionable system of apartheid, South Africa did have a functioning legal system and a community of lawyers ready, willing, and able to defend apartheid opponents like Nelson Mandela, Steve Biko, and Oliver Tambo. With support from the Ford Foundation, we underwrote their efforts.

We didn't just write checks. In 1974, Edie and I left our then-three little kids with her sister Ruth and traveled to South Africa as part of a biracial group of lawyers. Our goal? To encourage the Johannesburg Bar to create an organization like the Lawyers' Committee to provide pro bono legal services. At the Johannesburg airport, security officials separated our Black colleagues from the group and made them travel to the city in separate taxis. Each was then officially designated an "Honorary White," which meant they could stay in the same hotel and eat in the same restaurants as us for the duration of their stay. Edie and I were appalled and could only imagine how it must have felt for them to be declared "white" for the week. We went along because we believed it was the best way to promote change.

During our trip, we met with Arthur Chaskalson, a brilliant young lawyer who was representing Nelson Mandela, then imprisoned at Robben Island. Twenty years later President Mandela appointed Chaskalson chief justice of the Constitutional Court of South Africa. We also met a *Rand Daily Mail* columnist who asked us to deliver some papers to a *New York Times* reporter during our return stopover in Nairobi. Feeling like characters in a John le Carré novel, we accepted the mission and handed the papers to *New York Times* reporter Charles Mohr. Coincidentally, Charlie and his wife Norma later became our next-door neighbors in Maryland (more about Norma later). We had no idea what was in that envelope. Like good spies, we never asked, but Charlie assured us that the information we had delivered was critical to an important story he was writing.

In addition to working on those big political issues, I took every chance I got to work alongside some of the nation's finest trial lawyers as they litigated civil rights cases across the country. Watching them in action taught me so much about how to question witnesses—what to ask, and what not to ask. It also taught me that lawsuits are both dramas and sagas. By drama, I mean that a lawsuit isn't a dry, theoretical exercise. It's a contest. To win, you need to tell a story to convince someone—be it a judge, a panel of judges, or a jury—to care about the legal issues and ultimately to see them your way. By saga, I mean that each case traces its own meandering path, moving from a trial court to an appeals court, maybe to a state supreme court, and perhaps even to the US Supreme Court. Some lawsuits take more than one trip up and down the legal ladder. The whole thing can take years.

Litigation is not for the impatient, the faint of heart, or the financially strapped. All this I learned at the feet of the masters.

Of all the big cases I worked on at the National Lawyers' Committee, it was one of the smallest that was personally most meaningful. In Opelika, Alabama, a little city in the middle of the state, pregnant public school teachers were forced to quit when they began to "show." Although Edie never taught in Opelika, Chicago Public Schools had the exact same policy, and she would have been fired during her first pregnancy had she still been working there. Our class action lawsuit in Opelika brought that nonsense to an end—at least there. Not only that, but the judge who ruled in our favor was the great Frank Johnson, whose judicial career has always been a bright beacon for me.

As you by now understand, I grew up in the Lawyers' Committee. It was where I refined my legal skills and where I found many of my lifelong mentors and role models. It was also where I met the senators, civil rights leaders, members of the Kennedy and Johnson administrations, and future members of the Carter and Clinton administrations who were so consequential twenty years later when I was being considered for the federal bench. More advice to young lawyers: Attach yourself to an organization whose mission you care about and where you can find mentors and role models. They will inspire you, give meaning to your career, and help you down the road in ways you can't possibly anticipate.

———

After two years with the National Lawyers' Committee, another opportunity came knocking. It was Hogan & Hartson (now known as Hogan Lovells), one of Washington's oldest and most prominent law firms, and they wanted me to work in their pro bono practice. The offer was irresistible—again, right place, right time—and a logical next step. Hogan was the first major firm to establish a separate practice group devoted exclusively to pro bono work. They called it the Community Services Department (CSD), and it was truly groundbreaking. While lots of law firms, including my old firm Sidley, did pro bono work, only Hogan had a dedicated staff—at that time, a partner and two associates—working exclusively on pro bono cases. Its first leader, John Ferren, had founded a neighborhood law office for low-income clients while teaching at Harvard Law School. At Loeb's Delicatessen on 15th Street, home to D.C.'s best roast beef sandwiches and biggest chocolate chip cookies, John and I sealed the deal. I was headed back to private practice.

For the next few years, until Jimmy Carter took office in 1977, Hogan's Community Services Department was my home. It was the best of both worlds, allowing me to do the kind of work I'd done at the Lawyers' Committee but with the resources of an elite law firm. And I didn't have to do any fundraising! I took referrals from my old friends at the Lawyers' Committee, found my own civil rights causes to pursue, and, best of all, had two gifted associates working with me full-time—plus many others who weren't part of the Community Services Department but who took on pro bono cases in their spare time. And for the first time, I wasn't in just a coordinating role or playing second fiddle to a law firm partner who was leading the charge. Now *I* was that law firm partner.

I worked on many significant cases during my time at Hogan, but by far the most important arose from an economic boycott in Port Gibson, Mississippi. That case ultimately made it all the way to the Supreme Court. Even compared to Cairo, Port Gibson had a melancholy history. It was the town that General Ulysses S. Grant, during the Vicksburg campaign of the Civil War, proclaimed "too beautiful to burn." Those words appear throughout Port Gibson even now, including on every police uniform.

Beautiful as it was, Port Gibson had an ugly side—a long history of blatant racism. On the eve of the Civil War, enslaved residents outnumbered the free four to one. A century later, as the *Washington Post* described it, "unemployment, inadequate housing, and intimidation of voters were the order of the day" for the town's Black residents.

In the 1960s, the NAACP organized economic boycotts of white merchants across Mississippi. In Port Gibson they focused on businesses that refused to hire Black employees and to call Black patrons by normal respectful titles like "Mister," rather than "Boy." Among other things, they demanded the desegregation of the schools and county hospital, the hiring of Black police officers, and the selection of Black people for jury duty. The boycott had its intended effect, hitting racist business owners where it hurt. George Hudson, who owned Piggly Wiggly, the largest grocery store in town, complained to the *New York Times*, "We're not getting any colored trade." Instead of acceding to the NAACP's demands, Hudson and the other merchants fought back. Supported by the White Citizens Council (a country club version of the Ku Klux Klan), a group of local businesses—four grocery stores, two car dealers, several variety, hardware, and auto parts stores, as well as a gas station, a pharmacy, a laundry, and a liquor store—filed a multimillion-dollar antitrust case against the NAACP and 146 individual picketers. Their boycott, the merchants argued, was an anticompetitive conspiracy that interfered with their lawful business activity.

That was the setting of my next act. The dramatis personae included the boycotters themselves, mostly poor, many unemployed, and all struggling under the weight of Mississippi's harshly segregated society. Julia Jones was the daughter of sharecroppers. Frank Davis worked at the Piggly Wiggly until George Hudson fired him for showing up late because of the boycott. Then there was Charles Evers, the NAACP's field secretary in Mississippi. Evers helped organize the boycott. He was also the brother of the assassinated civil rights leader Medgar Evers. Before assuming his slain brother's role, Charles Evers had been a bootlegger, a racketeer, a disc jockey, and a brothel owner in the Philippines. Years later, he would endorse Ronald Reagan and Donald Trump.

A central actor in the show was Dixon Pyles, the lawyer representing the merchants. Decades earlier, Pyles had helped defend Willie McGee, a Black man convicted of raping a white woman. At the time, Pyles was affiliated with the National Lawyers' Guild, an organization accused during the McCarthy era of being allied with the Communist Party. (I can't imagine there were many lawyers who worked for both the National Lawyers' Guild and the White Citizens' Council.) After two retrials, McGee was sentenced to death and executed by the state of Mississippi. The case sparked international outrage because of doubts over his guilt and because every member of the juries that convicted him was white. It was hard to believe that the defender of Willie McGee was the same Pyles I saw in action in Mississippi. He had been hired because of his experience representing striking union members, which made him an expert on boycotts. And he seemed to have no problem switching teams. He was a thoroughly practical man. "The only thing I can't forgive in a client is insolvency," he said.

As it turned out, this was no one-act play. The merchants had filed their lawsuit in 1969. They wanted the boycott to stop and, of course, they wanted money—in particular, the earnings they claimed they'd lost when the boycott had its intended effect. Seven years later, after nearly eight months of trial and testimony from 144 witnesses, a state judge ruled that the boycott had been unlawful and had interfered with the merchants' businesses. For their trouble, the judge awarded them $1.25 million, a financial hit that threatened the very existence of the NAACP. A *New York Times* editorial called it "the judicial equivalent of an old-fashioned Mississippi lynching."

The verdict came as no surprise. The NAACP knew from the very start that it was doomed in the Mississippi courts, where many judges ran for election on openly racist platforms and rubbed elbows with the very merchants who'd filed suit. But it believed it could get that verdict overturned in an appeals court, where the judges acted more like judges and might recognize that its boycott was lawful—and, indeed, protected by the First Amendment. The problem was getting there, which is why I first entered the scene.

Under Mississippi law, the NAACP could appeal only if it posted a bond equal to 125 percent of the judgment within thirty days of the verdict. That meant it would have to put down more than $1.5 million in cash to exercise its right to judicial review of the verdict that had been unfairly entered against it. The NAACP didn't have anything like that kind of money, despite a major public fundraising campaign, a $100,000 contribution from Muhammad Ali, and hundreds of envelopes that arrived in the mail from supporters, each containing a few dollars in cash. The trial had been well handled by a fine team from the Lawyers' Committee, who'd simply run up against a biased judge. The NAACP wanted help. It needed lawyers who could come up with some creative way to get them the appeal they deserved without bankrupting the whole organization. They asked my good friend Jim Robertson and me to step in.

We jumped at the chance. Jim was another lawyer who had responded to JFK's clarion call. Inspired by the Lawyers' Committee and its mission, he left his law firm, moved his entire family to Jackson, and became the Lawyers' Committee's chief counsel in one of its most important battlegrounds. "I wasn't a radical or a long-haired hippie," Jim liked to say. "I was the delegate from the establishment who believed in the rule of law." Jim was another person whose path crossed mine more than once. Years later, Jim, like Lou and me, became a federal judge in Washington.

We put our heads together and worked out a plan. This was about something bigger than one problematic verdict; it was about access to the legal system for *all*, regardless of the amount of money someone happened to have in their bank account. That's what we planned to argue in the Mississippi Supreme Court. But given the hostility of the state's courts to anything civil rights—and especially anything involving the NAACP—we knew federal court was our only hope. So that's where we planned to file if (or, really, when) the Mississippi courts rejected our argument.

Jim and I spent a few weeks in D.C. drafting the briefs for the Mississippi Supreme Court and the pleadings we knew we would have to file in federal court. Our legal theory was that the bond requirement violated the NAACP's First Amendment rights to protest and to access the courts for redress. To help explain why that mattered, our written submissions included a sworn declaration from Daniel "Chappie" James, the Tuskegee Airman who became the first African American to reach the rank of four-star general. In 1945, James had led a group of young Black Air Force officers in an unsuccessful attempt to integrate an all-white officers' club. The NAACP had defended them on various charges and saved their careers. There was no better way to dramatize the importance of the NAACP's work.

Days before the filing deadline, Jim and I flew to Jackson to meet with our team, which was headquartered in a former grocery store. We were ready for battle. On the day the bond was due, Jim made our First Amendment argument to the Mississippi Supreme Court. He did as well as anyone could have. But we lost, just as we'd anticipated. By then, two of our lawyers and I were already racing across the Mississippi Delta in an Avis rental car (with me riding shotgun), arriving in Oxford just in time to file a motion for emergency relief and argue our case at the federal courthouse. We were trailed the entire way by an ABC-TV van. This time, it was my turn to argue. And this time, we won. Judge Orma Smith issued an order that excused the NAACP from posting the massive bond until he could sift through the merits of our claim and determine whether the bond requirement was constitutional. It likely helped that the Justice Department—President Nixon's, no less—had notified Judge Smith that it agreed with our position. This only confirmed Dixon Pyles's view, as he told the judge, that the Feds "treated Mississippi as a conquered territory." The night before, I'd overheard the hotel's desk clerk ask Pyles how he planned to argue the case. (Oxford was a small enough town that we were all staying at the same place.) "I'm going to stand up and moan and groan," he replied. That's about what he did.

Quite apart from Judge Smith's ruling, I was struck by his kindness to me during my court appearance. I still wasn't using a white cane and was doing everything I could to downplay my vision problem. Our lawyers in Jackson had figured it out. Unprompted, some of them even read papers aloud to me. I still rang up large phone bills back to D.C., where my secretary handled most of the reading and all my dictated memos. To help me prepare for the argument, she had recorded onto cassettes the contents of key documents. I'd memorized most of them, along with the relevant statutes and key cases.

When the clerk called our case, I walked to the lectern, holding the sleeve of one of my colleagues. I presented my argument without notes and answered Judge Smith's questions. It was the most important argument of my career, and my voice trembled as I tried to convey how much was on the line for the NAACP, for the First Amendment, and for the legal system more broadly. The work I'd put in committing everything to memory gave me confidence. I knew the answer to every one of Judge Smith's questions.

When he granted our motion at the end of the hearing, Judge Smith asked that I prepare an order for him to sign. It needed to be done quickly because the bond was due in just a few hours, so his law clerk invited us to use the judge's private library. I accepted, we drafted the order, and handed it to the clerk, expecting the Judge to make whatever revisions he wanted and issue the order. But that isn't what happened. A few minutes later the clerk invited us into Judge Smith's chambers. Greeting us with a friendly "Hi," Judge Smith explained that he'd made some minimal changes to the order. Instead of just showing us those revisions, he read the revised order aloud. He must have noticed that I had been helped to the lectern, and that when we entered chambers I continually touched my colleague's elbow. He said not a word about it. I was appreciative as much for his grace in handling the situation without comment as for his kindness in reading the order aloud.

Judge Smith was another of those principled and courageous Southern judges who enforced the Constitution and the civil rights laws even at great personal risk. There's a story about Judge Smith that says a lot about the man. When he first took the bench, he referred to Black people in his courtroom as "nigras." He presumably didn't think twice about it, any more than most white people in Mississippi did at the time. But when later presiding in a different case, he noticed that Aaron Henry of the Mississippi NAACP (later one of my Port Gibson clients) seemed uncomfortable at the mention of the word. The judge took him aside to ask what the problem was. "Judge, you can't call Black people that," Henry said. Judge Smith never used the word again. Would that all judges, and justices, rise above their own biases in the performance of their judicial duties. What a privilege to appear before someone who lived that ideal.

As a consequence of Judge Smith's ruling, which he eventually made permanent, the NAACP and the boycotters were able to appeal the antitrust judgment to the Mississippi Supreme Court. Yet again, that court ruled against them. They were vindicated six years later, however, when, in the summer of 1982, the US Supreme Court ruled that boycotts in the service of social justice and human rights are protected expression under the speech, assembly, and petition clauses of the First Amendment. The case, *NAACP v. Claiborne Hardware*, stands as an unequivocal affirmation of First Amendment rights. "One of the foundations of our society," wrote Justice John Paul Stevens for the Court, "is the right of individuals to combine with other persons in pursuit of a common goal by lawful means." After all, that is exactly what the colonists did when they boycotted the Stamp Act of 1765 and the Tea Act of 1773. Like those revolutionary protests, the Port Gibson boycott "included elements of criminality and elements of majesty." It was constitutionally protected speech through and through.

I'd helped with some of the Supreme Court briefing but watched from the sidelines as Lloyd Cutler brilliantly argued the case. The Court's decision was announced the same day that three thousand delegates had gathered for the NAACP's seventy-third national convention in Boston. "Members joyfully and tearfully transformed their meeting for a time into a cross between an emotional church service and a rowdy political convention," the *New York Times* reported. "As delegates sang 'We Shall Overcome,' Mississippi members paraded through the aisles and up to the stage, holding high a signpost bearing the name of their state. Then, with a flourish, the organist played 'Amazing Grace.'"

Amazing indeed. Not only did the Port Gibson boycotters prevail in the Supreme Court of the United States, but they also prevailed in Mississippi. Thanks to the powerful Voting Rights Act of 1965, two boycotters were elected to positions in Claiborne County that Black people had not held since Reconstruction: Julia Jones as circuit clerk and Frank Davis as sheriff.

More than forty years later, *Claiborne Hardware* endures as a touchstone of the unique American right to protest enshrined in our Constitution's very first amendment. Over the years, the Supreme Court has announced many important First Amendment rulings that have protected and defined the essence of our free society, from guaranteeing the right to criticize the government even during wartime, to protecting the right to burn the American flag. *Claiborne Hardware* belongs in that pantheon.

The part I played in *Claiborne Hardware* remains one of my proudest accomplishments. At one point, I even considered moving my family to Port Gibson so I could write a book about the case. I didn't get much further than the title: "Too Beautiful to Burn." Publishers didn't bite, but at least I got a chapter title for this memoir. I've never forgotten my time in Mississippi. A few years ago, I returned there with Edie as part of a civil rights tour of the Deep South. In addition to Birmingham, Montgomery, Selma, and Memphis, we visited Oxford, where my old friend Curtis Wilkie, the respected journalist and historian of the South, arranged for us to visit the courthouse where I'd appeared before Judge Smith.

We found that times have changed. The federal courthouse now belongs to the town, and the courtroom is used for traffic cases. Even so, it gave me goose bumps to be back in the building where many years ago I'd fought so hard for something I'd deeply believed in. Standing again at the lectern, now completely blind, I was reminded of what motivated me all those years ago: those courageous lawyers in the Kennedy Justice Department who had fought for justice in Mississippi and Alabama, sometimes in this very courtroom. It reminded me of why President Kennedy had challenged the legal profession to create the Lawyers' Committee in the first place. When Jim and I worked on the Port Gibson case, we were partners in major law firms, using the resources of our firms to defend the constitutional rights of the NAACP and the Port Gibson boycotters. We were heeding the President's call.

CHAPTER 7

"Those Who Have and Those Who Have Not"

BY 1974, I HAD BEEN LEGALLY BLIND FOR OVER A DECADE. BE-cause I still had some peripheral vision, I could usually get around on my own. But more and more, I needed to hang on to a companion's arm when navigating a new place or a busy street. Reading on my own was by then a thing of the past. The large fonts, thick black markers, and other tricks that had gotten me through school were no longer enough. Now I relied on my secretary to read material aloud to me.

Despite my ever-shrinking visual field, I still kept up the ruse that I was just like everyone else. And most of the time, I still got away with it. My family of course knew, and most everyone at the Lawyers' Committee had figured it out. But I hadn't yet accepted the fact that I had a disability, and I certainly didn't want the world to see me that way. For that reason, I absolutely refused to use a white cane. I was well past the point at which I needed one to navigate safely. But tapping a cane in front of me felt like making an official announcement that I was blind, and I wasn't ready to do that. Did I fear that people would treat me differently if I used a cane? Yes. Did I fear that if I used a cane I would have to acknowledge that someday I would be totally blind? Maybe. Was holding off on getting a cane doing a number on my shins? Absolutely. Trying to piece together my mental and emotional state during that period is difficult. Hindsight is twenty-twenty, but memory isn't. I think the truth is that I was deeply in denial and just trying my best to get through each day as it came.

Anyway, my limited vision wasn't limiting my professional dreams. To the contrary, as my vision clouded, the path I wanted to pursue was only becoming clearer. Fully committed to the cause, I'd just won one of the most significant cases of my career. It felt like I was gaining steam. Beginning with my summer jobs in the Kennedy administration, I'd always wanted to pursue civil rights work from within the government. But with Richard Nixon in office, there was no place in his administration for either civil rights or me. Besides, I was happy at Hogan, where I was making more of a difference from my post in private practice than I'd ever thought possible. Even so, I still believed in the power of government to do good and hoped that someday I'd get the chance to be part of it.

That opportunity came sooner, and in a different form, than I'd expected, at a place called the Legal Services Corporation (LSC). The mission of the LSC—an independent nonprofit created by Congress and run with government funds—was to ensure that the poor had access to the civil legal system, just like the wealthy. But the LSC had a target on its back from the start, and before it could begin fulfilling that mission, it had to weather a barrage of political attacks. That's where I came in.

But I'm getting ahead of myself. To understand the political fight that consumed the early years of the LSC, you need to know where it came from. The LSC has its origins in President Lyndon Johnson's War on Poverty. In service of that "war," Congress created the Office of Economic Opportunity (OEO), a new federal agency intended to improve and coordinate health care, education, employment, and other social services for the poor. It was a nice idea, and some of its programs continue today under the auspices of the Department of Health and Human Services. But improving the lives of America's poor is a big job. OEO's first director, Sargent Shriver (JFK's brother-in-law), recognized that ensuring access to legal services was an indispensable piece of the project. After all, what good are laws and regulations intended to benefit the poor if the people they're intended to help have no means of enforcing them?

Historically, Legal Aid Societies around the country were both scarce and poorly funded, so OEO set up a network of publicly funded neighborhood law offices. Hundreds of lawyers began representing poor people in their disputes with landlords, stores, hospitals, banks, and government agencies, to name just a few. In addition to those neighborhood offices, OEO established about a dozen "backup centers" that concentrated on substantive legal subjects. Often housed in welcoming law schools, the backup centers included the Center for Law and Education at Harvard, the Youth Law Center in San Francisco, the National Senior Citizens Law Center in Los Angeles, and the Indian Law Support Center in Boulder. These centers were vibrant intellectual hotbeds of reform where subject-matter specialists developed creative, big-picture strategies and worked together with lawyers in neighborhood law offices as they assisted people with their day-to-day problems.

Shriver saw civil legal assistance as a means to an end: the end of poverty. Running OEO, he said, gave him "a new appreciation of the contribution legal services can make not simply to get poor people out of a specific jam but to get poor people out of poverty once and for all." Shriver's recognition that lawyers had a role to play in ending poverty echoed what Louis Brandeis, the great Boston lawyer and future Supreme Court justice, had said in 1905. Fearing that lawyers had "allowed themselves to become adjuncts of great corporations," Brandeis warned of an "ever-increasing contest between those who have and those who have not" unless lawyers started fulfilling "the obligation to use their powers for the protection of the people." The new network of neighborhood law offices and backup centers was the government's attempt to shift the balance of power.

A power shift, however, wasn't good news for those who benefited from the status quo. Shriver's new interest in federally funded legal services was controversial from the jump. He had plenty of support, including from the American Bar Association, which, despite considerable internal opposition, had long supported federally funded legal services. The ABA president at the time was Lewis Powell Jr., later appointed to the Supreme Court by Nixon. The epitome of the courtly Virginia gentleman, Powell was the kind of centrist, incrementalist, and institutionalist that defined Republican politics for decades. (Today, he'd be called a RINO.) With Powell's leadership, the ABA's efforts produced broad bipartisan support within the legal community.

Not everyone believed that giving poor people government-funded lawyers was a good idea. When legal services lawyers began suing government agencies and powerful corporations, political opposition grew. President Nixon wanted OEO legal services gone. "The idea that government would subsidize suits against the government is absolutely repugnant to me," he railed, "and I want nothing to do with it." He wasn't alone. Ronald Reagan rose to prominence in part by demagoguing "welfare queens" and the legal services lawyers who represented them. Reagan loved Big Agriculture almost as much as he reviled the farmworkers who picked grapes for it. And California Rural Legal Assistance—the bête noire of Reagan's gubernatorial tenure, as he told it—was funded by OEO.

To its credit, Congress stayed the course. In 1974, to insulate OEO legal services from political interference, it created the Legal Services Corporation, a private nonprofit corporation funded by the government but insulated from political whims. Embroiled in Watergate, President Nixon grudgingly went along, believing that an amendment to the bill would defund the pesky backup centers he so despised. He signed it the day after the Supreme Court ordered him to release the tapes that ended his presidency two weeks later.

The statute creating the LSC gave the new corporation ninety days to take over the legal services program from OEO. Reenter Louis Oberdorfer, then on sabbatical from his law firm, and me, then running Hogan's Community Services Department. The LSC's newly confirmed board asked Lou to serve as the organization's interim president, and me to serve as its general counsel. Once again, right place, right time. It wasn't the Justice Department's Civil Rights Division, where I'd always hoped to work. Nor was it technically even the government (despite its government funding). But it was a golden opportunity for Lou and me to help make the legal system work for everyone, and I didn't even have to leave Hogan to do it. So off we went on our next adventure.

Working with Lou in the LSC's threadbare Washington offices, I got to see how a real leader operates: gentle but indefatigable; always teaching, never lecturing; relentlessly "peeling the onion," as he put it, to get to the heart of an issue. He had a way of helping others recognize their own errors, instead of just pointing them out. You'd go in to see Lou, he'd softly ask some questions, and somehow by the end you understood exactly what was needed and walked away thinking that it had been your idea all along.

I had a lot to learn. I knew the civil rights laws backward and forward but hadn't spent so much as a minute counseling corporate clients. The single class I taught at Michigan about the nonprofit tax exemption, which I'd never imagined might come in handy, now seemed like my most relevant experience. Good thing I wasn't alone. Hogan had every kind of lawyer under the sun, and we needed their help to get the LSC up and running. The firm's corporate lawyers helped us draft our internal regulations. Its nonprofit and regulatory experts helped us figure out how to funnel congressional appropriations into the LSC's coffers. And its tax lawyers helped us put together the LSC's tax-exempt application, which I walked across town to hand-deliver to the IRS. It was exactly the kind of cross-disciplinary collaboration Hogan's Community Services Department was made for.

Sometimes, my own legal skills even came in handy. One early question was whether the backup centers could continue operating in light of the amendment Nixon believed would kill them. Determined to save the centers, I wrote an internal legal memorandum showing that the sloppily drafted amendment didn't preclude funding the centers after all. Sure, some who voted for the amendment—and the president who signed it into law—assumed that the language they'd chosen would defund the centers.

What mattered, I explained, were the words they actually wrote. And those words didn't cover the backup centers at all. I was a textualist long before the word became the clarion call of so-called legal conservatives. If Richard Nixon had still been paying attention, he would have been horrified. Several of the backup centers he so loathed remain alive and well today.

My Hogan colleagues and I also represented the LSC in a case involving an obscure legal question and a person who was not the least bit obscure. The obscure question was whether the president has constitutional authority to make "recess appointments" to the LSC's board—in other words, to appoint board members without Senate approval. The not-so-obscure person at the heart of the dispute was none other than Hillary Rodham Clinton. You see, Reagan had never let go of his enmity toward the LSC. "Of all the social programs growing out of the Great Society," *Time* magazine wrote, "there is none that Ronald Reagan dislikes more than the Legal Services Corporation." In 1982, he made a series of recess appointments in an attempt to weaken the LSC by replacing board members dedicated to its mission with others committed to its destruction. Clinton was one of the dedicated ones, and Reagan wanted her gone.

We sued on behalf of Clinton and the other board members Reagan sought to replace. We argued that because the LSC was a private corporation, the president had no authority to make recess appointments to its board. The case ended up before the D.C. Circuit, the very court on which I'd later serve. But the court never had to rule because, by the time the case was ready for decision, Reagan had renominated the new board members, who were quickly confirmed by the Senate. Our recess appointment argument had become moot, and Clinton lost her board seat, much to the dismay of everyone at the LSC. Apparently Clinton never forgot it. At a White House reception seventeen years later, the First

Lady brought me over to meet the president. "Bill," she laughed, "this is the lawyer who lost that LSC case!"

———◦◦◦———

If there's a thread running through my career, it winds around the obligation of lawyers to ensure that everyone has access to our legal system. From Robert Kennedy's plea "Where are all the lawyers?" to my two stints with the Lawyers' Committee, to the Port Gibson case, to my judicial opinions concerning Guantanamo detainees you'll hear about later on, and even to the writing of this memoir, I've worked to make equal justice under law a reality, not just a mission statement. Creating the Legal Services Corporation was a step in that direction. Over the years, the LSC has helped countless mothers and children escape domestic violence, seniors keep their housing, consumers protect themselves from predatory lending, and veterans apply for disability benefits. Of course, Ronald Reagan wasn't the last of its political troubles. The LSC has never been given as much funding as it needs, and it has faced regular threats of defunding altogether. Donald Trump repeatedly called for its abolition. Even so, the LSC's value has become so widely accepted that its continued existence is no longer in question. I hope.

Despite the successes of the Legal Services Corporation and other organizations working to bring justice to those who need it most, we still have a long way to go. Today, 90 percent of low-income people who need the help of a lawyer still can't get one. In large part, that's a funding problem. The LSC needs much more money to serve all eligible clients. (The US spends far less per capita on public civil legal aid than many European countries.) It's also a problem because of the limits Congress has imposed on what LSC lawyers can do for their clients. For starters, they can't file class action, abortion, or certain desegregation cases;

they can't represent their clients in deportation hearings; and they can't petition Congress on behalf of their clients. Never mind that class actions are supposed to be a vehicle for bringing justice to the masses; that bodily autonomy and equal treatment are (or, at least in the case of bodily autonomy, were) constitutional rights; or that the legislature, like the courts, is supposed to be open to all.

In *Gideon v. Wainwright*, the Supreme Court, in one of its finest moments, ruled unanimously that the Sixth Amendment, which guarantees a right to counsel in criminal cases, requires the government to pay for a lawyer for any criminal defendant unable to afford one. That ruling transformed the criminal justice system for the better. Although public defenders are woefully under-resourced, they're there, seeking to ensure in every criminal case that the defendant has a voice and that the government respects that defendant's rights. Were I in charge of the world, I'd extend *Gideon* to civil matters, guaranteeing lawyers for poor people facing eviction, victimized by predatory lenders, or sued for failing to make car or medical payments, just to name a few. But courts can't make that happen because the Sixth Amendment says nothing about civil cases. Congress could do it, of course. But if Congress won't adequately fund the LSC as it is, there's no way it will take the leap to civil *Gideon*. Fortunately, some states and cities have taken up the fight. Most states, for example, provide counsel to indigent parents in custody cases, and some states and cities provide counsel to poor tenants facing eviction. That's a start, but nowhere near enough.

There is, however, an institution capable of ensuring that every poor person who needs a lawyer gets one: the legal profession itself. Unlike people who run airlines, deliver packages, make smartphones, or operate any other commercial business, lawyers must not measure their success merely by how well they serve those able to pay their bills. As officers of the court, lawyers have a broader responsibility to ensure that the courts work for everyone. In addition, lawyers enjoy a monopoly on the practice of law. No one can practice law who doesn't pass the examinations the profession administers and obey the ethical standards it establishes. With this great privilege, along with the enormous profits it yields, comes great responsibility. As gatekeeper to the legal system, the profession itself has an obligation to ensure that those gates are open not just to those who can afford to pay attorney fees, but to everyone entitled to the law's protection. Robert Kennedy said as much in a celebrated speech at the University of Chicago Law School at the end of my first year. Only when we've "created in fact a system of equal justice for all," he exhorted us, "will our profession have lived up to its responsibilities...to make law not only the guardian, but the agent of freedom." In photos of the event you can see a very young David Tatel in the back.

The suggestion that the legal profession should itself undertake to provide a lawyer to everyone who needs one is no pipe dream. According to the Census Bureau, the profession's gross revenues are approaching nearly half a trillion dollars a year. Just 0.3 percent of that—that is, three cents for every ten dollars earned—would enable the Legal Services Corporation to serve every client it now turns away. The country's hundred largest law firms alone could double the LSC's budget with contributions of less than half a percent of their gross revenue. And the $12 million in signing bonuses that law firms paid their newly hired Supreme Court law clerks in 2022 could have funded roughly 150 legal services lawyers in Washington, D.C.—enough to enable the program to handle another ten thousand cases in a single year.

Regardless of their political views, lawyers should be able to agree that access to the legal system ought not depend on the size of one's wallet. It is a bedrock American principle that we all enjoy the same rights—from the lofty, like the right to speak freely, to the more mundane, like the right to accurate Social Security payments. But rights are hollow promises if people can't go to court to vindicate them. How can we, as a society, insist that people resolve their disputes with each other and with their own government through the legal process, yet deny the poor access to the very system we insist they use? The rule of law cannot long live if it works only for the wealthy.

CHAPTER 8

Becoming Blind

THERE ARE FEW THINGS I LOVE MORE THAN READING, AND especially bedtime stories to our children and grandchildren. But by the mid-seventies, when I was director of the National Lawyers' Committee, I could no longer see the words on a page. As I faced the reality that I'd never be able to read on my own again, it felt like I was losing that part of my life forever. At work I had my secretary, who read briefs, cases, and other legal materials aloud. But asking her to read me a novel didn't seem like a particularly good use of her time. And while I'm sure my secretary was an excellent bedtime story reader, listening to her read children's books over the speakerphone to my kids and me wasn't exactly the kind of cozy experience I had in mind.

That's when I discovered free "Talking Books" produced by the Library of Congress. I could order them by mail, and they arrived in a box labeled "Free Materials for the Blind." At first, I resisted.

I still didn't think of myself as "blind" and didn't want to be using resources meant for actual blind people. But Talking Books were too useful to ignore. Vinyl records halfway between the size of a 45 and a 78, they played on a boxy green record player supplied by my local library. It was simple enough to use on my own, with a big on/off switch, an even bigger knob for volume, and a jack for headphones. Professional actors did the reading. All I had to do was put the record on the turntable, switch the thing on, and place the needle on the record. Some books came on five or six records. Robert Caro's *The Power Broker* needed dozens. Later the books came on floppy disks, then cassette tapes, then CDs, each format with its own new machine. Now, I download them wirelessly.

The Talking Books program dates to the 1935 Works Progress Administration under FDR—a wonderful example of the government helping people who need help. As my sight dimmed, I'd been reading fewer and fewer books. Talking Books changed the game. For the first time in a long time, I could read on my own.

It was actually even better than that. In the Department of Silver Linings, if I unplugged my headphones Edie and I could listen to audiobooks together. Now, of course, audiobooks are a huge industry, and many people experience the great pleasure of reading right alongside their family and friends—or while sitting in traffic. But back then, they were available to only a special few of us. Edie and I are always reading at least one book together when we're driving or walking or sitting by the fireside. It's like a book club, except that we're on exactly the same page and can pause anytime to discuss a particularly interesting passage.

Audiobooks also connected me intimately with my children and grandchildren, who've all become virtuoso listeners. What could be better than snuggling with a child in a cozy chair while reading *Make Way for Ducklings, Charlotte's Web,* or *The Chronicles of Narnia* through the speaker or a shared set of earphones? My grandchildren found untangling those annoying cords endlessly entertaining.

Shortly after Talking Books, I discovered the amazing Kurzweil Reading Machine, invented by computer genius Ray Kurzweil. It converted print into speech, which, at the time, seemed a miracle. The first machine, developed in the early seventies, was the size of a large Xerox machine and cost $30,000. Out of the question for me. But over time the machines got smaller and less expensive. Hogan ultimately bought me a $5,500 version that was the size of a desktop printer. To use it, I'd put a document or book face down on the glass plate, close the cover, push a button, and a synthetic voice would speak the words on the page. Then I'd open the lid and place the next page on the glass. It was slow going. But the machine worked quite well, except when it came to multicolumned pages, like those in *The New Yorker*, where the columns were so close together that the machine read right across each line, disregarding the narrow break between columns. Hannah Arendt was hard enough to read with her sentences in proper order. We fixed the problem by drawing vertical ink lines between the columns. Like most technology, the Kurzweil Reader became more advanced and user-friendly. It kept getting smaller and cheaper, too. Today it's a free app on my iPhone.

Around the time I got my first Kurzweil Reading Machine I finally bit the bullet and learned Braille. When I say it didn't come easily to me, I mean it. Law school was a breeze compared to trying to decipher the small raised dots on a page simply by sliding my fingers across them. Those dots represent letters of the alphabet, numbers, and punctuation. I needed to learn what each configuration represented, which was hard enough. Even harder (at least for me), was figuring out with just my fingertips what each configuration actually was. I kept having the same problem my Kurzweil Reader had with the *New Yorker* columns: I'd miss the place where one letter ended and the next began.

Exasperated but determined, I hired a tutor named Bertha. Every Wednesday afternoon, I took a taxi to her apartment in Langley Park, Maryland. We sat at her kitchen table with her furry guide dog, Tanya, at our feet. Our lessons reminded me of Hebrew School. I enjoyed neither, but I eventually got better at Braille than I ever did at Hebrew, though not by much. I could read the Braille labels on the boxes of Talking Books records, which was some help. Full sentences and paragraphs, however, still took forever to decipher. And by the time I reached the end of a paragraph, I'd usually forget how it began.

Bertha also taught me to type Braille, which was somewhat easier because I didn't have to decipher any raised dots with my fingertips. I learned on a ten-pound metal machine called a Perkins Brailler, which was sort of like a typewriter, but with six keys, one space bar, and a bell that dinged seven spaces before the end of each line. To type, I'd depress keys in combinations that signified letters. Just one key for "a," two keys at the same time for "b," a different two together for "c," and so on. I was more enthusiastic about my Braille typing lessons than my Braille reading lessons in part because I'd never learned to type on a standard keyboard. Back in the fifties, girls learned typing and boys took shop, so I learned to craft a top-notch walnut ashtray, which came in handy exactly never. But typing? No way.

Today, the iPhone is magic for people who are blind. (Apple paid me nothing to say that. And I mean no offense to other smartphone manufacturers. While I'm sure Google and Samsung's phones are also great for blind people, I've been an iPhone enthusiast for years.) The iPhone's VoiceOver function reads aloud everything that appears on the screen. With it, I can listen to newspapers and books, send and receive emails, and search the web. I activate VoiceOver in Settings, then control it by swiping and tapping the screen. Swiping right takes me from app to app; a double tap opens the app I want; a two-finger down swipe starts it reading; and a z-shaped squiggle is equivalent to the back button. I can speed up the reading, too. It's all unbelievably cool—and completely transformative for people who are blind. It's also free (well, "free" assuming you've already shelled out for the device), as VoiceOver comes embedded in every iPhone's operating system. That means I can use an iPhone right out of the box, just like a sighted person.

I sometimes think about how different my life and Edie's might have been if today's technology were available back then. As my vision waned, Edie, busy mothering our four small children, did much of the reading that Siri now does. We started bright and early each day with the morning papers. Until technology caught up, I'd gather them from our front porch every morning for Edie to read aloud to me. We'd usually get through the major news and editorial pages before the kids woke up. In the evenings, after the kids went to bed, we'd catch up on the newest magazines. I loved Edie's curating: she read aloud only what she knew interested me. Now, with the iPhone and other technologies, I can read by myself, though I skip *New Yorker* fiction unless Edie recommends it.

Throughout my thirties I was traveling a lot, usually on my own. This presented challenges—some comical, some dangerous. When I was at Sidley in Chicago, I regularly commuted to New York. I'd leave in the early morning and usually return to Chicago the same evening. I could manage the airport and taxis. When I stayed overnight, I always used the same hotel,

The Madison on Park Avenue, which had a brightly lit lobby and large numerals on the guest room doors. The bellhops and waiters all knew me. Even though I wasn't yet using a white cane, they lent a hand when they thought I needed it. They never asked, they just helped.

What I remember most about those New York trips were the flights home. Until 1970 United ran an all first-class Caravelle (a now-defunct French jetliner) that left Newark at 5 p.m. Hard to believe, but those flights were men-only. In its full-page newspaper ads, United called them "Executive Flights" and a "Club in the Sky!" Fasten your seat belts for the words that followed: "What we give men is an opportunity to get away from women. We don't regard it as segregation—we regard it rather as a little luxury." On board, the only women (all "stunning," according to my travel companions) were "stewardesses" who served martinis and sirloin and handed out the free cigars that everybody besides me happily accepted and then proceeded to smoke right there in the cabin. My clothes reeked for days. I never heard anyone complain about the smoke, much less the exclusion of women. Once, as we waited to board our flight to Chicago, a woman ran up to the gate hoping to nab an open seat. "I missed my flight," she told the gate agent. "Any chance I can get on this one?" "I'm sorry, ma'am," the gate agent replied. "This is a men-only flight." She didn't get mad. She didn't even seem surprised. She was just embarrassed about her mistake. "Oh, I'm so sorry," she said and hurried off in search of a flight that would abide her presence.

Finding airport pay phones (this was way before cell phones, of course) was a special challenge. At D.C.'s National Airport—which I knew cold, down to where each gate was for the cities I visited frequently—I got really good at detecting phone banks. As I walked down the concourse, I listened to the conversations and comings and goings around me. I'd stop when I could hear "telephone talk" along one side of the concourse. To find an empty phone, I'd linger behind the talkers, listening for a gap between them or else someone saying "goodbye." Lo and behold, I'd find myself a vacant pay phone.

Many times I needed help getting where I was going, and because I was never quick to ask for it, I often benefited from the kindness of strangers who noticed my plight. To all of those Good Samaritans who helped me get wherever I was going: Thank you. Over the years, there were truly too many to count. I'll give you just one example, someone who helped me find my way home from New York after my job interview with the National Lawyers' Committee.

I made it to the interview without a hitch. That was a flight I knew well, and when I landed at LaGuardia I grabbed a cab to the Bedford-Stuyvesant neighborhood of Brooklyn. I followed some other walkers into the building, where I met with the Committee's cochair, John Doar, who had run the Justice Department's Civil Rights Division under Robert Kennedy and who later was chief counsel to the congressional committee that recommended the impeachment of Richard Nixon. The trouble started as soon as I headed for home. I exited the building into a large plaza set back from the street. I tried to get my bearings by listening for traffic, but I was all turned around and couldn't find the curb. A teenage boy came to my rescue. "Hey, Mister," he asked, "what are you doing?" "I'm headed for the airport," I responded. "I'm trying to catch a cab." "Well, you won't get one here," he said. Apparently, I was nowhere near the road. But the young man offered to take me there.

I accepted, and we chatted along the way. We talked about the weather and sports. I didn't explain why I needed help, though he must have understood. When we got to the street, I held up my hand. My new friend got a kick out of that. "That's a garbage truck, man. And that one's a delivery van." He took me around the corner, found me a taxi, and said, "Good luck!"

I didn't know the young man's name, where he came from, or where he was going. But the encounter has stayed with me. Something about the way he treated me—like there was nothing wrong with me—stood out. I learned something about human kindness that day, and something about my own discomfort with blindness, too. I hadn't asked for help, and still couldn't bring myself to admit my condition to anyone, let alone to a stranger. Still, this teenager clearly understood that something was wrong, but he didn't ask. He just lent a hand.

———

People sometimes ask what I experience with my eyes open. What do I see? It's hard to explain. It's not total darkness. It's not a void. It's like a thick, drab fog. Sometimes I think I'm aware of light, particularly outdoors on a sunny day, although maybe what I'm perceiving is just the sun's warmth. I can't tell whether the lights in the house are on or off. I can't see shapes, faces, objects, or even movement. It's just the same thick fog, extending to infinity in every direction.

But I do know what many things look like because I had my vision for so long. I still have vivid visual memories of growing up: the gray mouse that met its demise in the trap in our pantry; the brown and white cow my grandfather slaughtered in his butcher shop right in front of me; my mother's long white Pall Mall cigarettes; the gigantic steaming locomotives at Union Station; Passover Seders with my aunts and uncles sitting around my grandparents' huge table; the gaudy circus next to the railroad tracks; the model boat with our handmade brass fittings and varnished deck; El Misti; that toaster! I can also still see images of my parents' love for each other: Dad tossing little Mom in the big waves of the Atlantic on the Jersey Shore; the two of them walking hand in hand on the beach; the candles they lit as they danced to "The Blue Danube" in our living room. All are lasting snapshots of my childhood. I draw on that glossary of images when I listen to others and conjure up a picture of what they're describing. After all, "seeing" happens not in our eyes, but in our brains.

For my entire adult life, Edie, whose shiny auburn hair and bright blue eyes are embedded in my memory, has been my Describer-in-Chief. We've spent so much of our lives together that we have a deep reservoir of shared experiences she can draw on to help me see what she sees. "The woman at dinner looked a lot like my sister," she might say. Or she might tell me that a sandy beach we're visiting is even whiter than our Bermuda honeymoon beaches, and that the sky is the same blue as her eyes. She can't describe everything, of course, so she focuses on the details she knows I'll find interesting, curating images for me in much the same way she once curated *The New Yorker*.

My children and grandchildren have been describing things for me since they were very little, and they've grown into full-fledged audible artists. They all have their own descriptive styles. "It's dark blue and light green mixed together. I don't even have that color in my crayon box," little Emily said as we stood hand in hand on the rim of Crater Lake. When Rebecca and I cross-country skied on the Mall, she painted the picture for me: "Dad, on our right there's a huge oak tree. Its branches look like arms reaching in every direction, and every black branch is piled with snow. It's just beautiful, all sparkling in the sun." My then-six-year-old granddaughter Maya, perched in my lap as we sat on the dock, cupped my ear with her little hands and whispered, "Poppa, *shhhhh.*

There's a mama deer across the pond with a tiny baby fawn. It's even smaller than my little brother." Later she sketched a picture of the scene and traced my finger along the lines she'd drawn.

When my family describes these images to me, in my mind I definitely see them. I see the brown and white cows on gently sloping hills, the fallen tree snags deep in the forest, the bright yellow daffodils along the side of the highway, the swooping heron at the pond at sunrise, and the distant mountains lit up orange at sunset. My whole family uses words precisely and even poetically, choosing just the right adjectives and adverbs to let me see what they see. Constantly describing the world that I can't see myself seems to have made them all into great describers — and terrific writers.

In 1991, with the help of my son Josh's precise narration, I was the scribe on a fantastic sailing adventure in the British Virgin Islands skippered by a good friend and crewed by his son, two nephews, and Josh. At the end of each day, I'd add to our ship's log from what Josh and the others told me, as well as what I could hear, smell, and feel — and whatever Blackbeard allusions I could come up with. Tapping away on my little Braille computer, I'd quiz the boys for more details, suggesting descriptions that they'd verify or refute. My log recorded, "A huge orange setting sun over sparkling turquoise seas ... endless white beaches ... hummingbirds in the trees ... an underwater array of blue and yellow zebrafish ... a dark, isolated cove that seems like the perfect spot for pirates." It was as if I'd seen those things myself. Being blind amid an all-male crew and their strewn laundry and beer cans also had its upside. "What you can't see can't bother you," I wrote in an entry intended for our absent women.

I've also been asked whether I dream in pictures. The answer is yes. In most of them, my vision is twenty-twenty, and I see the world in Technicolor. But in my nightmares, everything is black and white, and I'm blind and anxious, often about finding the right airport gate or getting lost in the dark.

———◆◆◆———

In writing this memoir, Edie and I have talked about my career, my blindness, and the effects of both of those things on our family more than we ever did in the past sixty years. I'm sorry to say that for *many* of those years, I was a far less attentive, empathetic, and forthright person than I hope I am now. Back then, I was consumed with becoming an excellent lawyer, meeting my mentors' expectations, and furthering the causes that I believed in. At the same time, it took an enormous amount of energy and effort—both deliberate and unconscious—to compensate for my waning vision. And the less I could see, the less I was able to help with even the small things around the house. I relied entirely on Edie to tend the home fires, which she did so well, and which allowed me to enjoy my time with the kids when I was home.

Edie thinks that as the women's movement of the 1960s and '70s unfolded, we were lucky that she was content to focus on parenting while our kids were young. "Maybe it wouldn't have worked if we both were Type A professionals intent on establishing ourselves right then," she says. She kept on teaching part-time through the births of our first three children. But after our fourth child, even part-time work became impossible to manage, so she gave up teaching for a time, and with it, her professional identity. None of that was easy. For a while she felt like she was known only as "David's wife" and "the kids' Mommy," roles she adored, but which defined only a small part of who she is. Of course, she eventually made many new friends and carved out a meaningful life of her own. She never forgot her professional passions and the difference she wanted to make in children's lives. When the kids were older, Edie returned to school for her PhD, and Dr. Tatel resumed teaching, this time at the university level. Then for years she worked as a teacher coach.

Edie is a very social person, but she's also very private. Although she did confide her occasional despair to her sisters, few others would have suspected how much she was going through. Parenting four small children is hard enough. Add to that mix a husband who not only had an extremely demanding work and travel schedule but who also needed more and more help and you'll begin to understand what Edie was dealing with. One of the few times she brought up her worries with a good friend, it convinced her that most other people just didn't understand. When a recent eye exam disclosed that my vision loss was accelerating, Edie called her friend that evening and tried to express her anguish. "Oh, I know just what you mean," the friend replied. "My husband can't see very well, either, without his glasses." She offered no shoulder to cry on. She asked no questions. That good friend was demoted to the reserve list.

So my disability was not mine alone. We shared it. Edie, our children, and eventually their spouses and our grandchildren—we were all in it together. It touched all of our lives. It was simultaneously a challenge and completely normal. Edie and I were both aware of—and worried about—the hassles and hazards we faced every day. At the same time, our adjustments became routine, and often even unconscious. Our kids, of course, knew nothing else. Blindness bound us tightly together. We read together. We walked together—a "Dad Walk," the kids called it. We held hands. We *still* hold hands. When Vixen isn't guiding me, even my youngest grandchildren naturally reach for my hand.

I adored taking my kids with me on business trips. They each came with me to New York. The shuttle flights that had become routine to me were thrilling to them. Even the taxi rides into the city excited them. We went to the top of the Empire State

Building, found Eloise at the Plaza, watched the skaters at Rockefeller Center, and navigated lunch at the automat. Those times together were precious. As we walked through the city, I trusted them completely. We'd navigate together, with the kids confirming the numbers on the street signs we passed. When it came time to cross, I'd remind them to look both ways. When they said they were sure it was safe, we stepped out together into the street. My life was quite literally in the children's hands.

Over the years, we went on many other excursions where the children were my eyes. Rebecca led me on snowshoes across a frozen lake with little Olivia, our first granddaughter, marching behind in our tracks. Emily took me to the top of Pikes Peak. Josh guided me bouldering and rock climbing. Stephanie and I went camping in the Bitterroot Range. (We'd both thought Edie was coming, too, but she feigned illness at the last minute, which I learned years later had been her real plan all along.) Stephanie was totally in charge of the route, our meals, and me. Later she said that she hadn't been at all worried about my blindness, but the repeated lightning strikes up in the mountains had sure given her a fright.

As I look at my adult children today, I see Edie. They share her optimism, her cheerfulness, and most importantly, her amazing parenting skills. I couldn't be prouder.

I love Edie. Edie loves me. We love each other's varied interests, strong opinions, and boundless curiosity. We share hopes and dreams, fears and nightmares. We're in it for the long haul. But how wearisome it must be for Edie to live with this blind person! The nuisances are both tedious and maddening, petty and profound. Just ask her. She'll first focus on the bright side. You'll never catch me preening in the mirror, and I never criticize her clothes or hair or how dinner looks on the plate. But then again, I also can't say that her hair looks nice. I can't play pickleball or help choose paint colors or get her out of computer hell. I can't drive. Body language goes only one way, since she can see me but I can't see her.

But Edie doesn't feel sorry for herself at all. She's always seen the bigger picture—that life is uncertain, that there are many, many physical and mental conditions worse than blindness, and that all kinds of people live alone without anyone to compliment their clothes, hold their hands, or help choose a new rug. She likes to say, "We never know what's on the menu of life." Do you see why I love her so?

As saintly as Edie is, I can still drive her nuts when I yell for help with problems of my own making. Where are my shoes? (Unnecessary, if I'd put them away.) Are my socks the same color? (Unnecessary, if I'd kept the black socks and white socks in their separate drawers.) Where is the aspirin? (Unnecessary again, if I'd placed the bottle back on the shelf where it belonged.) And on, and on, and on. In fairness to myself, I'm usually super organized all day at work because I have to be. But I'm not always as careful at home. When Edie was getting our young kids ready for school and chaos reigned in the kitchen, it didn't help to have me hollering, "Where are my keys/headset/briefcase?" Living with me is definitely a challenge.

Edie and I sometimes wonder if everything she does to help me enables some of my bad habits. Perhaps so. But just as often as she says, "Let me help," she says, "Why don't you do it yourself?" When I need something that she's sure I can handle on my own, she'll say—sometimes with a smile in her voice—"David, pretend you're alone." She keeps reminding me that I'm not helpless. That push and pull is just part of our marriage.

———◦○◦———

Over the years, we've worked out strategies to make both of our lives easier. First and foremost, we try to make our home a predictable environment, which increases the chances I'll be able to navigate by myself. No cabinets left open to knock my head into. No shoes or dog toys on the floor. In our fridge, milk is always on the right; yogurt is on the top shelf to the right; fruit in the left bin, vegetables in the right bin; dog treats in the bottom right drawer. No containers left open to spill.

To reduce the hazard and frustration of knocked-over cups and shattered glasses, we found never-leak thermoses and heavy, broad-based coffee mugs that are really hard to knock over—though I've done it—and that I can microwave myself (I like my coffee very hot). We replaced my stemmed wineglass with a heavy lowball that has a fighting chance if it hits the floor, and we placed little sticky bumps onto pill bottles and the recycle bins. Then there are the dreaded touch screens. They're everywhere, and super frustrating for blind people. We try to make them usable by sticking bumps onto the microwave's "start" and "stop" buttons, the security system's control panel, the gym's elliptical and treadmill, and so on. But the bumps sometimes fall off, and when I encounter a new touch screen on my own, even Vixen can't help me.

Raised dots, especially raised Braille dots, do work fine on playing cards, though, and we buy decks that are already embossed. Even with my limited Braille skills, I can distinguish a four of hearts from a ten of spades. Until they become flattened, those dots let me play endless games of Go Fish, Cheat, and Texas Hold'em with the kids and grandkids. I'm particularly good at blackjack. On one family trip to Las Vegas, fifteen-year-old Emily and I went alone to the gaming floor. With no bumps on the cards, she acted as my eyes—which is why they didn't kick her out. I'd sold the outing to Edie as a chance to teach Emily the perils of gambling. We won ten hands in a row, and I split our $150 winnings with her. Some lesson.

As my eyesight waned, what really helped is how my memory developed. In the casino, I needed Emily to tell me only once what cards were in our hand. It became easier and easier to memorize long speeches, charts, and data. I could retain whole statutes and judicial opinions in my mind. If the person reading to me accidentally skips a paragraph, I notice. Frank Bruni had the same experience when he suddenly lost all the vision in one eye. Describing how his other senses took over, he wrote, "Parts of my brain had clicked into overdrive—as an adaptation to, and compensation for, the injury to my vision." The same thing happened to me. I find myself constantly marveling at the adaptability of the human brain. Shirley Hufstedler, a onetime federal judge and Secretary of Education (and who would've been President Carter's first nominee to the Supreme Court, if he'd gotten one), once graciously said of me: "Because he can't see people, he sees through them. He picks up nuances that those of us who are sighted cannot."

Of all of my workarounds, my ears are the most important. Sound is my best friend, and I thank my lucky stars every day that my hearing is as good as it is. The rhythm of traffic, the sounds of voices, the swish of an arriving subway train—such auditory cues substitute for visual ones. Sometimes, though, sound itself is a problem. In a Metro station, the PA announcements can be so loud that, before I got Vixen, it was hard to know when a train was arriving. Loud restaurants and parties, the noise of a crowd, a band, an air conditioner—they're all tough for me. With all that sound—and without access to the lip movements and facial expressions that sighted people depend on to decipher who's saying what—I can get pretty lost. Once, when I was overwhelmed by the din of a cheerful crowd to the point of feeling under attack, I found a wall and glued myself to it. I kept my phone to my ear, pretending to be talking. When Edie noticed where I'd gone, we swiftly found our coats and then the door.

As you've by now surmised, the toughest part of living with blindness—at least for me—isn't worrying about getting hit by a bus or falling down a flight of stairs. Those are genuine concerns, and I do worry about them. But it's the little stuff—like tripping on things, bending over to pat Vixen and smacking my face on a countertop, or bumping into a half-open door—that frustrate me the most. I truly hate half-open doors. The scars on my forehead bear witness to my many encounters with them. And then there are the small indignities that don't leave visible scars, but that hurt nevertheless. Store clerks, ticket agents, and flight attendants often treat me as if I'm invisible, speaking to Edie when they're really questioning me: "What size is he?" "Where would he like to sit?" "Would he like a safety demonstration?" It's as if being blind means I can't hear. A thousand times, Edie's replied, "Please ask him."

As I've grown more comfortable with my blindness, I've started asking others to make easy changes that would make life better for me and for others who can't see. (My teenage self could never have imagined.) Sometimes the results are delightful. I was so excited, for example, when baseball finally returned to Washington in 2005. The new Nationals Park was beautiful, and I couldn't wait to attend my first D.C. ball game in more than thirty years. But there was one big problem. When I turned on my transistor radio to hear the play-by-play commentary, I discovered that the Nats had introduced a fifteen-second delay, apparently to keep cussing by fans and players off the air. I'd hear the crack of the bat and the roar of the crowd, but not until fifteen long seconds later did I find out that Ryan Zimmerman had just hit a walk-off homer. Maybe it sounds like a small thing, but to me it was infuriating. Fifteen seconds is a long time to hear everybody screaming with joy while I have no idea what's going on. Of course, I could have asked my friends, but that's not the same. I'm a huge baseball fan and I wanted to be able to enjoy an afternoon at the ballpark just like everyone else.

I wrote letter after letter to the Nats. They never answered. Some time later, though, I happened to meet a member of the family that owns the ball club. After praising the team, I took my shot and told him about my problem with that darn fifteen-second delay. This was apparently the first he'd heard of it. He promised to look into it. I appreciated his hearing me out but didn't imagine much would come of it. To my great surprise, a few days later I got a call from a Nats vice president who said that if I let him know the day before I was going to a game, he'd get rid of the delay. It worked like a charm, and as far as I know, the FCC never complained. Now, in its gift shop, the team sells dedicated earpieces for any fan who wants to hear the play-by-play in real time. I take full credit for this brilliant technology.

———◈———

All the technology and adaptations are great. But they pale in significance to the power of my marriage itself. When Edie agreed to marry me, she didn't know — and couldn't know — what she was signing up for. She knew what I had told her: that I had an eye disease that probably meant I'd lose some vision and that causes blindness in some people. When she and I reflect on how we've endured, as we've done in constructing this chronicle, Edie says that even in times of family turmoil — and there certainly was some turmoil — it rarely occurred to her to abandon the marriage. For my part, it's impossible to imagine how I could have gotten by without her. Perhaps for that reason, I never entertained the idea that she might give up on me, despite the cascading burdens that I knew I imposed. We were in it for life. "Even if love doesn't conquer all," Edie says, "it helps a lot."

Edie and I have been at this so long that our ways of being together are both subtle and unconscious. Our friend Debby Shipler called it a dance. "When you see David and Edie walking toward you in a crowd," she wrote, "they step easily together, greeting friends. You see David greeting others by name. When you get closer, if you look carefully, you can see the quiet whisper that he hears. When you join them on an outing, David puts on his coat and walks to the door. If you're still looking carefully, you can see Edie's quiet hand on his back. When they walk down the steps, if you are very near, you might hear a whispered caution. But you must pay attention to see this lovely dance. It barely shows, yet happens, most likely, a thousand times a day."

That dance is one aspect of my blindness that's actually helped our marriage. Because I didn't have a cane for years and I didn't get Vixen for decades, it was Edie's hand that usually guided me on the street, through Back to School Nights, airports, and restaurants. Even if we argue during dessert, we still hold hands on the way out the door. It's tough to stay mad for long at the person you love if you're holding hands.

CHAPTER 9

Turning Points

T HE FIRST TIME I TOLD SOMEONE IN MY WORK LIFE ABOUT the possibility I might become completely blind was in 1974, during my job interview at Hogan & Hartson. Edie and I had discussed how I should handle the issue, and we both agreed that, for the first time in my life, I'd try just being open and honest. By that point, it felt like I didn't have much choice. But I'd carried the secret for so long and rehearsed the words so many times in my head that it felt like a relief to just say them. "I have retinitis pigmentosa, and I don't know how much longer I'll be able to see," I explained to the partner, Bob Kapp. I remember the conversation very well because it was so difficult, personally and professionally. It was a turning point. With those words, I abandoned my carefully nurtured identity as a person without a disability and acknowledged the reality that I might actually become completely blind.

I remember the exact words Bob said in response. He didn't ask whether I could do the work. He didn't pry. He didn't even seem to feel sorry for me. He asked just one question: "What help will you need?" Those five simple words changed everything. The defenses I'd hidden behind for so many years, the worry that my declining vision would prevent me from getting a good job — all gone in an instant. I explained that all I'd need was a full-time secretary who could also read aloud to me. "Consider it done," Bob replied. That's how I met Jana Frieslander, my invaluable secretary who would be with me for the next forty-three years, from Hogan to the Carter administration, and ultimately to the federal courthouse.

I just as distinctly remember returning home that evening to tell Edie what had happened, and our feeling of relief. At long last, I'd admitted my blindness to someone outside our little family bubble, and, in so doing, started on my long journey toward accepting it myself. I was thirty-two years old.

As I wrote this book, I asked some longtime friends when they first noticed that I had a vision problem. One college friend said she remembered when we were both sitting on the Diag — the large plaza in the center of Michigan's campus, and a social crossroads — and someone said hello. I had no idea who it was. At that moment it dawned on her that I had a problem with my eyes. Another Michigan friend wondered why I ignored a waiter standing at my elbow. Was David just absent-minded? Rude? Or was there an issue here? A fellow associate at Sidley recalled that he first noticed something was off when we were walking down busy La-Salle Street and I kept touching his arm with my elbow. He figured that it was the only way I wouldn't lose him. It was one of the clever ploys that I thought no one noticed. None of these friends, sensitive to my privacy, ever said a word about what they suspected.

People who knew me less well were more likely to have been tricked. Joe Rauh, a celebrated D.C. civil rights lawyer, met with me twice to vet me before I went to work for the Carter administration. Later, he told a reporter in amazement that he didn't know I had a visual disability. Countless others I came across professionally didn't catch on, either. My eyes looked just like anybody else's. I didn't wear dark glasses. I looked at the person I was talking to or at the object that was producing sound. My face was expressive. And with all my various tactics, I was good enough at evading detection that most people during the early years of my legal career never had any idea that I had a problem.

My deceit came at a cost. Indeed, some old friends I checked in with while writing this book said my behavior in those years sometimes seemed aloof or downright rude. One told me that when he went to shake my hand at the theater, I ignored him. "I thought that was quite odd," he told me, adding that "not until later did I realize that it stemmed from your visual disability." That story was no outlier. I'm sure there were countless unacknowledged handshakes, unanswered waves hello, and unreciprocated nods. I was so busy convincing myself that no one could tell what I was up to that I didn't realize I might be alienating or offending people I cared about.

Another turning point came on the ski slopes, of all places. Our children were home with Edie's mom, so it was just the two of us and the mountain for a whole week. The morning was magnificent, with bluebird skies and pillows of fresh powder blanketing the slopes. We rode the chairlift up the mountain from Snowmass Village. But as we started down Banzai Ridge, I realized I was having trouble seeing other skiers. They were like those little white dots in the peripheral vision test—sometimes visible, sometimes not. I pulled over to the side of the trail, and Edie stopped to see what was wrong. When I told her I couldn't make out the other skiers, she threw her arms around me. We stood absolutely still for minutes, holding each other close. Then, putting our skis into a beginner's snowplow, we inched our way to the bottom—the slowest, saddest, and, I feared, final ski run of my life. Edie and I were both devastated. I loved skiing. We loved skiing together. My whole life seemed to be headed downhill, and not down a ski slope. By the time we finally reached the bottom, I'd consigned myself to a week of reading in the Silvertree Hotel.

As luck would have it, though, Edie had just skimmed a hotel magazine article about a program for blind skiers called BOLD (Blind Outdoor Leisure Development). The program was brand-new, created by a group of skiers to assist Jean Eymere, a former member of the French ski team who had lost his sight due to diabetes and who ran a small hotel in Aspen. His friends were determined that blindness wasn't going to keep Jean off the slopes. BOLD's basic idea was as simple as it was, well, bold: A guide would ski behind the blind skier and call out turns; the blind skier just had to listen and follow instructions—instantly, without question. Edie gave them a call and the very next morning, Retired Colonel John Hayes knocked on our door. He'd been part of the storied 10th Mountain Division that skied across Norway during World War II. His command to us: "Let's go skiing!" And off we went. All the way down the mountain, John stayed right on my tail, shouting "Left...TURN!" "Right...TURN!" "Hard left!" "Easy right!" "Bump ahead!" "Stop!!" As Edie later put it, "BOLD swung open a door that we thought had slammed shut." By the end of the week, I was skiing confidently again.

Every BOLD skier wore a bright orange bib with BLIND SKIER emblazoned on it. The guide's orange bib read GUIDE.

Even so, not everyone got the message. One afternoon, after a fast trip down the Big Burn, John and I, both wearing our distinctive bibs, were greeted by a woman: "It's so nice to see you two blind guys skiing together!"

Nowadays most resorts have "adaptive" ski programs for disabled skiers. But back then, there was nothing like it. BOLD was a pioneer, and as one of their first participants, I was, too. For years I skied with John and other BOLD guides—until my kids Josh and Emily took over. When we glided off the lift, one of them would take my hand and draw on my palm a rough map of our route downhill. Then we'd set off, and they'd ski right behind me, shouting out turns. Later we used a two-way radio headset, which meant that nobody else on the slopes could hear their commands. They were amazing: Emily on her snowboard, and Josh on his telemarks. I couldn't see them, but I could feel their confidence and strength. Josh says he always felt privileged to ski with me. "What's better than a father's one hundred percent trust in his son? Plus we got to skip the lift lines, watch other skiers stare at us, and meet other ski guides, the coolest ski-bum dudes ever."

<hr />

Just as Jean Eymere's friends didn't let blindness stop him from skiing, my friends didn't let blindness stop me from running. I had begun jogging when Edie and I lived in Chicago's Hyde Park, but that didn't last long. One day, while running on 57th Street, I tripped and fell over a short iron lawn fence that eluded my peripheral vision. Scraped hands and knees warned me that my running career might be over before it had really begun. I didn't tell Edie about my accident, but I stopped running on sidewalks and streets. When we moved to D.C., I discovered I could run safely on the concrete track at the Y while Edie and the kids swam in the pool. It was perfect: There were no obstacles or traffic, and for a while I could make out the edges of the track where the cement changed to grass. Sometimes little Rebecca even ran a few laps with me.

My running world expanded dramatically when, through our babysitting co-op, I met Lawrence O'Rourke, the D.C. bureau chief of the long-departed *Philadelphia Bulletin*. Larry was an avid runner and offered to go running with me. Initially, we ran side-by-side as I held his arm, but we soon switched to tethering ourselves together at our elbows with a long shoelace. Larry would call out obstacles like curbs and potholes. In time we barely noticed the shoelace. Others joined us, including Peter Osnos of the *Washington Post* (and later, founder of *Public Affairs*), my internist David Lawrenz (everyone should run with their own doctor), a psychiatrist, a retired CIA agent, and a few others. We'd gather in front of my house at 5:45 a.m. and run for an hour, discussing politics, books, family, and the cosmos. We talked so loudly at that early hour that we got a few complaints from neighbors who heard us through their open windows. They could have come along! Dr. Lawrenz's scruffy mutt Dicey regularly accompanied us unleashed, a problem only when she wouldn't stay on the paths as we ran through fancy Chevy Chase Country Club. We ignored the club's warning to keep the dog off the greens until one morning when we found a Chevy Chase Village Police stakeout awaiting us. They warned us that if we entered again—with or without Dicey—we would be arrested. We found a new running route after that. Fortunately, this brush with the law didn't come up at my confirmation hearing.

Our group ran three marathons together—two Marine Corps and one New York City. When a cranky back ended my running career, I switched to swimming and, eventually, to long walks with Vixen. But the many years of early-morning running with dear friends helped prove that losing my sight wasn't going to be the end of the world.

―――――•◦•―――――

Other turning points in my life resulted directly from new technologies. Back in the Neolithic era, before the iPhone roamed the earth, the Dictaphone (for readers under forty, this onetime ubiquitous device was a small tape recorder) was considered high-tech. I got really good at it. For me it worked two ways: the regular way, which just meant dictating letters and briefs for my secretary to type; and the other way, which meant using it to listen to court decisions and memos that my secretary read aloud and recorded. I used that little machine with its tiny tapes for just about everything: to record my to-do list, to keep track of book recommendations, and to maintain time sheets.

Then came computers. Thanks to screen-reading software, many blind people use them with great ease and accuracy. But not me, because I never learned to type. Remember my walnut ashtray? Fortunately, Bertha had taught me to type Braille, so I could use a specialized computer made for Braille writers, which improved my life immeasurably. The Braille 'n Speak computer that our kids dubbed "Dad's Fisher-Price toy" was a purple machine about the size of a flat tissue box, with seven black rectangular buttons (six Braille keys and a space bar). It really did look like a kid's toy. As I typed, the machine spoke each word through either its speaker or my earphones. Its voice was high-pitched and tinny, but I got used to it. It was a vast improvement over the Dictaphone for taking notes, drafting memos and briefs, and maintaining my to-do list. My secretary and I could share materials, but the process was cumbersome, as everything first had to be copied onto a floppy disk. I ended up with piles of floppies stacked high on my desk, and struggled to keep track of which was which.

Although primitive, the Braille 'n Speak revolutionized my day-to-day life. I became so dependent on it that I started to worry about how on earth I'd cope if the company that made it stopped servicing it—or worse, since I wore them out and needed regular replacements, stopped selling them entirely. That dreaded day came sooner than I feared. For a few years I'd gotten by with a stash of used machines I'd bought on eBay and hoarded away in a file cabinet. I even found a fellow in rural New Hampshire whose hobby, oddly enough, was repairing Braille 'n Speaks. Roger was a computer wizard, but at some point even he couldn't keep my poor little old machines going.

The time had finally come for a new computer. For the non-typing visually impaired, a dwindling population, the brand-new VoiceNote was the latest and greatest in computing technology. It took me about two minutes with the machine to realize that my fears had been misplaced. Newer was, in fact, better. The VoiceNote did email, searched the web, and had a far better voice than the Braille 'n Speak. I relied on the VoiceNote for years before it, too, was orphaned. The company that made it stopped servicing it, and around the same time Google decided the device was too insecure to handle Gmail. I panicked. Without a computer, would I have to return to the old days of dependence on others? Another new device came to the rescue just in the nick of time. The BrailleSense is virtually identical to a PC except for the Braille keys and the voice reading everything aloud. I used my BrailleSense to write the very book you're now reading.

It's difficult to overstate the extent to which the world's transition to digital everything has given me reading independence. For example, using an iPhone app called Voice Dream Reader, on my own I can read articles, briefs, memos, and virtually anything else.

I can even read Supreme Court decisions—including reversals of my opinions—within minutes after they've been issued. The app reads it aloud to me at any speed, and in any voice I choose (lately I've been listening to "Alexander"). The voice is so authentic that I can hear the "reader" breathing. What a joy to be able to work on my own, especially in the middle of the night.

Thanks to a terrific service called Newsline, run by the National Federation of the Blind (NFB) and free to anyone with a documented medical need, I can read just about any newspaper or magazine whenever I want. Every night hundreds of newspapers and publications from around the world download their digital feed to an NFB computer in Baltimore. When I wake up in the morning, I open the NFB app on my iPhone and—presto!—my favorite newspapers are all there.

The papers also automatically download to my Victor Reader, another device I've integrated into my daily life. Slightly larger than a smartphone, the Victor Reader has physical buttons arranged like a telephone keypad, plus a few other keys for adding bookmarks, announcing the date and time, and finding text. I can easily move between and within publications by pressing the buttons. Number 6 takes me from newspaper to newspaper; 0 opens the newspaper I've selected; and once inside, 6 moves me from article to article. That's how I read my favorite papers, magazines, podcasts, and my huge audio library.

As a prodigious consumer of audiobooks, I have some pretty strong views about what makes for a good read. I greatly prefer readers who speak with clarity and fluency, but no excessive drama. I want the words on the page, not a theatrical performance. Just like a sighted reader, I want to interpret the author's words myself.

For new books, the best way to instant gratification is Bookshare (also free to the blind). When a book review lures me in, I can download the book immediately onto my iPhone or Victor Reader and start reading right away. It's a synthetic voice, but I use it so often that it's now an old friend.

Some technologies pair blind people with human volunteers in helpful ways. One of my favorites, Be My Eyes, connects sight-impaired people with one of millions of volunteers who help out during live video calls. I open the app, hit "Call a Volunteer," and within a minute or two a friendly voice says, "Hello, may I help you?" Before Vixen and I go out for a nighttime walk, I can ask, "Is Vixen's collar light on?" and the volunteer, looking through my iPhone camera, can tell me yes or no. I can ask if I'm about to open a bottle of aspirin or acetaminophen, if this tie goes with that shirt, or if my shoes are the same color. The volunteers are cheerful and the service is completely free. Be My Eyes recently added a new function, Be My AI, powered by Chat GPT-4. I take a picture with my cell phone and within seconds a clear synthetic voice describes the scene in detail. "The picture shows a German shepherd dog lying on a blanket with a pastel-colored pattern. The dog appears relaxed and is looking toward the camera with its mouth slightly open, as if it's panting or smiling. The blanket is on a wooden floor, and behind the dog there is a dark wooden cabinet and a red armchair. The room gives a cozy, lived-in feel." Through a chat function, I can follow up with a question. "Where is the dog's bowl?" Within seconds, it answers, "The dog's bowl is not visible in the picture provided. Would you like to take another picture that includes the area where the bowl usually is?" I take another picture, and AI finds the bowl. Amazing, and so helpful.

One of the very best new technologies is one I get to use only once a year. It has to do with voting. For decades, I could vote only with the help of an assistant. There was no way I was going to vote with a stranger, so Edie always stepped in to help. After signing an affidavit swearing that she wouldn't influence my vote, she'd accompany me into the voting booth, read the names of all the candidates and issues, and vote as I directed. I love spending time with my wife, but not in the voting booth. Thanks to two important laws, the Americans with Disabilities Act (ADA) and the Help America Vote Act, I now vote all by myself. Wearing earphones and using a keypad attached to a regular voting machine, I listen to the audible ballot and cast my vote — all in secret. At long last I feel like a full citizen.

Although technology has come a long way, it's far from perfect. Specialized computers for the blind can fail, and when they do, it's super frustrating. Freezing text, disappearing files, Bluetooth glitches, and every nightmare that plagues regular computer users are all magnified, time-consuming frustrations for me. I can feel pretty helpless at times.

Also, good hardware and software will take you only so far. Federal law requires government websites to be accessible to the visually impaired, but most are not. The situation is even worse for nongovernment websites, most of which are entirely inaccessible to the blind. The iPhone has the same problem. As good as VoiceOver is, Apple depends on third-party app developers to make their apps compatible with VoiceOver. The software development tools they need to make their apps accessible are free and readily available on the Apple website. Yet only a tiny percentage of the more than 1.5 million apps in the App Store are compatible with VoiceOver. For the blind, the websites and apps that no one has bothered to make accessible simply don't exist.

Rideshare apps are a great technology, especially for blind people, since we can't drive. But there's a huge problem. Even though federal and state laws require drivers to allow guide dogs, a survey by the National Federation of the Blind found that almost

25 percent of blind people with guide dogs are regularly rejected by drivers. I experienced this myself on the very day I was writing this chapter. Edie and I were visiting our friend Rabbi Lauren Holtzblatt to learn about how the Old Testament deals with blindness. The answer was even better than I'd hoped: Leviticus 19:14 commands: "Before the blind: thou shalt not place a stumbling block." That means that the sighted have a responsibility to clear the way for the blind, both literally and metaphorically.

Ten short minutes later, Lyft—apparently unaware of Leviticus, much less the law—placed a serious stumbling block in my way. No sooner had Vixen and I hopped into the back seat than the driver began shouting. "Get out! Get out!" "The dog's dirty!" "The dog will pee in my car!" Vixen was as insulted as I was. This went on for several minutes. The driver even got out of his car. Edie tried calmly explaining that Vixen is a guide dog, that the law requires the driver to take us, and that Vixen is very well trained. Nothing helped. We finally gave up, and Edie rearranged her day so she could drive us to the courthouse. It was humiliating. And what would have happened if I'd been alone, as are many blind people with guide dogs?

That Lyft driver sure tangled with the wrong guy. I filed a complaint on the Lyft website, then called my friends at the *Washington Post*. Within a week the paper ran a huge front-page Metro story, including a big picture of Vixen. The 23-point bold headline blared, "A Federal Judge Was Refused a Lyft Ride with His Guide Dog. He's Not Alone." Lyft offered me a ten-dollar credit, but I rejected it. I didn't want compensation. I want Lyft and every rideshare driver to obey the law and welcome blind passengers with guide dogs into their cars.

CHAPTER 10

"It's Just Politics"

SHORTLY AFTER JIMMY CARTER'S INAUGURATION IN 1977, I was skiing in Colorado when a ski patroller nabbed me on the slopes to tell me that I had an emergency phone call waiting for me at the base. My bright orange BLIND SKIER bib made me easy to find. On the line was an aide to Joseph Califano Jr., Carter's new Secretary of Health, Education, and Welfare, also known as HEW. At the time, HEW was where all of the most exciting work was getting done. After all, what could be better than providing health, education, and welfare for everyone? Califano wanted me to lead the HEW agency called the Office for Civil Rights (OCR). OCR had a sweeping mandate to enforce civil rights, and its most important work in those years was enforcing the Supreme Court's ruling in *Brown v. Board of Education* that racially segregated schooling is unconstitutional. Supreme Court rulings are important, but they're sometimes just words on a page until someone does the hard work of enforcing them. For *Brown v. Board of Education,* that someone was OCR.

OCR faced a serious uphill battle. Immediately after the triumph of *Brown* in 1954, the three branches of government had worked together to begin desegregating schools, even in the face of massive Southern resistance. Four short years after *Brown,* the Supreme Court unanimously ordered schools desegregated in Little Rock, Arkansas. The justices felt so strongly about the issue—and were so dismayed by Little Rock's resistance to its prior ruling—that their decision was not only unanimous, but for the first time in history, every one of them signed the opinion. President Eisenhower then dispatched troops to Little Rock to enforce the Court's order. Troubled by the continued defiance of *Brown* and recognizing that more insidious forms of racial discrimination were on the rise, Congress enacted Title VI of the Civil Rights Act of 1964, which prohibits entities receiving federal funds—including school districts and universities—from discriminating on the basis of race. The cost of a violation? Loss of those all-important federal funds. With the government firing on all three of its cylinders, it finally seemed like racial segregation was on the run. Throughout the South, thousands of Black and white children began attending school together for the very first time.

Progress faltered, however, when Richard Nixon became president. Nixon was in no hurry to enforce *Brown,* and he particularly hated the idea of busing students from one place to another to achieve integration. While the Supreme Court remained committed to desegregation, Nixon used his considerable power to cut back enforcement, making good on the racial cynicism he had ridden into office. At Nixon's command, OCR took pressure off Southern school districts, did virtually nothing about still-segregated colleges and universities, and ignored thousands of individual complaints about discrimination. When Leon Panetta, Nixon's OCR director (and later President Clinton's chief of staff and President Obama's secretary of defense), tried to stand up to the president and do his job, he was forced to resign. The NAACP Legal Defense and Education Fund and other civil rights organizations sued, and in a case known as *Adams v. Richardson*, the Court ordered OCR to enforce the civil rights laws. Even so, the Nixon and short-lived Ford administrations did little to comply.

When Carter was elected, he promised to change all that. To make good on that promise, he needed OCR kicked back into gear. Joe Califano was fully on board with Carter's agenda. He wanted me because of my experience on the front lines of civil rights cases, and because my selection, according to Califano, would herald that "HEW was once again serious about civil rights." I'd be a "symbol" of HEW's new ambitions, he told me. And he knew I was dedicated to the principle that all students in America have an equal right to education, no matter the color of their skin. I couldn't say no.

I took the job, my first in government since my two summers during the Kennedy administration. Never once in Califano's many press statements did he mention that I had a visual disability. That was my doing. Right before Califano announced my appointment, his PR folks called me at home to ask whether the Secretary could mention my limited vision. I didn't think twice before saying no. I now very much regret that decision. By hiding my failing eyesight and clinging to the notion that my personal struggles were irrelevant to my career, I scotched an opportunity for my success to inspire others.

With my family at my side, I was thrilled to be sworn in to my new role by Justice Thurgood Marshall, who had argued and won *Brown* in the Supreme Court. At the time, OCR had more than eight hundred lawyers and investigators, one hundred or so in Washington and the rest spread throughout ten regional offices across the country. I couldn't believe that all of those civil servants now worked for me. During my first few weeks on the job, Califano invited the entire HEW senior staff to screen the new movie *Star Wars*. "In that film," Califano said, "it's obvious who the good guys and bad guys are. That won't be true in the work you are all about to undertake." He sure was right about that.

———

At the top of the stack of papers on my new very big desk were draft letters terminating federal funding to six rural school districts in Texas and Arkansas because of their Title VI violations. Their offense? Firing nearly every Black teacher during the desegregation process. The unlawful discrimination in those districts was so egregious that even Nixon's and Ford's hamstrung OCRs had found that they had violated Title VI. All that remained was for HEW's top brass to bring down the hammer and terminate federal funding. The letters that would do that were ready to go. But Califano's predecessor never sent them, leaving OCR's Title VI enforcement efforts in limbo for years.

It wasn't as simple as just putting those letters in the mail. Although the school districts had blatantly violated Title VI, cutting off federal funds was like dropping an atom bomb: Everyone gets hurt—especially, in this case, the very children the funds were supposed to help. Califano wanted to give the districts one last chance before lighting that fuse. He sent me off to Texas and Arkansas. If I came back without having convinced the districts to make things right, we'd have no choice but to cut off their funding.

It was my first trip as OCR director. By that time, getting around on my own had become challenging, and I certainly couldn't navigate in new places. So I took my reader along. Why wasn't I using a white cane? Even as I clung to the last gasps of my fading vision, I cared more about how other people saw me than about how well I was getting by. Walking around tapping a cane was a declaration of blindness that I still wasn't prepared to make. I'm sure people wondered why this Washington bureaucrat was holding on to his assistant's arm, but they never asked. I didn't think anyone noticed. My colleagues and friends played along, respecting my desire not to make my vision an issue.

Plus, I enjoyed the company of my reader. My first one was a recent college graduate full of excitement and curiosity about the work we were doing. We began every morning with the *Washington Post* and the *New York Times*, which weren't yet accessible to me on my own. A neighbor who also worked at OCR usually drove me to work in her little red VW bug. We'd pick up my reader along the way, he'd jump in, squeeze into the back seat, and read the newspapers aloud all the way in. During the day, he hung out in my office reading memos, mail, and reports to me. I held his elbow as we moved from meeting to meeting while he warned me under his breath about stairs, curbs, and other hazards. In the evenings, he'd sometimes come to our house after dinner to catch up on work, especially to help me respond to letters from members of Congress. When I traveled, which was often, my reader came too. He would read to me on the plane, sometimes to the chagrin of passengers seated nearby.

On that first OCR trip, my reader and I walked into some of the most impoverished school districts in the country. In both Texas and Arkansas, we sat down with administrators — sometimes in small, stifling trailers — to try to hammer out a deal. I didn't want to cut off funds to those schools any more than their administrators didn't want us to. Quite the opposite. Visiting those schools revealed how badly the funds were needed. But that was the very real threat I was there to deliver: Make every one of those fired Black teachers whole or we'd be left with no choice. One of the districts immediately relented. It was a victory for the teachers (who got their back pay), for the schools (who kept their funding), and above all for the students they served. But the other districts resisted, requiring further enforcement actions and demonstrating how far we still had to go.

The next thing on my desk was even more daunting: the huge backlog of individual complaints left by the Nixon and Ford administrations. The *Adams* order had set deadlines for OCR to finish processing those complaints, but it was immediately clear to me that hitting the deadlines with our existing staff would be impossible. So I returned to court, and the judge gave us more time. Not wanting me to come back asking for yet another extension, though, he entered an unusual order requiring us to make enough hires to clear the backlog. The White House bureaucrats responsible for our budget were none too pleased, but I went to Congress anyway, explained what the judge had ordered, and voilà, Congress gave us enough money to hire another 850 investigators, doubling OCR's size. For their part, the civil rights groups that had brought the *Adams* cases, all represented by my friends in the civil rights community, were also not pleased that I'd asked for more time. But they trusted me. And sure enough, by the time I left OCR two and a half years later, the backlog was virtually gone. OCR was back to work. That didn't stop the civil rights groups from keeping the pressure on, of course. That was as it should be. They were our antagonists, but they also were participants in a legal process. There's no way we could have made all that progress without them nipping at our heels. It's a perfect example of how insiders and outsiders can work together, accomplishing what each separately cannot.

During my time at OCR I faced two defining dramas, each involving desegregation and each still echoing today. One involved Chicago's racially segregated public schools, and the other North Carolina's segregated public university system. Both illustrate the promise and perils of federally driven school desegregation.

In Chicago, most Black children attended Black schools, and most white children attended white schools. Although no law required segregation, a series of deliberate, concerted actions by both private and public entities meant that, as a practical matter, Chicago's public schools were racially segregated. At the heart of the problem was residential segregation, the result of decades of discriminatory housing practices such as racial covenants, redlining, and steering. The cycle became a vicious one as businesses and landlords divested from Black neighborhoods, and white residents—along with their tax dollars—fled to the suburbs.

Residential segregation led invariably to school segregation, and Chicago school officials made a bad problem worse. They constantly manipulated school boundaries to make sure kids in predominantly Black neighborhoods stayed in predominantly Black schools. When Black schools became overcrowded, they erected temporary trailer classrooms—called "Willis Wagons" for Chicago school superintendent Benjamin Willis, then the fourth-highest-paid public official in the United States—rather than divert the overflow to white schools with space to spare. Edie knew all about Willis Wagons. Back in the late sixties she taught tenth-grade English in a Willis Wagon at Harlan High School, where the city was desperately trying to make more room for Black students rather than simply shift them to the nearest white school. Apparently no one in Chicago seems to have appreciated the irony of segregating a school named for John Marshall Harlan, the courageous justice whose 1896 dissent in *Plessy v. Ferguson* declared that racial segregation violated the Fourteenth Amendment and laid the groundwork for *Brown's* holding that "in the field of public education, the doctrine of 'separate but equal' has no place."

Racial segregation in Chicago wasn't news to me or to anyone else paying attention. I vividly remembered the crumbling walls and overworked teachers of the inner-city schools I'd visited as a young lawyer in the aftermath of the riots. When Martin Luther King brought the civil rights struggle to the North, he was shocked by the city's entrenched segregation. After being attacked by a rock-throwing mob in Marquette Park, he declared, "The people of Mississippi ought to come to Chicago to learn how to hate." OCR had received many complaints about Chicago's segregated schools. But it never did anything about them.

I was determined to change that, but our political options were limited. Even though the Supreme Court had ruled that federal courts could order busing to remedy segregation, Congress passed a law, cosponsored by then-Senator Joe Biden, that prohibited OCR from requiring busing as a condition of receiving federal funds. The law's other sponsor, Tom Eagleton of Missouri, called to say that I shouldn't take it personally. "It's just politics," he told me. He was obviously under pressure from home, where desegregation cases were heating up in St. Louis and Kansas City—two cities that would eventually consume a decade of my life.

Although Eagleton-Biden meant we couldn't order busing, OCR still had to enforce Title VI, and I worked for nearly a year to amass the evidence we'd need to proceed against Chicago. Under Title VI, we didn't have to prove intentional discrimination by the city—that they'd done this on purpose—only the fact of segregation. I knew, though, that Chicago officials *had* segregated the city's schools on purpose. And I wanted Califano, and the public at large, to understand that Chicago schools were as bad if not worse than many in the South. The subtler forms of discrimination at work in Chicago, I believed, were potentially even more dangerous than the more obvious ones lingering in the South. To prove the point, I prepared a set of dramatic posters detailing how the school system, year after year, revised district boundaries and located Willis Wagons to preserve segregation. In the Secretary's huge conference room, I walked Califano and fifty other HEW officials through the evidence I'd amassed. I couldn't see any of the charts, but with my reader's help I had memorized them. Years later, one attendee who remembered my presentation told me that he had no idea that I couldn't see the graphics I used to prove my case. The audience was rapt, as was Califano. "Go get 'em, David," he concluded.

I tried everything to convince city leaders. Stripped of our power to compel busing, however, I was negotiating with one hand tied behind my back. Officials understood that we couldn't force them to bus students, and they were willing to bet that President Carter, facing reelection, would ultimately take their side. Offering Chicago a carrot worked no better than the Title VI stick. Unlike Southern school systems, which accepted additional federal funding under the Emergency School Aid Act in exchange for desegregating, not even millions of federal dollars could entice Chicago's white leadership to allow Black kids to attend white schools.

By 1979, it was clear that a negotiated resolution wasn't going to happen. We had no leverage. Chicago politicians had dug in. Public opinion wasn't with us. Eventually, HEW referred the stalemate to the Justice Department, which, unbound by Eagleton-Biden, could sue to force Chicago to desegregate. But the Justice Department punted, just as Chicago officials had anticipated. The presidential election was fast approaching, and if

Ronald Reagan took the White House, everyone understood that OCR would revert to the days of Nixonian resistance. Six weeks before Election Day, the Justice Department settled the case in exchange for a meaningless promise that the city would propose a desegregation plan by the following March. The subtext? They had simply given up.

By March, President Reagan had taken office, and over the next few years, the city and Reagan's Justice Department agreed to an array of purely voluntary measures. A few school boundaries were tweaked. A few new magnet schools were established, though mostly in white areas, imposing the burden of commuting onto Black students. Busing was out entirely. In short, nothing meaningful had changed. In the NAACP's words, "An elephant labored and produced a mouse."

After so much time and drama, the nation's third-largest school system remained profoundly segregated and had committed to do almost nothing to change that. In the ensuing decades, things only got worse. Today, Chicago schools are the third most segregated in the country. Some neighborhoods are even more segregated than they were when I made those damning posters so many years ago.

North Carolina's sixteen-campus university system was the battleground for my other major desegregation fight. Before *Brown*, the North Carolina higher education system, like others in the South, was segregated by law. Separate meant profoundly unequal. *Brown* forced white colleges to open their doors to Black students, but it didn't remedy the extreme inequality between historically white universities and historically Black ones.

"Didn't have enough books, didn't have enough space, didn't have enough facilities" is how Floyd McKissick, a civil rights leader who marched with Dr. King, described the historically Black North Carolina law school he'd attended after serving in the army during World War II. That school was no exception. Across the state, historically Black universities lagged far behind historically white universities on almost every relevant metric. Whereas UNC-Chapel Hill and ten other state schools with almost entirely white student bodies were well-funded exemplars of higher learning, the state's five historically Black colleges and universities (HBCUs) were decrepit. They lacked basic libraries, laboratories, and athletic facilities. One library had only six microfilm readers for five thousand students and a book catalog that was grossly lacking. The university's biology lab had only a single autoclave sterilizer (broken for years); the chemistry lab's hot and cold rooms were inoperative. The business school at the historically Black NC Agricultural and Technical State University? Two rooms in a decrepit building equipped with old typewriters. The business school at Chapel Hill? A palace.

Desegregating universities required a different tool kit than desegregating K-12 schools. You couldn't bus and you couldn't adjust attendance areas. The only way to desegregate state higher education systems was to strengthen the Black schools to make them more attractive to white students, give financial incentives to white students to attend Black schools (and vice versa), and eliminate unnecessarily duplicated courses. The latter tactic had proven effective in other Southern states, including President Carter's Georgia. If the same courses were taught both at a historically white school and at the HBCU nearby, white students had no reason to take a class at the HBCU. But if some courses were taught only at the HBCU, those classes would integrate naturally.

North Carolina's governor, Jim Hunt, was ready to negotiate. Chapel Hill, however, didn't want any settlement with OCR to limit its program offerings; the HBCUs worried about being assimilated out of existence. Stalemate. Although the state was willing to give more resources to its Black schools and even to offer incentives to attend them, it balked at eliminating duplicate programs. Chapel Hill wouldn't budge. And we were getting slammed in the local papers, which thought the feds were sticking their nose where it didn't belong. The "university should yield no more to Califano," one paper declared. To move state officials, we needed public support, and to get public support, we needed the local press. One day when I was sipping coffee with Joe in his office, he remarked that the influential *Raleigh News & Observer* and other local papers had no idea that the conditions at the HBCUs were so dreadful. If reporters knew the facts, then maybe (just maybe) they'd be on our side.

I'd already dealt extensively with reporters while at OCR, as well as in my time with the Lawyers' Committee. I had learned that ignoring reporters often meant bad press, while letting them in could yield accolades. But handling reporters is a fine art, and I was still an apprentice. I'd recently learned an important lesson when I told a *Washington Post* reporter "on background" that the Eagleton-Biden anti-busing provision was a really bad idea. The next day, the *Post* ran a front-page story attributing my views to a "high-ranking civil rights official." First thing the next morning, Eileen Shanahan, Califano's formidable press secretary (and former *New York Times* economics reporter), hauled me into her office. "David," she said, "you need a lesson about dealing with the press." Apparently there's a difference between "background" and "deep background." Who knew? Now I spell out my expectations about anonymity in plain English and speak only with reporters I trust. I was never burned again.

Winning over the North Carolina papers, however, would require a creative press strategy. I called up every one of the reporters who had been publishing critical pieces and invited them to join me on a three-day tour of the HBCUs. I knew the presidents at each school from our months of negotiations. They had become accustomed to seeing me touching my aide's elbow as we walked, and probably also noticed him read to me from time to time. They never asked about it, but during our tours they went out of their way to vividly describe their facilities as they showed us around. The descriptions were meant for my benefit, but they hammered home the campuses' shortcomings for the reporters. It's one thing to see a run-down chemistry lab, but quite another to also learn that the Bunsen burners and autoclaves needed repair and that most of the chemical storage units in the back were empty. One reporter remarked, "We sure are lucky to have Tatel along—we might not have noticed those things." Each evening, I met with editorial boards. Soon enough, the stories turned around. "The blunt truth often hurts," stated a lead editorial in the *News & Observer* right after our visit, and the blunt truth was that the HBCUs had been woefully neglected. "My heart aches," said Governor Hunt, to see "some of the buildings these children have to go to school in."

We had exposed North Carolina to the depressing truth. But it wasn't enough. Leaders of the white universities (especially Chapel Hill) remained dug in, and newly inaugurated President Reagan immediately agreed to a settlement far worse than what we in the Carter administration had repeatedly rejected. The federal government failed the students of North Carolina just as it failed the students of Chicago.

Our unsuccessful efforts in North Carolina and Chicago revealed the weakness at the heart of Title VI. HEW and its successor agency, the Department of Education, operate like federal ATM machines. Congress appropriates billions for them to distribute to educational institutions throughout the country, and politicians at both ends of the money hose benefit from the flow. But OCR—whose job it is to make sure that schools receiving federal cash hold up their end of the deal—is the skunk at the picnic, threatening to shut off the flow to universities and school districts that violate the law. While members of Congress eagerly proclaim their support for broad civil rights laws, they change their tune when funding for their constituents is threatened. In the real world, money sometimes matters more than the law.

———

Chicago and North Carolina weren't the only cases during my tenure at OCR that presented difficult questions about race and education. Affirmative action—the idea that schools could consider race during their admissions processes in order to foster a diverse educational environment—was as controversial then as it is now. The issue came to a head in a case called *Regents of the University of California v. Bakke*. A white student, Allan Bakke, had been rejected by the medical school of the University of California at Davis. Bakke claimed unconstitutional racial discrimination. We at HEW were stunned when we learned that Carter's own Justice Department was preparing an amicus brief urging the Supreme Court to declare that race-conscious affirmative action plans were presumptively unconstitutional. Luckily, the White House, especially Vice President Walter Mondale, agreed with us. After a series of extremely tense meetings, we convinced the Justice Department to change direction and file a brief that supported affirmative action. It worked. In *Bakke*, the Supreme Court ruled that colleges have a compelling interest in fostering a diverse student body and that they could consider race as one factor among many in their admissions process.

Forty-five years later, a very different Supreme Court overruled *Bakke* without even acknowledging that it was doing so. More about that case and its implications for the rule of law in Chapter 18, but it merits mention here because the case involved none other than the University of North Carolina at Chapel Hill. Decades after my unsuccessful struggle with Chapel Hill, the university had finally adopted an affirmative action plan to increase its minority enrollment and strenuously defended that plan in court. How ironic that a university that had so long fought the federal government and resisted desegregation has now been stripped of its most effective tool for achieving racial diversity. Similarly ironic is that the very institution that ordered the elimination of separate-but-equal education in the first place, the Supreme Court of the United States, has now proclaimed that taking race into account in an effort to achieve racial diversity is unconstitutional.

In the beginning, the Civil Rights Movement was all about race. But by the late 1960s the movement had expanded, and by the time I joined OCR the office was beginning to grapple with discrimination based on disability and gender. Both forms of discrimination were still commonplace.

Although the revolutionary Americans with Disabilities Act was more than a decade away, its progenitor, Section 504 of the Rehabilitation Act, was signed into law in 1973. Modeled on Title VI, Section 504 prohibits colleges, school districts, and other institutions receiving federal funds from discriminating on the basis of disability. Before its passage, people with disabilities were barely second-class citizens. Only one in five children with disabilities completed a public education, and 1.8 million were barred from attending public schools altogether. What better evidence that we needed Section 504 than that the federal official in charge of enforcing it—me—was downplaying his own disability because of shame and the fear of discrimination?

The Nixon administration had done virtually nothing to enforce Section 504. It had even refused to issue the disability-discrimination regulations that career officials had already drafted. The last HEW secretary before Carter took office, David Mathews, actually skedaddled out of town with the regulations to avoid being held in contempt of court. By the time Califano took charge of HEW, the disability rights community was demanding action. Energized by the victories of the Civil Rights Movement, they even picketed Califano's home. Joe later recalled that he was petrified that his golden retriever would bite a demonstrator. "Califano's Dog Bites Blind Man" wasn't the kind of headline he was hoping for.

One of my first acts as OCR director was to hand-deliver the long-awaited Section 504 regulations to Califano to sign. Thus began our campaign to give life and meaning to the statute's lofty promises. Tricky questions about the new law's scope cropped up almost immediately. The most fundamental question was unique to the disability rights arena: Did the principle of nondiscrimination require only that funding recipients treat people with disabilities the same as people without? Or did it obligate them to provide accommodations to ensure truly equal access? We believed the law required accommodations. After all, what good is it to tell wheelchair users that they are welcome inside a government building if the only way in is a flight of stairs? But answering the accommodations question yielded only more questions. What percentage of facilities had to be accessible? Every building? Only new buildings? Was every playground in America required to install a water fountain accessible from a wheelchair? What about subtitles for the deaf? Braille dots for the blind? Were alcoholics and drug addicts "disabled"? The law itself answered none of those questions. It was OCR's job to fill in the details.

Progress was slow. In response to the new regulations, one university announced that it didn't need ramps because its football players could carry wheelchair-using students up the stairs to their classes. Another said it didn't need to provide an ASL interpreter because deaf students could just read lips. Still another wouldn't let any "handicapped" students participate in contact sports. We issued policy statements making it clear that such evasions wouldn't fly and, slowly, stopped hearing excuses. Most universities wanted to comply—they just needed help. We published guidance about how to install ramps in old buildings, where to obtain Braille textbooks, and when to deploy interpreters in classrooms. It was nice to be working with schools rather than against them. Together, we transformed the lives of millions of disabled Americans and laid the groundwork for the even more transformative ADA. Thanks to Section 504—and, later, the ADA and the Individuals with Disabilities Education Act—schools are now much better places for disabled students than they once were. Most students with disabilities now graduate from high school, and nearly one in five undergraduates reports having a disability. That's real progress, but problems persist. Students with disabilities continue to be suspended and expelled at far higher rates than other students. And after they graduate, their struggles continue. People with disabilities are more than twice as likely to be unemployed as people without disabilities.

Even as I downplayed my own disability, I was surprised at how deeply I felt about Section 504. Although I didn't think of myself as disabled, I understood what it would mean for blind students to be given, for the first time, a textbook they could read without help. I understood how it might feel for wheelchair-using students to be able, for the first time, to enter their school buildings on their own. Even more, I understood what it was like to be invisible—and then finally to be seen. This fight, I realized, was my own.

The women's rights movement was well underway before I started at OCR, but the country still had a long way to go. Remember the men-only flights in the 1970s? The movement's biggest victory to date had been the enactment of a law called Title IX, which prohibits education programs that receive federal funds from discriminating on the basis of sex, just like Title VI prohibits them from discriminating on the basis of race. The passage of Title IX, which was buried in a broader statute called the Education Amendments Act of 1972, didn't grab many headlines. In its front-page story on the statute, the *New York Times* included only a bullet point about Title IX. But sometimes Congress does hide elephants in mouseholes. Title IX gave OCR the tool it needed to prevent schools from discriminating against their students on the basis of gender.

I'm sure you won't be surprised at this point to learn that the Nixon administration had done virtually nothing to enforce Title IX. The Ford administration had done a bit better, reluctantly issuing regulations that covered admissions, recruitment, scholarships, sports, and extracurriculars in both K-12 and higher education. But its OCR had done little to enforce those regulations.

From the moment I became OCR director, women's groups were banging down my door demanding change. I was with them and so was Califano. It wasn't going to be easy to fulfill the promise of gender equality in education, and we knew we needed to start by listening. So we invited representatives of leading women's groups to share their concerns and ideas. We all gathered in the Secretary's Conference Room. Only Califano was missing. Tied up at the White House, he kept everyone waiting for nearly two hours, so it was almost five o'clock when we finally got started. The meeting was tense. The groups were rightfully dismayed by OCR's failure to enforce Title IX in the past and fairly skeptical of our intentions to change. We tried to listen more than we spoke, but it wasn't going very well. Then, suddenly, in walked my secretary, who deposited into my lap our twelve-month-old Emily, along with her bottle and blanket. I had promised to babysit while Edie took our other three children to see the IMAX film *To Fly!* across the street at the Air and Space Museum. I cuddled Emily and gave her the bottle. After the applause died down, the meeting continued. Baby Emily's presence cut the tension, and we started making progress. I know some thought it was a setup, that I'd planned to win them over by caring for my daughter during our meeting. I assure you I wasn't so clever. On her way out the door, Marcia Greenberger, founder of the National Women's Law Center, asked whether I was planning to bring my ironing next time.

As I soon learned, gender equality is more complicated than just requiring that schools treat girls and boys alike. Issues around athletics proved particularly difficult. Title IX required "equivalent" funding for women's sports, but did "equivalent" funding mean fifty-fifty, even in schools where few women were participating? Did schools need to create a women's team for every sport for which it had a men's team? What about intercollegiate football and basketball, which produced so much revenue compared to other sports? The big football universities lobbied hard to get Congress to exempt football from Title IX. One congressman summoned me to a breakfast meeting with Notre Dame's football coach and several football boosters, some of whom were priests. They began by saying grace, offering a prayer for "the future of intercollegiate football." I figured we were in trouble because they had God on their side and all I had was the law.

This time, the law prevailed. We convened a meeting of college presidents and football coaches in Washington. Tempers were running hot. Even the suggestion that football powerhouses might have to share their money with women's sports got the footballers riled up. Sitting across the table from me was legendary

Penn State football coach Joe Paterno. I couldn't see him, but I sure could feel the daggers. My deputy, Cindy Brown, who was both highly respected in the women's movement and an avid football fan, led a series of follow-up meetings around the country. She then produced a policy statement, issued after we left office, that still governs intercollegiate sports today. Most importantly, it requires that universities equitably distribute funds among men's and women's teams, including with respect to coaching, equipment, travel, and even locker rooms.

In the now more than fifty years since its passage, Title IX and the regulatory guidance we helped promulgate have dramatically altered the landscape of school sports. Female participation in organized athletics has surged at both the K-12 and collegiate levels. At some Olympics, American women now win more medals than the men. It was never just about sports. Women's strides toward equality on the basketball court and the playing field helped catapult them into boardrooms and other places of power across America. Just ask Wall Street: 94 percent of female C-suite executives played sports, more than 50 percent of them at the collegiate level. As one magazine put it, Title IX was the "37 words that changed everything."

———

You've now heard about most of what I was up to at OCR— fighting discrimination on the basis of race, disability, and gender. But there's one more, somewhat less glamorous fight I took on during my tenure. OCR's guidance documents, press releases, public reports, and letters were the tools of our trade, but those documents were so full of jargon and bureaucratese that they were almost indecipherable. How could recipients of federal funds possibly figure out what we expected of them if we weren't saying it clearly? We had a writing problem, and I set out to fix it.

Fortunately, our next-door neighbor, Norma Mohr, was a gifted writer, and she agreed to come to our rescue. She ran a weekly "Writing 101" class and compiled her lessons in a book called *Civil Writing* that would've pleased Strunk and White. Here are some of my favorites:

> Avoid "sneaky whiches": "Which" and "that" do not mean the same thing.
> Using the passive voice is like walking backward.
> Don't use words like "identifiability": This eight-syllable ogre is not a word.
> A period is a bureaucrat's best friend.

The results were instantaneous. Instead of "Ramps which can be used by people confined in wheelchairs should be installed by funding recipients in locations with high identifiability," we wrote, "Funding recipients should install wheelchair ramps in clearly visible locations." Our writing became crisp, clear, and jargon-free. We received far fewer inquiries from confused stakeholders. And OCR staffers were proud of their work. It was a win-win for everyone.

Particularly for me. When I became a judge, I kept a copy of *Civil Writing* in my chambers right next to Strunk & White and *The Chicago Manual of Style,* and I never forgot Norma's lessons. In one opinion, I explained that Congress had used "which" when it meant "that," and that the grammatical mistake made a difference. In another, I warned a federal agency that its use of the passive voice in the phrase "if a persuasive showing is made" left us unable to determine who exactly was supposed to be making that persuasive showing. In still another, I used a sentence diagram, a skill I learned in Mrs. Schict's fifth-grade class. The case involved identity theft. The law imposed a mandatory two-year prison term on anyone who "knowingly...uses, without lawful authority, a means of identification of another person." The government claimed that "knowingly" modified only "a means of identification," but not "of another person"—such that it would theoretically apply to a defendant who didn't know the ID she was using belonged to someone else. I disagreed. My opinion included a sentence diagram demonstrating that the word "knowingly" modified the verb that follows it ("uses") and, given the context, was best read to carry through the rest of the sentence, including the phrase "of another person." Here's the diagram:

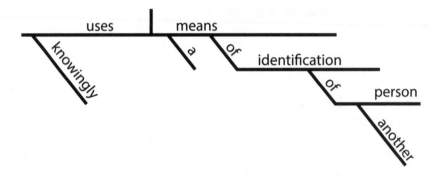

To my knowledge, this was the first federal court opinion that included a sentence diagram. Perhaps it's no coincidence that a blind judge did that first. Because I can't see the words on the page, I often parse complex text by creating diagrams in my head. It worked in the fifth grade when I could see, and it works even better now.

In the spring of 1979, two years into my tenure, I felt like OCR had gotten its groove back. We were making real strides against race-, disability-, and gender-based discrimination in schools across the country. We were writing better, too.

But all that progress wasn't to continue. Times were tough for the country, with long gas lines and double-digit inflation. President Carter, approaching a reelection campaign, had gone off to Camp David to consult with national leaders. When he came down from the mountain, he asked his entire Cabinet to resign. Califano's was one of five resignations he accepted.

His replacement was Patricia Harris, then–Secretary of the Department of Housing and Urban Development (HUD). Harris and I got off to a rocky start. To ease the transition, Harris's people directed department heads like me to prepare binders of briefing materials for her. We were given precise rules: The binders had to be just so, with particular kinds of tabs, executive summaries, and specific materials. Although I thought it all a bit excessive, I cared about OCR and wanted Harris to succeed. At our first transition meeting in Harris's HUD office, she sat on one side of the table, I sat on the other, and dozens of staffers surrounded us. I could still see well enough to make out shapes and movement and was startled when Harris stood up and proceeded to dress me down. "I gave you specific instructions about how to do these briefing books!" she said, waving a book at me. "This book doesn't have tabs. This book doesn't have executive summaries!" Except it did have all those things. Harris was waving the wrong book. Then she proceeded to lecture me in front of my entire staff about how badly OCR was handling Chicago and North Carolina. It was obviously a setup designed to show the White House that Harris would be a different kind of Secretary. But it backfired on her.

When I got back to HEW, Califano was eager to hear what had happened. I gave him the full report. He immediately picked up the phone and called his friend, who just happened to be the executive editor of the *Washington Post*. The next day, the front page blared, "Harris Is Reported Sharply Critical of HEW's Rights

Chief." Harris looked bad, but the wound was self-inflicted. In any event, the writing was on the wall. I knew that Harris wanted to hire her own people. Within a week of our explosive first meeting, I asked to meet with her. I entered her office and handed her my letter of resignation. Holding it for just a moment, she let it drop to the floor, sighed, and asked me to stay on to help with the transition. I'm glad I did. Despite our rough start, Harris came to trust me, and I her. When my successor finally arrived, Harris came to my office, thanked me, and gave me a big hug. As we walked down the hall to the press conference, she held my hand the whole way. During the announcement, she never let go.

I thought what my team accomplished at OCR was government at its finest. How sad that today so many people believe that government itself is the problem. President Carter certainly contributed to that perception by telling audiences that the American people were "better than their government." Ronald Reagan later doubled down with his cynical gag: "The nine most terrifying words in the English language are 'I'm from the government, and I'm here to help!'" I never thought that was very funny. The government makes mistakes, of course. But as I first learned in my summer jobs at the Labor Department and then again at OCR, with good people at the helm there's no more powerful force for good. We were indeed from the government, and we were in fact there to help.

CHAPTER 11

A Tale of Two Cities

O N THE DAY THE *POST* RAN THE STORY ABOUT MY CONFRON-tation with Secretary Harris, Hogan's managing partner called. "Sounds like you need a job," he said. He was right. I did need a job. But I'd caught the education bug big time. Although the Chicago and North Carolina cases sometimes made me want to pull my hair out, I'd become deeply committed to the cause of desegregation. I couldn't think of anything more important for children, and for our country. I wanted to keep doing that work if at all possible.

So I made a pitch to Hogan: How about establishing a new practice group dedicated to education? I'd found at OCR that many school districts wanted to desegregate their school systems but lacked the legal and technical know-how to make it happen. The expertise of a big D.C. law firm could definitely help. We could represent school districts trying to live up to the ideals of a desegregated America. And we could help them with their other day-to-day legal problems, too. Based on my OCR experience, I thought we could also do the same for colleges and universities. I didn't know for certain whether an education practice could make money. After all, no other major law firm had one. But I believed that we could. Multimillion-dollar corporations retained D.C. law firms, so why not multimillion-dollar school districts and universities?

Hogan was all in. In early 1980, we launched the firm's brand-new education group, with me at the helm. While I'd worked in private practice before, this was the first time I was responsible for developing business—and for turning a profit. So I started pounding the pavement, reaching out to contacts I had developed over the years with school superintendents, university presidents, Washington-based education associations, and even governors. Although some of those officials had previously been my adversaries, we'd always maintained cordial relations. More advice to young lawyers: Treat everyone with respect, especially those at the opposing counsel's table.

It worked. The education group thrived, growing to eight lawyers working full-time on education matters. We also relied on the expertise of other partners and associates eager to pitch in. Because my fingerprints were all over desegregation efforts across the country, that inevitably became a cornerstone of my Hogan practice. But we didn't work only on desegregation. We also handled controversies about free speech, school finance, scientific research, and gender and disability discrimination, just to name a few. It was satisfying work, and we even made money.

———

I learned about what would become our first and biggest case in a roundabout way. In March 1980, Edie, the kids, and I were returning to Washington from a Colorado ski trip, and while changing planes in St. Louis, Edie pointed to a newspaper box and said, "David, check out this headline: 'Federal Appeals Court Orders Desegregation in City Schools.'" According to the article, the court had ordered the St. Louis school system to pursue the possibility of including nearby white suburban districts in the desegregation process. Neither of us knew then that within a month I'd be deeply involved in that very case.

At the time of *Brown v. Board of Education*, St. Louis operated the second-largest segregated public school system in the US. Like other southern and border states, Missouri had a "racially dual school system," meaning that schools were racially segregated by law. Since 1929, at the height of Jim Crow, Missouri law specifically required that "separate free schools shall be established for the education of children of African descent; and it shall be unlawful for any colored child to attend any white school, or any white child to attend a colored school." After *Brown* there could be no more "white schools" or "colored schools," but in the more than two decades since *Brown*, St. Louis had done little to desegregate its schools.

Enter Minnie Liddell, a Black seamstress who just wanted a quality education for her five children. When they were assigned to a shabby old school miles from her home rather than the brand-new school right in her neighborhood, Liddell decided to sue. She became a folk hero almost overnight. "A MOTHER ON THE MARCH," a headline in the *St. Louis Post-Dispatch* blared. After filing her lawsuit, Liddell said she just "began to walk and ring doorbells to see if other parents were as upset by this as I was." As it turned out, they were. Once the word began to spread, Liddell got so many phone calls that she installed a second line.

By the time we got involved, there were no longer enough white students in St. Louis to desegregate the city's schools. The school system was 75 percent Black, and most Black students attended virtually all-Black schools. The city was surrounded by twenty-three suburbs whose schools were mostly white. Those suburban schools had better teachers, better resources, and offered a better education. Very separate, but not at all equal. The only way to desegregate St. Louis, civil rights advocates and the courts recognized, was to include its white suburbs in the project.

But they faced a major obstacle: the Supreme Court of the United States. In 1974, the Court had ruled in *Milliken v. Bradley* that federal courts couldn't order an interdistrict desegregation plan—meaning a plan that transfers students between the city and suburban school districts—unless either the suburban districts or the state had contributed to the racial segregation in the city's schools. According to *Milliken*, "local control" over "neighborhood" schools—that is, white schools—was paramount. Suburban districts could be required to take Black students and give up some of their white ones only if they or the state shared at least some of the blame for the problem. *Milliken* had been the Civil Rights Movement's first major loss in a school desegregation case. It seemed to suggest that separate but equal was okay as long as the separation was between a city and its suburbs. The vote was 5–4, with all four Nixon-appointed justices in the majority. Justice Thurgood Marshall, who two decades earlier had argued and won *Brown* (and who had sworn me in at OCR), warned in his dissent that *Milliken* reflected "a perceived public mood that we have gone far enough in enforcing the Constitution's guarantee of equal justice."

Satisfying *Milliken* would be challenging, but city leaders believed that including the white suburbs was the only path to desegregation. The superintendent said as much to one of the experts in the case, who replied that he knew just the person for the job. "I'll introduce you to David Tatel," he told the superintendent.

He did, the school district hired me, and we went to work. If St. Louis was ready to desegregate its schools, my Hogan colleagues and I were ready to help.

We began by joining forces with the superb team of NAACP lawyers who had just won the court order requiring St. Louis to pursue a metropolitan-wide remedy. Together we set about exploring the causes of school segregation in the St. Louis metropolitan area. We hired historians, educators, and demographers. After months delving deep into dusty archives and interviewing dozens of witnesses, we uncovered volumes of evidence that the suburban districts and the state of Missouri had been a "substantial cause of inter-district segregation"—exactly what *Milliken* required us to prove.

The evidence was compelling. Both before and after *Brown*, suburban school districts, supported by the state of Missouri, routinely transferred Black students away from white districts and into Black ones. This forced Black students to travel miles, passing white schools along the way. In their public statements, the districts were remarkably candid about what was really going on. One district advertised that a boundary change would "take all the colored out of this District." Another wrote that consolidation would be appropriate only between districts with "populations of…the same general type." Still another maintained that reorganization would be acceptable only if the new districts "include elements of the population with a high degree of homogeneity."

As in Chicago, discriminatory housing policies masterminded by the state and other government agencies were also to blame. Racially restrictive covenants blanketed the metropolitan area, public housing was built primarily in Black neighborhoods, and real estate agents steered Black clients away from white neighborhoods. The racially segregated housing that resulted virtually guaranteed racially segregated school districts.

Armed with all this evidence, which showed a century-long campaign by state officials and suburban school districts to preserve a racially segregated school system, we sued the state and the suburban districts simultaneously. The judge was impressed by the evidence we'd amassed and made it clear to the suburban districts that if they went to trial and lost, he would have no choice but to create a single metropolitan-wide school system. That got their attention, and brought them to the negotiating table. I then spent weeks in a giant conference room on the third floor of the old federal courthouse negotiating with dozens of lawyers representing the state, suburban school districts, and the NAACP. The judge told us we couldn't stop talking until we reached a deal.

Few of the other lawyers in the room had ever worked with a blind person. While they were always professional and rarely asked questions about my eyesight or white cane (yes, I eventually did get a cane—more about that in the next chapter), they were fascinated with my Braille 'n Speak computer. I was happy to answer their questions. In time, they began reading material aloud to me without being asked and offering a hand during lunch breaks. Like many sighted people who talk to a blind person for the first time, they were eager to tell me about their cousin who couldn't see three feet in front of herself. I didn't mind. They meant well, and we all soon became comfortable with each other. It reminded me of the time when I was leading a negotiating session on school desegregation in New York City during the Great Blackout of 1977. The running joke was "Tatel's got a big advantage since he's used to negotiating in the dark."

At one point during the St. Louis negotiations, I showed up with a cast on my right hand. While skiing, I had done a thumb plant that needed Gamekeeper's surgery. More than one conversation went like this:

"What happened to your hand, David?"

"I did a thumb plant on the slopes at Aspen."

"Wait...what!? You ski?!!"

The first five times I was asked, I was delighted to explain that indeed I did. By the sixth, a thumbs-up with my cast became my reply.

After weeks of tense negotiations, we agreed on a desegregation plan for St. Louis. It had three parts. First, the suburban districts would accept specific numbers of Black students from the city. Second, the city's Black schools would be strengthened with smaller classes, enriched programs, and improved facilities. And third, the city would establish magnet schools to attract white students into the city. Almost all of that would be funded by the state of Missouri.

The St. Louis plan became the longest-running voluntary desegregation program in US history. In its heyday, around thirteen thousand Black city students voluntarily transferred to suburban schools every year, and almost fifteen hundred white suburban students voluntarily attended the city's magnet schools. It was a wonderful accomplishment and proof that our small but growing education group could, as I had hoped, make a difference in students' lives.

It had taken almost three years to build our case and forge that deal. During those years, at least once a week I took the 7 a.m. TWA flight from Washington to St. Louis (again, for readers under forty, TWA = Trans World Airlines). I spent countless nights in the dreary old Mayfair Hotel. Times have changed. TWA's last flight was in 2001, and the Mayfair is now the fancy Magnolia. Even the product of our hard work, St. Louis's voluntary student transfer program, is now history.

The interplay between city and suburban districts became a recurring theme in my education practice at Hogan. Word got around about our success in St. Louis, and school districts across the country with similar problems came knocking. On my office wall I put up a map of the United States that bristled with a growing number of red pins marking each city where we represented school boards. Most people who fly across the country and look out the window think of folks they know or things they've done in the cities below. Me? I think about each city's school desegregation case.

One of those cases was in Missouri's other big city, Kansas City. The most interesting thing about that case was how we became involved. It all started in early 1984, when I received a telephone call out of the blue. "My name is Irv Hockaday," the caller explained, "and I'm the president of Hallmark Cards." (Yes, "When You Care Enough to Send the Very Best!") If you're wondering why Hallmark needed an education lawyer, so was I. "We have a metropolitan school desegregation case here in Kansas City," Hockaday explained. "Would you come out to meet with us?" What, I wondered, did greeting cards have to do with the school system? I was curious enough to go to Kansas City to find out.

A fancy car picked me up at the airport and took me directly to the company's executive suite. At lunch with Hockaday and other executives I learned that Hallmark supported the ongoing desegregation litigation. They believed that integrated schools were good for the city, for the company, and for all its employees. Hallmark wanted to know what it could do to help, and thought hiring me might be a good first step. Can you imagine what would happen if a major American corporation said something like that today? "Woke capitalism," Fox News would scream. "Concentrate on your greeting cards and your stock price," pundits would lecture, "and stay out of this diversity stuff." Fortunately for Hallmark, back then the nation respected good corporate citizenship, and I was thrilled to work with the company to advance the cause of desegregation in Kansas City.

I'll mention just one other metropolitan school desegregation case, this one in Milwaukee, Wisconsin. As in St. Louis, the school board was under a court order to desegregate its schools and there were too few white students left to desegregate the system fully. As in St. Louis, the school board retained me to explore the possibility of including the surrounding suburban school districts in the desegregation process. Also as in St. Louis, the evidence we uncovered confirmed that the city's segregated schools were no accident. Over the years, white suburban school districts had worked diligently to exclude Black students, choosing to close their schools entirely rather than include Black kids from the city. At the same time, zoning laws, racial covenants, redlining, and the location of public housing all worked in concert to create a racially segregated metropolitan area. Milwaukee was just four hundred miles from the Canadian border, but it sure looked a lot like the Old South. As in St. Louis, we sued both the state and the suburban districts on the school board's behalf, and as in St. Louis, we negotiated a voluntary interdistrict desegregation program funded by the state. For much of the 1980s and 1990s, the program thrived, successfully diversifying Milwaukee area schools for all its children.

The St. Louis and Milwaukee settlements were models of successful voluntary desegregation. As a result of those agreements, thousands of students attended integrated schools. Millions of dollars of state funding went toward better facilities and additional resources for children of all races. The educational benefits were profound. Research shows that Black students who attend desegregated, better-resourced schools experience greater educational achievement, attend college and complete their degrees at higher rates, are more likely to attend selective colleges, and have higher earnings throughout their careers. Those benefits are not all-or-nothing. The longer Black students attend such schools, the better the outcomes. Research also shows that desegregation benefits white students in many ways. They demonstrate increased empathy, commitment to justice, and other positive social-emotional traits, while having no detrimental effect on grades or test scores. It's a win-win for everyone.

Why did we succeed in Milwaukee and St. Louis but not in Chicago? I think there were three significant reasons: good judges, responsible political leaders, and a spirit of compromise. In the places we succeeded, desegregation was pursued through lawsuits initiated by ordinary citizens. That meant that federal judges were involved from the very beginning, and by allowing us to present our evidence against the state and suburbs, the judges in Milwaukee and St. Louis created an atmosphere that encouraged settlement. Those judges weren't the only public servants who did their duty. Imaginative and courageous civic leaders in both cities helped opposing parties find common ground. In Milwaukee, it was Governor Tommy Thompson, who became Secretary of Health and Human Services in the George W. Bush administration. He was friendly, open-minded, and pragmatic. He opposed mandatory busing but supported voluntary efforts, and he was willing to commit state money to make desegregation happen. In St. Louis, although the state's attorney general, John Ashcroft, was running for governor on an anti-busing platform, officials in Missouri's Department of Education strongly believed in the promise of a voluntary interdistrict desegregation plan. In both cities, we had allies on the other side of the table who were willing to work with us for the good of their constituents.

By contrast, in Chicago, desegregation efforts were initiated not by private parties suing in court, but by the federal government—that is, the Office for Civil Rights, i.e., me. Moreover, the anti-busing Eagleton-Biden amendment meant that we had little leverage. The federal court eventually did get involved, but too late to make a difference. Making matters worse, city officials from the mayor on down vehemently opposed desegregation. We had no allies at the state level, either. We could hardly get key government officials to answer our letters, let alone have a cordial and constructive conversation. If more cities had leadership like St. Louis's and Milwaukee's, our nation's experience with desegregation would have been quite different. People, not just the law, always matter.

But both people and the law change. By the turn of the century, our successful experiments in St. Louis and Milwaukee had pretty much ended, as had virtually all desegregation efforts throughout the country. Starting with the Nixon administration, the same three branches of government that had worked together to desegregate schools in the sixties and seventies conspired to bring all the progress we'd achieved to a screeching halt. Congress prohibited busing, Reagan let Chicago and North Carolina off the hook, and the Supreme Court made the only effective desegregation remedies—those that included white suburban school districts—extremely difficult to obtain. Years later, the Supreme Court even barred school districts from taking race into account at all, even to promote voluntary desegregation. Today's Court would have stopped the St. Louis and Milwaukee plans in their tracks.

Now, more than seventy years after *Brown*, and more than sixty after the passage of the Civil Rights Act, most non-white children in America again attend schools that are mostly non-white, and most white children attend schools that are mostly white. Since 1988, the high-water mark of desegregation, the nation's share of intensely segregated minority schools — the vast majority of which are poor, with less qualified teachers, and less challenging curricula — has tripled, rising from 6 percent to almost 18 percent. The three branches of government have, in effect, restored America's racially dual system of education. At their confirmation hearings, dozens of Trump judicial nominees even refused to say whether they thought *Brown* was rightly decided.

———

Not all my work at Hogan was education-related. In the late 1980s, for example, the same federal judge who presided over the *Adams* litigation appointed me to undertake an independent investigation of sexual harassment within the Securities and Exchange Commission. Having just settled an employment discrimination case against it, the SEC had agreed to submit to an independent investigation as part of the settlement. It was the first investigation into sexual harassment at a major federal agency. After undertaking an exhaustive examination of the agency's culture and history of pervasive harassment, I wrote a report that detailed my findings and included a list of recommendations for improvement.

Before issuing the report, however, I wanted to be sure that my recommendations would have the support of the chairman of the Equal Employment Opportunity Commission. At the time, that role was filled by none other than Clarence Thomas. I knew then–Chairman Thomas because he and I had both at one time headed OCR, I in the Carter administration and he in the Reagan administration. He reviewed an outline of my report and offered helpful suggestions to improve training for supervisory employees and to better structure the agency's internal Equal Employment Opportunity procedures. My final report, over three hundred pages, documented years of extensive sexual harassment throughout the agency. Our findings were confirmed when my then-reader delivered the document. In the elevator on her way to the chairman's office, she was hit on by a senior SEC employee. I should have filed a supplemental report.

⸺✦⸺

I cherished my fifteen years in Hogan's education group. My younger self could never have imagined that I'd be able to pursue in an elite law firm environment the same civil rights goals that I'd worked so hard to achieve at HEW. It would be wonderful if the revolving door between big law firms and the federal government worked that way more often.

CHAPTER 12

The White Cane

B Y NOW YOU KNOW HOW MUCH I DIDN'T WANT TO USE A white mobility cane. You also know that I did eventually get one. Here's the story of how that happened.

When I left OCR in 1979 and returned to Hogan, it meant that I no longer had a government-paid aide to travel with me. The situation soon came to a head when I was invited to attend an education conference in South Carolina with the governor. I'd have to travel solo and had no idea how I'd manage it. Looking from side to side no longer worked, as even my peripheral vision was pretty much gone. With the conference a month away, I bit the embarrassment bullet and decided the time had finally come to get a cane.

I should have just called the Columbia Lighthouse for the Blind, an organization that excels at teaching cane travel. But I still didn't feel like someone who needed an organization whose name included the dreaded word "blind." Fortunately, Edie had noticed at our community center a spry tap-dancing instructor, Ann Chapman, who was blind and used a cane. She agreed to teach me—and even offered to throw in some tap-dancing lessons for free. Perhaps regrettably, I passed on the tap dancing. But with Ann's encouragement, I bought my own cane, a white, foldable stick made of aluminum and fiberglass with a swiveling "marshmallow" at the end that helps the cane glide smoothly across sidewalk cracks. And I went to work on the difficult business of learning how to use it.

Ann lived just a block from us and taught me the basics of "cane travel"—how to swing the cane, when to tap, how fast to go—first in her living room, and then out in the neighborhood. What my instructor couldn't teach me was the emotional component. At the beginning, I practiced only at night, to avoid the possibility that someone I knew might see me and think that I was, well, blind. But as I grew more confident, the cane quickly became a real advantage. For the first time in a long time, I could walk around without holding someone's elbow. I was less likely to fall off curbs, less likely to trip over stuff, less likely to walk into a door or wall. I was safer. My shins were safer. Edie worried less. I went to South Carolina alone.

The cane was as much a symbolic change as anything else. It announced to the world that I was blind. That was the part that had scared me the most. But much to my surprise, I found that it was actually quite helpful. It meant, for example, that I could ask for directions without making up elaborate explanations of why I needed them. And without my having to ask, people introduced themselves. "Hi, David," they'd say as they approached me. "It's your neighbor Peter." So ceased my unintended rudeness, my ignoring people who tried to catch my eye, and my mistaking people for others. There was no more mystery about "Tatel's issues."

Edie remembers our conversation after my first week of commuting with a cane. "Guess what!" I told her. "People react totally differently to me brushing into them when I'm holding the cane." "No kidding," she sighed.

The cane was liberating in so many ways. All my subterfuges with maître d's, elevators, and the L7 bus became unnecessary. I didn't need to chat up the maître d' all the way to my table; I could just ask someone which elevator was arriving and would they please push 12; when a bus pulled in, it was easy to ask, "Is this the L7?" My cane allowed me to navigate the D.C. Metro entirely on my own. What a difference that cane made in how I moved through the world—and in how the world saw me.

I didn't even mind answering questions about the cane. One person I was standing next to, after inquiring if he could ask a question, said his mother was losing her sight and asked how she could get a cane. Feeling like an expert, I was happy to explain. On airplanes, seatmates often remarked, "Very cool the way it folds up," or "What's the ball at the end for?" One passenger told me I had a "nice golf club," and asked how I'd made it through security. I suspect he wasn't a very good golfer.

The cane let my family continue hiking, one of the things we love doing together. Sliding the marshmallow end along the ground doesn't work very well on a bumpy trail covered with leaves or rocks, so Edie or one of the kids would take one end while I hung on to the other, and away we'd go. Whoever was on the front end of the cane was responsible for telling me whatever I needed to know about the terrain. When a big rock was on the path, they would call out, "Step up, up, big up." Edie might say "Slippery!" at Little Devils Staircase in Shenandoah National

Park. She shouted "Steep!" all the way up the Schilthorn in Switzerland. At Colca Canyon in Peru, "Rocky, down" was her song. On the Appalachian Trail in Vermont, she'd just repeat "R&R," which means Rocks and Roots.

As I navigated airports and taxi lines with my cane, I discovered how helpful people could be. In St. Louis, a ticket agent at TWA Gate 38 always kept his eye out for me. After I landed, he'd often walk along with me through the concourse, chatting the whole way. In Milwaukee, the man at the newspaper stand at the bottom of the escalator always made sure I got a taxi. And then there were the random strangers who, seeing me with a cane, asked if they could be of assistance. Usually, I accepted their offers, except for the nice lady in San Francisco who asked in her pronounced British accent, "Sir, may I tie your shoe for you?" "Thank you," I replied—and tied it myself.

But some kinds of help are the kinds of help we all can do without, as the "Free to Be...You and Me" lyric goes. In St. Louis, our co-counsel, a Mr. Magoo–type, had better eyesight than me but was quite scatterbrained. After a long day of conferencing and brief writing, I was ready to return to D.C., and it turned out that Mr. Magoo was on the same flight. I made the mistake of following his lead: the inattentive leading the blind. Instead of relying on my cane, I held his arm as we rushed through the airport, got to the gate, and hopped on the plane. Soon after takeoff, the pilot announced, "Ladies and Gentlemen, our flight time to Columbus, Ohio, will be fifty-five minutes." Ugh. Gate procedures then were not what they are today.

———

Over the years, many people have asked, "How could a blind person be as successful as you've been?" Why didn't I just become a basket weaver as that clueless ophthalmologist suggested? I've thought about that question a lot.

One answer is that my parents were always behind me. They knew that something was wrong with my vision even though they didn't fully understand what it was. My dad never stopped showing me his complex formulas and intricate drawings, pointing out the stars and the planets, and letting me loose in his lab. My mom, worried as she was about my eyes, let me find my own limits, even if it worried her to see me behind the wheel of a car.

Another answer is that I was fortunate not to lose my sight entirely until I was an adult with a solid professional track record. I'd already succeeded at two universities, a law firm, and the Lawyers' Committee. I already had mentors and role models who cared about my success. It didn't hurt that I've always really liked gadgets and technology. And over and over I'd been in the right place at the right time. When I became completely blind, I already had a clear mission: I yearned to be a civil rights lawyer and to use my legal skills to make the world a better place. Basket weaving just wasn't going to cut it.

Perhaps the best answer is that my family has always been by my side. Edie and our four wonderful children have been my lifelines to the visual world. While there have been plenty of fears and frustrations along the way, my family's love, support, and encouragement have made my life—and definitely this book—possible.

CHAPTER 13

Benched

A LIFETIME SEAT ON THE NATION'S SECOND HIGHEST COURT, the opportunity to decide some of the most important legal issues facing our nation, the privilege of interpreting our two-and-a-half-century-old Constitution—all these make an appointment to the D.C. Circuit the apex of a legal career. But when I received that splendid job, it came as a consolation prize.

When Bill Clinton won the presidency in November 1992, I thought I finally had a shot at heading the Civil Rights Division at the Justice Department. But it wasn't to be. Clinton's political gifts didn't include filling positions expeditiously, and before anyone could be appointed to the Civil Rights Division, there had to be an Attorney General. That process alone ate up months. The President's first choice for AG was Judge Patricia Wald, the first woman ever to sit on the D.C. Circuit and the first woman ever to serve as its chief judge. She demurred, preferring, she later told me, the "contemplative life of the court." Also, the White House wouldn't have let her pick her own people, which for her was a deal-breaker. Clinton's next pick, Zoë Baird, was nixed because she hadn't paid Social Security taxes for her nanny, an undocumented immigrant. Next up was Judge Kimba Wood, who, it turned out, had a similar nanny problem. In retrospect, I expect it was no coincidence that the public's new obsession with the compensation of nannies and housekeepers coincided with a new push to appoint working mothers to federal office. The fourth time was the charm. Janet Reno—a state attorney from Florida who had no children (and no nanny)—became AG.

With Reno confirmed, Clinton turned his attention to filling the rest of the department's top positions. I was one of two finalists to lead the Civil Rights Division, but the White House chose Lani Guinier, a distinguished Harvard Law professor. I was disappointed, but I thought Guinier a fine choice. They offered to make me her deputy, but I declined. At this point in my career, I wanted to pitch, not catch. I watched from the sidelines as her nomination stalled. Republicans tagged her a "quota queen," a vicious and unfair label that combined a cartoonish notion of affirmative action with racist stereotypes about welfare queens. The label stuck, Democrats abandoned her, and the president ultimately did, too. In the interim, I was asked if I was interested in being commissioner of Social Security. That was a positively terrible idea. Edie and I hadn't paid taxes for our housekeeper, either. The headline ("Clinton Nominee for Social Security Commissioner Failed to Pay Social Security Taxes") would have written itself.

Then, in spring 1993, Justice Byron White announced his retirement from the Supreme Court. If Pat Wald had accepted the AG job, she probably would have been Clinton's first choice to fill the vacancy. Her decision to turn down the job was one of those "butterfly effects" that can change the world because it meant that President Clinton instead nominated Ruth Bader Ginsburg, a not-yet-"notorious" judge, who had served on the D.C. Circuit for thirteen years. Upon her confirmation, there would be a vacancy on the appeals court, and rumors circulated for a full year about who would be chosen to fill it.

For most federal circuit courts, home-state senators have a role, sometimes a veto, in deciding who gets nominated to fill such vacancies. The District of Columbia, of course, has no senators, so the White House alone controls the pipeline to the D.C. Circuit. I understand that my name was tossed into the ring by then–White House counsel Bernard Nussbaum and one of his deputies, Cheryl Mills, who had worked with me at Hogan. Perhaps my name was also on the list because, according to George Stephanopoulos in his own memoir, the White House had earlier considered me for the Supreme Court vacancy left by Justice White. They thought my personal story would make a "powerful statement."

When I learned I was on the list for the D.C. Circuit, I didn't play it cool. I let it be known to administration insiders and power brokers around town that I was interested. How did I "let it be known," you might wonder? D.C. can sometimes feel like a small town, and as in any small town, most everyone knows which front porch to visit for the latest gossip and who has the ear of the decision-makers. I basically told everyone I knew that I wanted the job, hoping someone would deliver the message.

Fortunately for me, Lloyd Cutler became White House counsel while the gossip mills were still spinning. I knew Cutler well. He had been in the East Room when President Kennedy launched the Lawyers' Committee, he'd hired me as director of the National Committee, and we'd worked together on the *Claiborne Hardware* case. With an advocate like Cutler on the inside, I felt like I had a real chance. Still, when the *Post* listed three front-runners for

Ginsburg's seat, my name was not among them. Don't believe everything you read in the papers.

Days after the *Post* article, the White House called to tell me that the president wanted to nominate me to the D.C. Circuit. It had come down to good friends, good timing, and good luck. I heard later that in the end the president just asked Cutler whom he should pick, and Cutler recommended me. He must have made a good case, because it was just a few weeks earlier at a White House reception that the First Lady had introduced me to the president as the fellow who lost her Legal Services Corporation case. It also didn't hurt that Vernon Jordan, another powerful Washington lawyer and Clinton confidant, had put in a good word on my behalf. He and I had met while I was OCR director when he'd helped me navigate some perilous political challenges, especially in North Carolina. Nobody was more persuasive than Vernon Jordan.

When the phone rang in the early evening, Edie and I were finishing the dinner dishes, and with the three older children away in college, only our youngest was still at home. Edie heard just my side of the conversation: "Oh, how wonderful...I'd be pleased to accept." Then she heard a lot of talk about schedules, announcements, and paperwork. "What was that all about?" Edie asked, though I suspected she'd already guessed. "It was the White House," I confirmed, "and believe it or not, the president has decided to nominate me to the D.C. Circuit." We hugged, put away the dishes, and went for a long, very quiet walk, absorbing the news and contemplating our new future. We told only our kids, which is probably when they began planning to buy the curly white judge wig they presented to me at my investiture.

I soon learned that being picked for the job was only the beginning. I filled out stacks of forms for the ABA (who'd decide whether I was technically qualified), the FBI (who'd decide whether I was a security risk), and the Senate Judiciary Committee (who'd decide whether I was politically palatable). I then began preparing for my formal nomination and confirmation process, which involved a few visits to the White House. I once ran into President Clinton briefly in the hall, but he never formally interviewed me. White House lawyers asked me general questions about judicial philosophy but nothing about abortion, affirmative action, or any other hot-button issue. Less important than how I would do the job, apparently, was whether I might cause problems for the president during the confirmation process. That part of the interview was deadly serious. A staff lawyer invited me into a private office, closed the door, and told me our discussion would never leave the room. "We're ready to go," he said, "but you need to tell me if there's anything in your background we don't know that would embarrass the president." I had nothing to report other than our failure to pay Social Security taxes for our housekeeper, which we'd already corrected. That issue had caused problems for so many nominees that the Senate Judiciary Committee had resolved that anyone could be nominated for a judgeship despite a tax issue involving a household worker so long as they retroactively paid the tax.

I was formally nominated the next morning, right before the Memorial Day weekend. In his announcement, the president lauded my "lifelong commitment to protecting and preserving the rights of all Americans" in both "the private sector and in public service." He said nothing about my vision, though the press reported that I would be the first blind person to serve as a federal appellate judge. I spent much of the summer preparing for my confirmation hearing. Justice Department lawyers grilled me, as did my partners at the firm. In many ways it was like getting ready for any job interview, working through my résumé to make sure that I remembered and could speak sensibly about the jobs I'd held and the cases I'd worked on. In other ways it was totally different. A Justice Department lawyer would play the role of a hostile senator, pepper me with questions, and give me feedback on my answers. Those practice questions mostly related to mutterings from conservative interest groups about my civil rights record. I had been labeled pro-busing, which sounded better than "quota queen" but stoked the same fears. Some also said I was too idealistic and insensitive to political realities. Pat Harris's criticism at OCR was dredged up. I prepared for all of those questions, though for the most part the answer was always the same: As a judge, I'd neutrally apply the law, and I couldn't comment on the merits of issues likely to come before me.

My nomination sailed through. Democrats controlled the Senate. Senator Ted Kennedy had introduced me around; Hogan partners like Frank Fahrenkopf, a past chairman of the Republican National Committee, had smoothed the way with GOP senators; and John Warner, a senator from Virginia, was a Hogan alumnus. They knew my work and my reputation, and helped convince their wary colleagues that I was no radical. My innocuous confirmation hearing lasted less than an hour. I was asked nothing about my blindness and didn't even get to use the answers I'd practiced to questions about busing. The most demanding question was from Senator Paul Simon: "You may have to rule on some legislation where you philosophically differ with the law. Is that going to be a major problem?" "It will not," I replied. "I fully understand the difference between advocacy and judging." There was of course only one right answer to that question. In the history of confirmations, I'm certain no one has ever bungled it.

This exchange reminds me of the best retort I ever heard at a confirmation hearing. President Carter had nominated Pat Wald for the D.C. Circuit—the very same Pat whose decision to decline the role of Attorney General led to RBG's nomination to the Supreme Court and mine to the D.C. Circuit. Pat, like Ruth, was a trailblazer for women in the law. Even before her nomination, she had become an influential voice on issues around juvenile justice, mental health, and legal services, despite taking ten years off to raise her five children. At her confirmation hearing, Bob Jones of Bob Jones University was called as a witness and accused Pat of being "an instrument of the devil." Senator Birch Bayh didn't miss a beat, asking Jones, "Have you ever met Mrs. Wald? Look behind you. Tell me if she looks like an instrument of the devil." Pat's five children were all there with their mom. The scene spoke for itself. Pat never had to say a word about "family values."

Happily, no one summoned the devil during my confirmation hearing. The Judiciary Committee unanimously approved me. A few weeks later, at one in the morning, the full Senate confirmed me without even a roll call. It was a different time. If I were nominated today, I'd be lucky to scrape by with a handful of GOP votes.

Back then, cell phones weren't yet ubiquitous. At the very moment the Senate voted to confirm me, I was on a delayed flight to Missoula, Montana, to go hiking with my son, Josh, who was in college there. I didn't find out about my confirmation until the next morning, when the White House Counsel's Office reached me at Josh's house. We celebrated over a cup of coffee, then hit the trail. At age fifty-two, I was about to become a federal judge.

Despite my best efforts, my blindness had become part of the narrative. As usual, I had tried to keep my vision out of the spotlight. At one point, Nan Aron, president of the Alliance for Justice, a powerful force in judicial nominations, told me that the Alliance would be putting out a statement supporting me and asked if the statement could reference my disability. I said no, just as I had years earlier when I was appointed OCR director.

Nevertheless, almost every paper that reported on my nomination and confirmation mentioned my blindness, sometimes in the headline. I hated that. Although I was proud of what I'd accomplished professionally, I didn't want my nomination attributed to my disability. I didn't think that the powerful reasons for appointing women, racial minorities, and other underrepresented groups to the courts applied to me. Even though my white cane meant the whole world could see that I was blind, I was still in denial.

Looking back, I regret my refusal to discuss my blindness and the shame I felt when others mentioned it. I now see that I was so wrapped up in my all-consuming effort to be "normal" that I missed another opportunity to be up front about my vision and help dispel stereotypes about the capabilities of people with disabilities. I also misunderstood what diversity is really about. I *wasn't* a judge who was just like everyone else, and the life experiences born from my blindness were valuable, not shameful. My presence on the court could help other people with disabilities in myriad ways. Indeed, if I'd had such a role model growing up, perhaps I never would have seen blindness as shameful in the first place.

My judicial career formally began with a ceremony called an investiture. Held in the huge sixth-floor ceremonial courtroom, it was packed with government officials, other judges, and my family and friends. The White House counsel read the Presidential Commission appointing me to serve "for good behavior," which is constitutional lingo meaning "for life, unless you really screw things up." Lou Oberdorfer, my mentor who'd become a federal district judge years earlier, administered the oath of office. I swore to "administer justice without respect to persons, and do equal right to the poor and to the rich." Then my four children "robed" me in the traditional black gown so I looked the part. And just like that, my new life began.

Everyone knows about the Supreme Court, but few know anything about what the Constitution calls the "inferior" courts. Let me pause here to take you on a tour of those courts—what they are, how they work, why they matter. Nearly every federal case begins in one of the ninety-four district courts across the country. (State cases are heard in the nation's fifty separate state court systems. If you want to learn about those, you'll have to read a different book.) The federal district courts are the trial courts you see on TV, the places where all the juicy stuff happens. District judges, like my friend Lou Oberdorfer, look at evidence, hear from witnesses, empanel juries, hold trials, sentence criminal defendants, and more. A single judge presides over each case. It's ultimately their job (sometimes with the help of a jury) to "find" the facts, which is just a legal way of saying they have to figure out what actually happened.

After a district court rules, the next step up the judicial ladder is a circuit court, otherwise known as a court of appeals. There are thirteen federal circuit courts, whose job is to review district court rulings for error. Don't like the verdict in your case or think the district judge got the law wrong? Then the circuit court is the right place for you. Circuit judges have more power than district judges, but their role is more limited. They don't hear testimony and don't do fact finding. Instead, circuit judges nearly always defer to the facts as the district court found them. They hear only from lawyers, who file written briefs and then appear before them for oral arguments. In reviewing those briefs and assessing the arguments, their job is to make sure that no error was made in the application of the law—which might come from the Constitution, a federal statute, or prior court rulings—to the facts. Unlike district judges, moreover, circuit judges don't work alone. They hear appeals in randomly selected panels of three judges, though on rare occasions the full court sits together. (This is known as sitting "en banc.") They issue their decisions in written opinions that explain their reasoning. When the judges hearing an appeal disagree, the dissenting judge writes an opinion explaining their contrary view.

If you're still not happy after the circuit court rules, the US Supreme Court is your last resort. The justices hear appeals from the circuit courts and from the fifty state supreme courts. All nine justices hear each case, and they have the final say about what the law means. But they don't take every case. Far from it. The modern Supreme Court "grants certiorari"—that is, agrees to review—in only a few dozen especially important cases each year. So in most cases, the circuit courts have the last word.

Remember the case in the Prologue of Daniel Lewis Lee's execution? Now you understand better what happened there. We on the appeals court had to wait for the district court to resolve the factual dispute about the effect of pentobarbital. Only after the district court made that finding could we apply the law (there, the Constitution's Cruel and Unusual Punishments Clause) and determine whether Lee's execution could go forward. Only after we'd made that determination could the parties ask the Supreme Court to hear the case. Of course, that's not what happened, because the Supreme Court short-circuited the process. But that's how it was supposed to work.

Each of the thirteen circuit courts has its own ethos, stemming in part from its geography. Judges on the very large Ninth Circuit, which usually sits in San Francisco and Pasadena, are spread out from Seattle to Phoenix, and from Alaska to Hawaii. Judges on the smaller Second Circuit, which sits in New York, live in Connecticut and Vermont as well as New York. The D.C. Circuit's geographical reach is the smallest, just the District of Columbia. That makes the court unique. For one thing, unlike larger circuits, all the D.C. appellate and district judges work out of the same courthouse on Constitution Avenue. That let us often have lunch together. (Mine was unvaryingly a turkey sandwich, iced tea, and a single oatmeal raisin cookie.) In the Judges' Dining Room, next to the cafeteria, we could talk informally, hear how other judges work, and empathize and socialize with each other. It's a safe place. A sign says, "No word spoken here shall ever be repeated outside these walls." The job of a judge is quite solitary, so I always enjoyed our lunchtime gatherings, though it could be a bit awkward when I sat next to a district judge whose ruling we'd reversed that morning.

The D.C. Circuit is unique in other ways as well. It was the first circuit court that Congress established and remained the only federal appellate court in the country (other than the Supreme Court) until the end of the nineteenth century. As the nation grew, the judicial system expanded. But the D.C. Circuit retained a special docket of cases involving the United States government. Most cases involving the president or Congress come through the D.C. Circuit. The court also hears nearly every case involving an alphabet soup of federal agencies, like the FCC, SEC, NLRB, EPA, and FAA. The D.C. Circuit has heard some of the most politically charged cases in American history, from President Truman's seizure of the steel mills to the Pentagon Papers to Watergate. Some cases, though less sensational, affect the lives of millions, as they raise questions about the availability of the internet, the safety of the skies, the quality of our air and water, and so on. Although the court's jurisdiction is geographically tiny, its reach and range are vast. That's why it's often called the second highest court in the land.

———

There are many wonderful things about being a federal judge. One I had to adjust to was the solitude that comes with the job.

After years in a busy private practice full of meetings, phone calls, networking, lunches, travel, and a built-in social life, I suddenly found myself mostly alone. The phone rarely rang. There were very few meetings and virtually no travel. And while I would hear cases with two other judges, we communicated almost entirely by memo. In time I thrived in my new environment. I liked the quiet, the court's predictable schedule, working with my law clerks, and the intellectual engagement with laws, writing, and collegial debate. When I needed company, I called a friend. Then I got a dog.

I was lucky that at least one friend was always close by: Lou Oberdorfer. We'd visit each other's chambers to discuss cases, history, politics, and the books we were reading. When the weather was nice, we continued our conversations on strolls down the Mall. Because of our special relationship, I recused myself from hearing appeals from any of Lou's cases. But that didn't stop Lou from reviewing mine. If I got a note from him with "YOUR OPINION" in the subject line, I knew I was in for it. Getting something past the Supreme Court was nothing compared to satisfying Judge Louis F. Oberdorfer.

One other perk of the job was the power to perform weddings (an especially unique honor before some states let just about anyone officiate). I've done ceremonies for friends, the children of friends, my law clerks, and all four of our children. There's just one wrinkle: Not all states allow federal judges to perform marriages. One way around this is to get a local judge to issue an order that grants a federal judge temporary authority to officiate. That's what I did for our daughters Rebecca (and her husband, Peter), Stephanie (and her husband, Christian), and Emily (and her husband, Noah). Another workaround is to perform the ceremony in a legal jurisdiction—say, my chambers in D.C.—and then reenact it at the wedding. Guests never know the difference.

I did that for our son, Josh (and his wife, Joanna), making it official in chambers, then doing it over again in Vermont thirty days later, the date they celebrate as their anniversary.

It's always a joy to be part of a happy wedding. Over the years a few couples who asked me to officiate at their weddings wanted to include their rabbis. I was fine with that, as long as the ceremony was First Amendment–compliant, with a high wall of separation between church and state. The rabbi chanted the prayers; I tied the knot.

The strangest wedding I ever performed was at Emily's request when she was a labor and delivery nurse at a hospital in California. One night, around 10 p.m. our time, she called to say she had a patient in labor. The baby was coming very early, and the parents hadn't had time to get married. "Can you do marriages over the phone?" Emily asked. "They really want to be married before the baby is born." "Of course not," I answered. "But I'm happy to do a ceremony now if the couple will promise, once the baby is born, to get a marriage license in California. And the next time I'm out there, I'll sign it." That's what we did. Emily was the photographer; Edie, on an extension phone, was the witness. Shortly after they committed "to love and to cherish till death do us part," and I declared them husband and wife, the baby arrived. A few weeks later Edie and I were in California. We had a lovely lunch with the couple and the baby, and I signed the license. The parents have since divorced. I can do weddings, but I can't assure happily-ever-afters.

CHAPTER 14

Behind the Scenes

AT THE D.C. CIRCUIT, LIKE ALL FEDERAL APPEALS COURTS, the judges neither select the cases they hear nor determine the composition of the three-judge panels that hear those cases. Instead, the court clerk assembles the panels and assigns cases to them at random. It's a three-step process, combining modern technology and a playground toy.

First, a computer program creates an oral argument schedule for the number of judges working in a given term, which on the D.C. Circuit runs from September through May. Judges get the summer to catch up on opinions, train new clerks, and prepare for the next term. In devising the argument schedule, the program aims to set enough argument dates that every appeal can be heard promptly, to balance each judge's workload, and to ensure that the three-judge panels vary throughout the year. The result is a complete argument schedule for the term, but with no judges' names or actual cases filled in. Schedule #5, for example, might involve hearing arguments on two days during the first week of September, on three days during the second week of October, and so on. But the program doesn't decide which judge is assigned to Schedule #5 or which cases will be heard on those days.

That's where the toy comes in. A court staffer fills a child's red sand pail with pingpong balls labeled with the names of each sitting judge, then draws balls to match judges to specific schedules. If someone says "Schedule #5" and then pulls the ball labeled "Tatel," I get assigned to Schedule #5. Those two steps are completed early in the year, so judges know their argument schedule for the full term in advance. But they don't yet know which cases they'll be hearing on argument days.

Specific cases are assigned at step three, which happens on a rolling basis over the course of the year. A few months in advance of each argument session, the Clerk's Office identifies all the cases that have been fully briefed and are ready to be argued. Then a software program assigns each of those cases to specific argument days. The program assigns about three cases per argument day, though that number has varied a bit over time.

Those assignments are almost entirely random, though the software can correct for workload imbalances or lumpy distributions of similar cases. The random assignment process is crucial to the integrity of the court system. Judges all wear the same black robes because it shouldn't make any difference which judge hears your case. I never doubted the D.C. Circuit's process for one second, though as you'll hear shortly, the sand pail occasionally dealt me cards I didn't see coming.

Judges know their sitting schedules and their fellow panel members months before a term begins, but they don't learn which specific cases they'll be hearing until six weeks before oral argument. Lawyers learn their argument date around the same time the judges do, but they don't learn which judges will be on their panel until a month before their court date. In many other circuits, lawyers don't know which judges will be on their panel until the actual day of oral argument. Either way, that means lawyers can't tailor their briefs to the views of any particular judge.

Oral arguments usually take place in our fifth-floor courtroom. At the front of the courtroom, the three judges sit behind an elevated "bench" that spans most of the room's width. It's so wide that to whisper to the judge in the next seat, you have to roll your chair over a few feet. Behind the bench, set into the pinkish-gray marble wall, is the bronze seal of the United States. In front of the bench are two big tables where the lawyers sit, and a lectern in the center where attorneys address the judges. On the side, to the judges' right, sits the courtroom deputy, who makes sure the lawyers are present and ready to go, calls each case for argument at the appropriate time, and, since the pandemic, coordinates any lawyers or judges participating remotely. To the judges' left sit the three law clerks working on that day's appeals. Most judges bring their computers to the bench for argument and can communicate directly with their law clerks through email and text. I didn't email my clerks from the bench, even though for the last few years I finally had a Braille computer that was capable of it. On the rare occasion I wanted something from my clerks during argument, I waved them up to the bench and whispered my questions.

The rest of the courtroom is for the public. Its six rows of wooden pews can hold around a hundred people. The walls of the room are dark wood, displaying portraits of circuit judges past and present. (The really old, dead ones get moved to the back corridor walls.) They all look pretty similar, mostly older white men depicted against muted backgrounds and surrounded by ornate gold frames. One stands out from the rest: Hanging in a plain silver frame on the south wall, right above Judge Robert Bork, is my portrait. Instead of muted colors, my background is the bright blue sky that was visible from my chambers' window. Another difference between my portrait and the stuffier ones? In mine, I'm smiling.

Those choices weren't accidental. Each judge's portrait is a gift from that judge's law clerks to the court, but the judges themselves (used to having their way) generally insist on choosing the artist and managing the production. Edie and I knew little about portraiture, so weren't even sure where to start. Working closely with a few of my more artistically minded law clerks, Edie began by contacting the National Portrait Gallery for help. The curator gave them a tour of the gallery, pointing out portraits in different styles, asking questions about what they wanted to achieve, and teaching them what qualities they might look for. She then suggested several artists for us to consider.

We selected Jon Friedman, both because his portraits are beautiful and because they reflect the personalities and life's work of his subject. Before painting me, Jon spent several days in chambers, read some of my opinions, attended an oral argument, and took lots of photographs as I worked. The final product was everything we'd hoped for. I'm told the image of a relaxed and smiling judge against the D.C. skyline gets my personality just right. Also visible in the portrait is an award from the Lawyers' Committee, a Lucite obelisk that depicts JFK in the East Room at the Committee's creation. Just next to the award are my earbuds in a little tangle on the table—both an exercise in realism (I can't tell you how much grief those tangled cords caused me in the pre-Bluetooth days) and a symbol of my blindness for anyone who knows to look. Were I to do the portrait today, Vixen would be front and center.

Oral arguments are always set for 9:30 in the morning. A few minutes earlier, the three judges assigned to the panel gather in the robing room, which is right behind the courtroom. It looks a bit like a locker room in a nice gym, with the judges' robes hanging in wooden closets adorned with little brass nameplates. By court tradition, previous tenants' names remain on the closets, with new judges' names added below—kind of like how winners are recorded on the Stanley Cup. My name is right below "R. B. Ginsburg." While we put on our robes, we schmoozed about the weather, sports, really anything other than the cases we were about to hear. Most of the time, oral argument is the first opportunity judges get to hear each other's views on a case.

At 9:30 sharp, the deputy calls the court into session, proclaiming, "Oyez, oyez, oyez. All persons having business before the honorable, the United States Court of Appeals for the District of Columbia Circuit, are admonished to draw near and give their attention, for the court is now sitting. God save the United States and this honorable court." With the bang of a gavel, the three judges enter the courtroom through a door behind the bench. The senior-most judge—which is to say, the chief judge or the active judge who's been on the court longest—sits in the middle, ready to preside. The next most-senior judge sits to that judge's right, with the most junior judge on the left. Before Vixen, when I was junior and had the longest walk, I'd run my finger along the back wall until I felt the piece of tape that I'd stuck there to signal I was right behind my chair. When I was second in seniority or presiding, I could get to my chair just using my cane. In later years, Vixen guided me. She knew which chair I'd be using that day because my law clerk had already placed a treat on my seat.

Oral arguments generally last between thirty and sixty minutes apiece. Each side is typically allotted ten to fifteen minutes at the lectern, though my court, unlike many others, allows arguments to continue as long as judges have questions. That meant that some arguments went on for hours. I never minded. For me, oral argument was the pinnacle of the appellate process. If you've never seen an appellate argument, I encourage you to attend one—they're open to the public. If you can't make it in person, you can listen in real time on the court's website. There's nothing quite like two well-prepared appellate lawyers arguing before three well-prepared judges peppering them with questions. Indeed, I often invited friends, particularly nonlawyers—to come see us in action. They always left impressed with the judicial system. Watching judges work together to try to understand the facts of a case, what the law requires, and any potential implications for other cases is really something to behold. It can bolster your faith in government.

All judges have their own approach to oral argument. I focused on the specific things I actually needed to know to decide the case. I'd ask questions about facts in the record that weren't clear. I'd ask questions about the nuances of the parties' legal arguments and, in particular, the reasons why those arguments might be wrong. I'd also ask about the implications of those arguments, often by using hypothetical questions. "I know in this case, counsel, that the defendant destroyed the evidence. But if he had only hidden it, would he still be guilty under your theory?" Those sorts of questions helped me tease out the precise rules the parties were advocating for and the potential implications of those rules for future cases. My questions were sometimes also designed to communicate with my colleagues, whose views about a case I rarely knew in advance. I might also ask an attorney a particular question not because I didn't know the answer, but because I wanted my colleagues to hear the lawyer answer it. Other judges did that, too.

Suffice to say that there was always a lot going on during arguments. They were great fun, but, wow, were they draining. I had to listen intently to the lawyers and to my colleagues to understand exactly what points they were trying to make, and I had to get in my questions without interrupting others. After a morning of arguments, I got very little done the rest of the day.

I'm often asked: What makes a good appellate lawyer? That's an easy one. Good lawyers know their case at least as well as the judges do. They know that when a judge asks a question, they should stop talking, think about the question, and answer it, preferably by starting with a simple yes or no. Good lawyers answer hypothetical questions rather than fight them. They almost never read from their notes. Above all, good lawyers understand that although their professional obligation is to represent their clients zealously, they are also officers of the court obligated to present their arguments accurately and honestly. Many lawyers who argued before me in the D.C. Circuit were fine appellate advocates. But I'm sorry to say that some—even those representing deep-pocketed clients in high-profile cases—were not always up to the task. That was disappointing. Good lawyers help judges do their jobs well; weak lawyers make it much harder.

During arguments, I used my Braille computer to listen to my notes about key issues in the case and the questions I wanted to ask. I'd keep one headphone in so I could hear those notes, and one out so I could hear the lawyers and my colleagues. In my last few years I graduated to a Bluetooth headset—no more tangled wires! My computer has a search function, which allows me to look things up on the fly. If, for example, a lawyer mentioned something about Section 36 of a statute, I would type "36" into the search function and presto, I'd hear the text of that provision through my headphone. One of my colleagues, Tom Griffith, liked to say that he wanted "one of those little black boxes that Tatel has, because it's got all the right answers."

When I joined the court, my new colleagues didn't make my blindness a big deal. Soon, they scarcely seemed to notice, which is just how I wanted it. My blindness became embedded in the culture of the court. If a lawyer referred to something without quoting it—for example, "Your Honor, please refer to Section 523b"—another judge would usually interject, "Counsel, please read it aloud." When I was the most senior judge on the panel and presided over the argument, the deputy sounded a subtle *beep* that I could hear from the bench since I couldn't see the red light that signaled the lawyer's time was up.

Only very occasionally did my blindness cause me trouble in the courtroom. At my very first argument, an important First Amendment case, I was so nervous that I left my headset in my pants pocket. I didn't realize it until I was seated behind the bench. In a packed courtroom, there was no way I was going to stand up, lift up my robe, and retrieve the headset. So I did the entire appeal by memory. After the argument in *US v. Microsoft*, an antitrust case that was heavily covered by the press, Edie overheard a reporter in the elevator saying that one of the judges had a hearing problem and used a "hearing assistance earphone." She quietly informed him that the judge was blind, not deaf, and, being Edie, answered all his questions about how my computer worked.

Does oral argument ever actually make any difference? People are sometimes skeptical, and I understand why. By the time judges get to oral argument, they've already studied the lengthy briefs from both sides. They've already looked at the statutes and cases on which those briefs rely. They've thought long and hard about the case. Don't judges have their minds made up already? How much can argument really add? I expect different judges would answer that question differently. For me, argument often mattered. Sometimes the lawyers' arguments would solidify my view about a case, particularly when the side I thought should lose couldn't give satisfactory answers to important questions. That increased my confidence that I hadn't missed anything and that the facts and the law were as I'd initially understood them. Quite often, lawyers' answers to my or my colleagues' questions gave me new information or ideas about how to write the opinion. It's one thing to know which side will win a case, but quite another to write an opinion explaining exactly why. And yes, once in a while, oral arguments changed my mind altogether.

After we were finished hearing the day's arguments, the three of us on the panel would return to the robing room, hang up our robes, then head across the hall to our airy conference room. Law books fill the shelves on two sides, and a long wooden table runs down the center of the room. In the middle of that table sits a small sculpture of the Scales of Justice. Natural light pours through the windows, which overlook the courthouse atrium. We again sat in assigned seats, with the most senior judge at the head of the table. Unlike at the Supreme Court (and most other appeals courts), on the D.C. Circuit the most junior judge speaks first and the most senior judge speaks last. This practice traces all the way back to the Sanhedrin, ancient Israel's governing tribunals where in capital cases the youngest rabbi spoke first so he wouldn't be swayed or intimidated by the views of his elders. Although the practice was designed to protect the newbies, I found it quite scary at the beginning. I was the most junior judge for three years, until Merrick Garland joined us, so I eventually got used to leading off.

Once each of us had a chance to share our initial thoughts, we all discussed the case together. That could take two minutes or two hours. We might pull books off the shelves and read key portions of relevant cases. Sometimes we'd take another look at the briefs and exhibits. A judge who consulted a book or document would usually just read it aloud so I could follow along. We'd listen to each other closely, and even if we arrived with differing views, very often we were able to reach consensus. It probably didn't hurt that during our conferences Vixen would snooze under the table, wander around the room, or settle in next to a judge who'd give her a tummy rub. The 2020 court photo of all the judges includes Vixen sitting next to me.

When we finished our discussion and our positions were clear, the presiding judge would usually decide who would write which opinion. In the spirit of collaboration, volunteers often got their choice. When we didn't all agree, the judge in the minority would write a dissenting opinion. It took weeks or even months for us to write those opinions, which become binding law in future cases and so must be crafted with great care. Once completed, draft opinions for both the majority and any dissent circulated by email for the other two judges to comment on. Most judges accepted a colleague's edits happily, and we continued circulating revised drafts until everyone was satisfied. (At our court, at least during my time on it, drafts didn't leak.) Once all three judges signed off on the opinion—the key phrase was "I am pleased to concur"—it was issued publicly, along with any dissent.

After conference, Vixen would guide me back to my chambers. Mine were on the fifth floor. They were spacious, with sweeping views of the Capitol, Constitution Avenue, the National Gallery of Art, and the distant Washington Monument. My office itself was filled with books, photos of my family, and mementos from my career. There was a couch, some comfortable chairs, and an adjacent small conference room. A computer monitor sat on my desk but faced outward for my reader and the law clerks to use. My judicial assistant sat right outside my door. Down the hall each clerk had an office with large windows that shared our incredible view. My reader sat at a desk at the end of the hall next to a large conference room with a big table where we'd often eat lunch as a group and where the clerks could gather to discuss the cases they were working on—or play trivia or Bananagrams or some other after-hours entertainment. Vixen had the run of the place. During the day she'd wander from sun spot to sun spot or settle right at my feet.

———•••———

Once back in chambers, I'd tell my clerks how we'd voted and which opinion I'd be writing. We'd get right to work. My chambers functioned as our own mini law firm. I adored working with my clerks, all recent law school graduates who would spend a year with me. Many then clerked for Supreme Court justices, and all went on to productive careers, including in law firms, government, and academia.

D.C. Circuit clerkships are competitive, so I had my pick of the nation's best and brightest young lawyers. They got to spend a year learning what goes on behind the scenes of an appellate court and helping me write opinions. In return, I got four brilliant assistants, all dedicated to the work of the court and jazzed about the possibilities of the legal system.

At lunchtime or day's end we'd sit around my desk or the big conference table discussing our cases. But that wasn't all we talked about. We discussed politics, breaking news, and the books we were reading (or wished we had time to read). We talked about music, movies, sports, and TV. And we talked about everything else going on in our lives. My clerks and readers gave me a window into youth and popular culture. I found them endlessly interesting. I wanted to know their views on free-speech controversies on college campuses, the increasing use of gender-neutral terms like "pregnant people," book banning, and the Kardashians. They'd read me their favorite tweets, try to explain what people were up to on TikTok, and describe the crowds that often gathered outside the courthouse on Constitution Avenue. Over the years it became unnerving to realize that while I kept getting older, the clerks always stayed the same age.

Occasionally, my clerks and I hosted guests in our chambers. A professor, reporter, or friend might stop by for lunch, or a former clerk would pop in for a visit. For a short time, we even hosted a Supreme Court justice. During the anthrax scare after 9/11, the justices were evacuated from the Supreme Court into our courthouse for almost a week. One of my law clerks, who would be clerking for Justice Sandra Day O'Connor the following year, asked if she could invite the justice to work in our chambers. I said of course. When the justice arrived I offered her my office. She declined, insisting on sharing with one of the clerks. She joined us all for lunch every day, which made my law clerks a bit nervous, but certainly enlivened our debates. I still think she was wrong in *Bush v. Gore*.

As much as I liked working with my clerks, I liked the process of selecting them less and less. For my first year, it was easy. When Abner Mikva, the court's chief judge, became President Clinton's White House counsel, he asked me to interview the clerks he had made offers to for the next two years. That worked out perfectly: His picks were excellent, and it meant I didn't have to worry about clerk hiring for a little while. At that time federal judges had agreed to interview applicants no earlier than March 1 of their second year of law school—an attempt to avoid judges jumping the gun on particularly promising students who had barely started law school. We were all deluged with hundreds of applications, which for many years arrived on paper. The people who delivered mail to chambers wheeled carts stacked high with envelopes. Batches of recommendations from law professors came in separately, so we'd spend hours attaching recommendation letters to the corresponding applications.

My current clerks would make the first cut. They sorted applications by law school and identified the top candidates. I'd then select a few finalists for in-person interviews. Top law school grades were a nonnegotiable prerequisite, but narrowing it down further proved much harder. I preferred applicants who had succeeded in rigorous undergraduate courses, especially science and math. Recommendations from professors I knew well and trusted were very helpful. I also liked applicants who were planning to clerk for a district judge before working on an appellate court. Experience outside the law, like working for a consulting firm or nonprofit, was also a plus. And I had a special affinity for Teach for America alumni because they had already demonstrated focus and perseverance. Besides, Edie had worked with TFA and was impressed with the corps members' dedication to public service.

This system was far from perfect. One problem was that with so many applications to sort through, judges (myself included) tended to focus on applications from elite schools, such as Harvard, Yale, Stanford, and my own Chicago. It was much harder to identify top candidates from other schools because most of the professors whose recommendations I trusted taught at the elite ones. During my first few years on the bench, I looked for applicants from lower-ranked schools. But given the ever-increasing number of applications, that quickly became overwhelming, so I tended to focus on the piles from the top schools. I know I missed many excellent applicants. I'd do it differently today.

Competition with other judges was another problem. "We're all type A+ by definition," another judge once explained. "We earn exactly the same amount of money. We have the same size offices, with the same size staff. We do the same work. The only way we can compete with each other is over law clerks." And compete we did—not always fairly. Some judges, never me, made "exploding offers" during interviews, or shortly afterward. "I'd like you to clerk for me," the judge would say, "but you need to accept right now." More "flexible" judges might inform candidates that they had one hour to decide, or that their offer would expire later that day. Other judges tried to game the system by scheduling four interviews at 8 a.m., blocking the applicants from early interviews with other judges. Some would schedule as many as a dozen interviews throughout the day, make exploding offers and, if accepted, cancel all the later interviews.

A legendary story around the courthouse illustrates how far judges would go to land a top law clerk. A candidate had lined up interviews with Ruth Ginsburg and Pat Wald, in that order. After finishing her interview with Ruth, the candidate went to Pat's chambers, where she waited to meet with the judge. While she was sitting there, Ruth called Pat's chambers, asked to speak with the candidate, and gave her an exploding offer. Legend says that the candidate accepted Ruth's offer on the spot, before Pat even had a chance to speak with her. Pat, as you might imagine, was none too pleased.

Some judges, usually self-proclaimed "conservatives" but a few others as well, refused to participate in the hiring plan at all. Calling it a "cartel" that would constrict their ability to hire "the best and the brightest," those judges interviewed and hired clerks before the plan's March 1 opening bell. One of those judges, Alex Kozinski of the Ninth Circuit (who years later resigned following allegations of sexual harassment), once joked to the *New York Times* that he began recruiting clerks "at birth." Very funny, but the headline for the story got it right when it referred to clerkship hiring as "lawless."

Maybe all's fair in love and clerk hiring, but I found these shenanigans troubling. Judges ought to recruit clerks more civilly than Division I schools go after athletes. Consider the system from the perspective of law students. These high-stakes interviews are likely their first contact with the federal judges whose opinions they have been reading in law school. To first- and second-year law students, federal judges are giants (trust me, I've been there). They hold all the power. How are students supposed to ask for more time to speak with their families or consider other offers when their judicial idols have just given them an exploding offer? How are they supposed to say no when a judge asks them to by-pass the hiring plan and interview early? What about the students who travel across the country on tight budgets for an interview only to be informed on arrival that the position has already been filled? Sure, we all wanted great law clerks. But there were plenty of outstanding candidates to go around. Does anyone seriously believe that students in the top 5 percent aren't just as capable as students in the top 1 percent? Or that students in a law school rated eighth in the nation aren't just as good as those in the number two law school?

Over the years we tried several schemes to improve things, but none of them completely solved the problem. In 2018 the courts developed a new hiring plan. Participating judges agreed not to interview applicants until after their second year of law school and not before a specific date in June. Exploding offers were banned, and all offers had to remain open for at least forty-eight hours. The new plan was a major improvement, though there still was no way to require every judge to participate. Our shift to an on-line database called OSCAR (Online System for Clerkship Application and Review) also helped, as it eliminated paperwork and simplified the sorting process.

During my last few years on the court, a new, secretive, and disturbing clerk-hiring plan emerged. Reflecting the growing ideological divisions in the courts, this new plan funnels selected law students to Trump-appointed and other conservative judges who agree to hire them. Unlike the official plan, which is public, open to all, and run by the judges themselves, the alternative plan is kept private, open only to students with particular viewpoints, and run by professors, students, and alumni affiliated with the Federalist Society, a conservative organization that has played an outsized role in the appointment of conservative judges. Also unlike the official plan, which is limited to students who have completed their second year of law school, the FedSoc plan identifies conservative-leaning students as early as their first few months of school. The FedSoc plan also doesn't end when a student secures a clerkship for a court of appeals or district court judge. Selected students often go on to clerk for right-leaning Supreme Court justices. They ultimately land in academia or big law firms, where they help mold and recruit the next generation of conservative law clerks. Some even become judges themselves and select the next round of clerks in their own image. The NCAA should be so good at identifying and developing top point guards.

Why is a secretive, ideologically skewed pipeline a problem? For one thing, it deprives judges like me of the opportunity to survey all the legal talent. I've never had an ideological filter for law clerks, and I value the opportunity to work with young lawyers whose policy views differ from mine. For another, it limits access to the career-defining federal court clerkships to a small subset of students who are invited in. Perhaps worst of all, many students themselves feel pressure to "pick a team" way too early. As first-years, they've barely learned what "originalism" is and are certainly in no position to decide whether that's the best or only way to interpret the Constitution. If I were a law school dean concerned about the education of young lawyers, I'd worry about a system that requires future lawyers to choose a legal philosophy and then structure their whole career around that choice when they can hardly tell a tort from a trademark. I would worry even more about sending the message that judging is all about ideology.

For those keeping score, like most federal judges of my generation I hired clerks who leaned left and clerks who leaned right. More of mine were left leaning, the result of some self-sorting combined with network effects. Finding clerks with the "right" politics, however, wasn't my goal. I never asked applicants about their political views. I wanted clerks who were bright, mature, engaged, and ready to work hard every day to help me find the right answer to difficult legal questions and draft clear and persuasive opinions. I wanted clerks who would challenge me to think differently and who weren't afraid to push back when they thought I'd gotten something wrong. And I wanted clerks who were interesting, who would be fun to spend every day with. If Antonin Scalia had applied to clerk in my chambers, I'd have hired him in an instant. I bet Pat Wald would have as well—unless RBG beat her to it. My clerks who went on to work for the Supreme Court did so mostly for the more liberal justices. Why were so few of my law clerks hired—or even interviewed—by the so-called conservative justices? You'd have to ask them.

———

By now you understand how I hired my law clerks, sometimes affectionately called "Tatel Tots." Each year, unlike other judges, I also hired a reader. I've had thirty-nine readers, many of whom were champion college debaters. Fast-speaking, fresh out of college, and bound for law school, debaters were perfect for the job. Several of them later became my law clerks, and some went on to clerk for Supreme Court justices.

Read the following lines aloud within ten seconds flat and you'll know what it's like to be my reader:

TATEL COMMA Circuit Judge COLON In *Shelby County v. Holder* ITALICS COMMA CITATION COMMA the Supreme Court raised serious questions about the continued constitutionality of Section 5 of the Voting Rights Act PERIOD Section 5 prohibits certain QUOTE covered jurisdictions CLOSE QUOTE from making any changes...

Did you read it all within ten seconds? Now try again, but this time without saying any of the punctuation. A bit easier, isn't it? Most of the time I don't want to hear punctuation because it distracts me from the content. And besides, most good readers signal commas, periods, question marks, and quotation marks through their voices. When I'm editing a document, though, I need to know for certain that the punctuation's there. I'm reliably informed that I can be an impatient listener. My readers say my favorite words are "Next sentence" and "Next paragraph." "Go back two pages" is also a popular one.

What did my law clerks and readers do? First they swore an oath of office, promising to "support and defend the Constitution of the United States." I explained to them that everything we do and say in chambers is confidential. I warned them to be especially careful when talking at parties or on the Metro, since there are ears everywhere. And then they got started. The law clerks' work consisted mostly of three things: writing documents called bench memos (before oral argument), drafting opinions (after argument), and spending hours reworking those opinions with me.

I'd start by assigning one clerk to each of my argument days. The same clerk would prepare bench memos for each of the cases we'd hear on a single day. That simplified the seating arrangements in the courtroom and helped smooth out workloads among the clerks. Each judge on the panel would usually be assigned to write the opinion in just one case, which meant each clerk usually left their sitting day with a single opinion-writing assignment. Once assigned sitting days, the clerks dug into their cases. They'd read all the briefs the parties had submitted, closely review the agency decision or district judge's ruling, read and analyze prior opinions addressing similar issues, and scrutinize the factual record. From all of that, they'd produce a bench memo, a ten- to twenty-page summary of the facts, the law, and the parties' arguments. The clerks also recommended how I should resolve the case and suggested some questions for oral argument. Bench memos were always a helpful starting point, but not much more than that.

Once I read the bench memo—that is, once my reader read it aloud to me—I'd read all the briefs and the key cases myself. Then the law clerk and I would sit down to discuss the case in detail. These discussions could last anywhere from a few minutes to a couple of days. In especially tricky cases, I'd loop my other law clerks into the discussion. The more brains, the better. Readers are right in the thick of all this, quickly learning every case themselves. After a year in my chambers reading all the briefs, memos, and opinions, they're more than ready for law school. I told my faculty friends that my readers should automatically get a year's credit, sort of like Advanced Placement for law school.

It was during our conversations that I might learn what other chambers were thinking about a case. My clerks would often talk to other judges' clerks, and those clerks sometimes shared their (or their judge's, if they had permission) preliminary views on a case. I gave my clerks only two rules about discussing cases with other chambers. First, they couldn't talk to other clerks until they'd developed their own views. I hired them and I wanted to know their thoughts, not those of the other clerks in the building. Second, they could share their own views about a case, but they couldn't share mine.

After I returned from conference with my opinion assignment, we'd get going on a draft right away. Writing opinions was the part of the job I loved best. It was deeply satisfying to take a complicated case and produce an opinion that explained the decision in a way that the litigants, other judges, and the public can understand and accept. Writing opinions was also the most important part of my job — and what distinguishes judges from other officials. The judiciary, after all, is the only branch of government that has to explain itself. Members of Congress just vote yea or nay, and presidents don't even have to disclose all the choices they make each day, much less explain their reasons for those choices. But while voters can approve or disapprove politicians' choices by deciding whether to reelect them, federal judges, with lifetime appointments, never face the voters. Instead, they must continually justify their authority by writing opinions that persuade the public that they are faithfully applying the law, not making policy. Alexander Hamilton was right when he observed at the Founding that judges possessed neither the "sword" nor the "purse," and that their power derived from "neither force nor will, but merely judgment."

I was intrigued at the end of the process how my opinion sometimes differed from my initial reaction when I first looked at a case. It was reassuring to know that all the work I'd put in trying to understand the facts and faithfully apply the law could lead me somewhere other than where my gut instincts first suggested. It meant I was acting as a judge, not just deciding cases based on which outcome I'd prefer. I also never lost sight of the fact that at the end of the process what I wrote in my opinions became binding law. If my opinion said, for example, that the Freedom of Information Act requires the government to turn over certain categories of records, the government would not only have to provide the records requested in that particular case, but also provide similar records in response to other requests going forward. That's why hypothetical questions were so useful at argument. They helped us understand the implications of our rulings for future cases.

Writing opinions was serious work, but it was also great fun for me, as well as for the law clerks. We'd start by talking through an outline at a high level—the facts I wanted to highlight, the legal points I wanted to make, and the counterarguments I wanted to address. Once we'd settled on an outline, my clerk would produce a first draft. It was a lot to ask of a young lawyer, but my clerks were almost always up to the task. It helped that I gave them a manual detailing substantive and stylistic guidelines. (Over the years the clerks updated the manual as my judicial style developed.) It also helped that they had each other and could work through difficult issues together.

After the clerk turned in a first draft, my reader would read it to me. First drafts are works in progress, so there were usually issues a clerk had missed or not gotten quite right. I dictated high-level comments and revisions and then asked the law clerk to do another draft. I'd then do the same all over again. We'd continue that way, rinse and repeat, with my comments getting more and more detailed as the draft started to take shape. Once I was satisfied that we had a solid draft, my law clerk would sub in for my reader and read the opinion aloud with me. We'd stop after almost every sentence to change a word, move a comma, or even rethink whole paragraphs. My reliance on others during the editing process was frustrating sometimes—and a big reason why I cared so much about hiring the very best law clerks. "Track changes" and "comment bubbles" are great editing tools, but they're designed for people who can see. I've come to believe that reading aloud has real advantages. It helps me write better, and because good writing is good thinking, it challenges me to think better. Reading text aloud helps me spot logical flaws, as well as grammar, language, and punctuation problems. Reading aloud also highlights unnecessary "little words" like *a, an, the,* and *so,* plus most forms of the verb "to be"—sentence clutter that clouds meaning. That process always took hours.

It wasn't uncommon for clerks, when speaking their own words, to suddenly stop and ask, "Did I really write that?" Same for me. That's why Edie always encouraged her students to read their own writing aloud. It's also why a quote from Roger Kahn's *The Boys of Summer,* one of my favorite baseball books, hovered on the wall above where my clerks sat: "When you write you must listen for sounds," Kahn wrote. "And there is a sound one word makes and there is the sound one word makes upon another and there is the sound of silences between words." In case my clerks hadn't already gotten the message, I also liked to tell them about how David Herbert Donald, the great Lincoln biographer, toiled away at his carrel in the stacks of the Harvard library, reading aloud each paragraph as he wrote. Eventually the librarians politely moved him to his own room. It's a good thing our talkative chambers were private.

When I was happy with the draft, I would set it aside for a few days before coming back to it one last time to finish the editing process myself. Using my Braille computer, I could read and edit the opinion without an intermediary reader. I didn't have to listen and translate, since I was getting the words directly. It let me think far more deeply.

What do Tatel opinions sound like? First, they get right to the point. Early in my career, a federal district judge in Washington, John Lewis Smith, taught me a big lesson. I had filed a motion asking him to allow me to file a brief that exceeded the court's page limits. "Son," he advised me, "I'm going to do you a favor. I'm going to deny this motion because I think you'll write a more persuasive brief if it's shorter." Sage advice, and also true for emails, letters, opinions—and memoirs. Chief Justice Earl Warren's landmark opinion desegregating schools in *Brown v. Board of Education* was only thirteen paragraphs long. My opinions are also known for their brevity.

The next thing you'll notice is that my opinions contain no footnotes. Not one. That's all Edie's doing. An outstanding writer, she played a major role in shaping my writing style. When I first became a judge, she asked me to promise her just one thing. I was expecting her to say something about making it home for family dinners or not getting too swept up in difficult cases. Not my Edie. What did she ask me to promise? No footnotes in my opinions! "If it's worth saying, it's worth saying in the text." Or as a colleague once observed, "If the gods wanted us to read footnotes, they'd have made our eyes vertical." In my more than seven hundred written opinions, I've never used one.

Full disclosure, though: In October 2003, I was invited to give the Madison Lecture at the NYU School of Law. Many Supreme Court justices, dating back to Hugo Black, have given the lecture, and the invitation is among the highest honors a judge can receive. My lecture was about judicial methodology and the rule of law in the context of Southern school desegregation. The speech, of course, contained no footnotes. But before agreeing to publish it, the school's law review insisted on footnotes. (Law reviews contain some good ideas; they don't contain much good writing.) So my law clerks went to work and added 296 footnotes. I wasn't happy about it, but I still think I kept my promise. Edie's directive covered only judicial opinions. She'd said nothing about speeches or law reviews. Call me a textualist.

———

I'm often asked how my blindness affects how I work. You've already heard how it affects my process, how I relied on my readers and clerks to read aloud to me. But does it also affect how I think? That's a good question. Even though I can't see, I definitely think visually. I don't know if my brain has always been wired that way, or if as I lost my sight I started using my mind's eye in new ways. But I do know that as I write or deeply edit, I "see" the actual words in my mind. It's as if the text—minus underlining, bolding, and italics—is actually there. And it stays there. My clerks were often amazed when they'd read me an opinion and I'd interject, "Please go back three paragraphs to the second sentence in that paragraph; it's inconsistent with what we're now reading." To me, those earlier paragraphs were still clear as day. One of my final steps in opinion writing was to have the law clerk read me the first sentence of each paragraph to confirm that it matched the version in my mind. So long as I kept my mental version of an opinion up to date, I could edit in my head—while walking with Vixen, working out, or lying awake at 3 a.m.

I do something similar when I read briefs. In my mind I visualize the steps of the parties' arguments: Major premises, minor premises, conclusions. That way I can literally see any gaps in the arguments. When I'm thinking about statutes, which usually have sections and subsections and sub-subsections, I imagine the text along a flight of stairs: Section 1 at the top, subsection (A) on the first step down, sub-subsection (i) on the second step, and so on. You've already heard about how I parse sentences in my mind using diagrams. When I heard oral argument, I digested the lawyers' spoken arguments in the same way I did their written ones. It was all the same to me.

My ability to visualize things in my mind comes in handy outside the courthouse, too. When someone gives me walking directions, for example, what appears in my mind is a map. Then, once Vixen and I are on our way, I see us progressing along that map like the little dot on a GPS system. My mental mapping system proved crucial in learning to use a guide dog (much more about that later). It also comes in handy when I'm driving some-where with Edie. Although Edie's always the driver, I'm usually Navigator-in-Chief, though I'm useless at spotting road signs and landmarks.

I've always wondered whether my need to have so much de-scribed to me might also be helpful in unexpected ways. I can't just glance at a photograph, chart, or graph, but as they're de-scribed to me, a picture begins to form in my mind and becomes more and more precise as the description continues. It's sort of like the old Paint By Numbers picture that emerged as more and more spaces got painted in. Does that process of thinking first and seeing second create a better and more lasting image than sighted people have? I don't know, but it may be that the extra process I go through—mentally translating what I hear into a picture—reinforces my ability to retain the information. Indeed, I often remember details that sighted people have long forgotten.

But here's the other side: Things that are not described to me are invisible. If I'm walking down a street, I see no buildings, no statues, no telephone poles, no flaming maple trees. Unless some-one has described them, to me they don't exist.

CHAPTER 15

The Art of Judging

WHEN I JOINED THE D.C. CIRCUIT, I'D NEVER BEEN A judge. As an advocate, I'd learned the language of litigation. I knew how to marshal facts, statutes, and precedent to my client's advantage. And I understood the role of the federal judge. But there were vast areas of law I knew little about. I'd never worked on a criminal case, nor did I know much about environmental regulation or labor law. Would I be able to master those new areas well enough to decide cutting-edge legal questions? Would I be able to work with my colleagues, many of whom had been judges for decades? When should I compromise in order to reach consensus, and when should I hold the line? What was my judicial philosophy? And most important, did I have what it takes to be a good judge?

There are no judicial test runs or training wheels. The day after I was sworn in I was assigned a full sitting schedule, so I had to learn as I went. Luckily, I had some good models. My new colleagues were happy to grab coffee or lunch with me and answer my questions about how they did their jobs. Several even offered to share bench memos to help me get up to speed on my first few cases while my law clerks and I were just settling in. Pat Wald, whom I already knew from our years together as public interest lawyers and whose chambers were next to mine, became my mentor. I knocked on her door whenever I had a question. She helped me think through many of the tricky issues new judges must grapple with: how to prepare for oral argument, how to persuade other judges to see it my way, how to offer feedback on other judges' draft opinions, when to stick my neck out and dissent. I called her Coach. The first time Pat dissented from one of my opinions, she sent me a sly note: "David, this will do wonders for your reputation."

As for my judicial philosophy, that came much more slowly. Remembering my promise to Edie, I once glibly told an assembly of law students that my only judicial philosophy was "No footnotes!" The comment drew some laughs, but it was a dodge. In the beginning, I don't think I had any overarching approach, other than a strong conviction from my time in practice that the most important job of the judge is to protect individual rights from what my Constitutional Law professor Philip Kurland had called "the Leviathan of government." I knew, however, that I needed something more. I needed a judicial North Star, a set of principles to guide my decision-making and to help separate my judicial obligation to faithfully apply the law from my personal views about right and wrong.

I looked for those principles first in judicial biographies, which I devoured while I prepared for my Senate confirmation hearing. The two that stuck with me were my friend Gerry Gunther's lovely book about Learned Hand, and John C. Jeffries's biography of Lewis F. Powell Jr. Learned Hand (yes, that was his real name) was the greatest appeals court judge never to reach the Supreme Court. He served first for many years as a district judge in New York City and then on the Second Circuit Court of Appeals for more than twenty-five years. Despite his decades of experience and peerless intellect, the hallmark of Hand's approach was self-skepticism. Agonizing over every decision, he was always able to see both sides of an issue. He described himself as "a conservative among liberals and a liberal among conservatives." Though progressive in his politics, Hand was a leading advocate for a philosophy known as "judicial restraint." To him, that meant that judges should stay humble and know their place. They should start with the presumption that legislators (who also take an oath to uphold the Constitution) know what they're doing. Judges should rule no more broadly than strictly required to resolve the particular dispute before them, respect agency expertise, and keep their personal views out of the courtroom. Skepticism, Hand said, was "my only gospel"—though, ever the fine writer, he added, "I don't want to make a dogma out of it."

Powell, who as ABA president had strongly supported legal services for the poor, was a Supreme Court justice from 1972 to 1987. I was drawn to his story because, like me, he'd gone directly from private practice to the bench. Also like me, he found his first year—the pace, the deluge of new issues, the isolation—especially challenging. "He had to learn every issue from the ground up," Jeffries wrote, "so he labored away at a mountain of paper that seemed to grow faster than he could digest." Powell went on to become a fine justice. His early struggles gave me hope that I, too, could master the job. Because Powell, like Hand, believed in judicial restraint, he frequently found himself in the middle of a divided Supreme Court (including in *Bakke*). He made some mistakes in his time on the Court, but he was unusual in that he later acknowledged at least some of them. And where there were two ways of resolving a case, one with sweeping implications and one narrower, Powell almost always took the latter course.

Hand and Powell were the kind of jurists I wanted to be. They played it straight. They strove to identify, and then ignore, their own predispositions. Above all, they believed in judicial restraint. As I soon learned, however, it was one thing to believe in judicial restraint and read biographies of judges who had tried to live up to that ideal, and quite another to put that belief into action and live up to it myself. In my early days, the humility and self-skepticism part came easily. I knew for certain I didn't know everything. So the tools of judicial restraint on which Hand and Powell had relied quickly became my best friends. Drafting narrow opinions, avoiding broad rulings except when necessary, and proceeding slowly and with caution sure sounded like good ideas to me. Deference to the judgments of elected officials, the fact-finding performed by district judges, and the opinions of subject-matter experts? That sounded all right, too. Judicial restraint was exactly the tool I needed to resolve close questions.

Over the years I became more and more confident in my judging. My reliance on the principles of deference, and my certainty that judges don't always know best, only grew over time. I added other principles of judicial restraint to my tool kit. For example, faithfulness to text is one way to put deference into practice. When interpreting a statute, start with what Congress actually wrote. I felt so strongly about this that I didn't read the parties' briefs until after I'd read the statute itself and parsed its language. Only then did I want to know the views of the parties and other courts. If you're interpreting something else—the Constitution, a state law, or a regulation—the same thing goes. By sticking to the text, judges make sure that they're applying the law, not making it.

So, too, for another core principle of judicial restraint: faithfulness to precedent, which means adhering to prior rulings by the Supreme Court or my own D.C. Circuit. Those prior rulings have the force of law and, much like statutes, demand judicial respect. The idea that judges must follow precedent has a wonky name: *stare decisis,* which literally means, "to stand by things decided." As you'll hear more about later, that principle is indispensable to the art of judging. It also often came in quite handy. The best way to deal with tricky questions, I quickly found, was to closely review older opinions dealing with similar issues. And it seemed to me most important in cases with a political valence. When judges appointed by a president from one party adhere to a decision made by judges appointed by a president from another, that sends a powerful signal to the public that judging is not just politics.

Taken together, the principles of judicial restraint limit what unelected judges can do. That's why it's called "restraint." Sometimes I found that frustrating. I thought I could see a better solution than what Congress, an agency, or the judges in earlier cases had devised, but judicial restraint meant there was nothing I could do about that. I had to follow the judgment of others because that's what judicial restraint required. Most days, however, the mantra of judicial restraint gave me confidence—confidence that I had the tools to resolve even the most difficult legal questions and confidence that I was doing my job as a judge. Above all, the principles of judicial restraint protect the separation of powers enshrined in our Constitution by keeping unelected judges from meddling in the work of policymakers elected by the people.

One of the greatest tests of a judge is to be able to produce an opinion that reaches a result different from what the judge would do as a member of Congress. Oliver Wendell Holmes Jr. put it this way: "It has given me great pleasure to sustain the constitutionality of laws that I believe to be as bad as possible, because I thereby helped to mark the difference between what I would forbid and what the Constitution permits." Although it was sometimes personally difficult to reach a result different from the one I'd have preferred, some of my proudest moments as a judge came when I did just that. It was then that I understood most clearly what it means to be a judge and felt most certain that judging was what I was doing.

I had two of those moments in a series of cases involving the decade-long struggle for the soul of the internet. For as long as there has been an internet, anyone who wants to use it must pay an internet provider, like Comcast or AT&T, for the pleasure. Those companies don't own the internet, of course. But they built the on-ramps, control incoming traffic, and charge a toll to anyone who passes through. For years, the existential question facing the internet has been whether those providers can discriminate among users based on who they are or where they're trying to go — or whether the internet must remain free and open to everyone, regardless of their identity or destination.

Say, for example, that our granddaughter Rae wants to show Edie a puppy video on YouTube. Rae copies the web address into her browser, Comcast transmits her request to YouTube, YouTube sends the video back to Comcast, and it makes its way to Rae's screen where she can show it to Edie (and maybe Vixen, too). Suppose, though, that Comcast decides to launch its own video website filled with its own puppy videos. That website brings in revenue only when people actually visit, so Comcast has every reason to direct puppy-video traffic to its own website instead of to YouTube. Comcast can't just send Rae to its own site when she types in a YouTube address. But what it can do is slow down all traffic to YouTube, so YouTube's videos are slow and laggy while its own site loads just fine.

The question whether it's okay for Comcast to slow down its transmission of YouTube videos to Rae's browser may not sound like a big deal, but it's really a question about the kind of internet we want to have. Should we treat Comcast like a telephone company, which has to handle all calls equally? Or is it more like FedEx, which is free to fast-track some packages and slow-walk others? This is a hotly debated issue, and like many issues in this country, the opposing sides tend to track along partisan lines. The *New York Times,* on the one hand, worried that without net neutrality, cable companies would destroy "Internet democracy" by creating a "two-tiered Internet with a fast lane and a slow lane." On the other hand, a *Wall Street Journal* column declared that mandating net neutrality would be like "neutering the 'net." I have strong views about this issue, too. Were I in Congress or on the Federal Communications Commission (FCC) — the agency responsible for regulating the telephone networks and radio airwaves — I'd fight hard for an open internet.

But I was a judge, not a policymaker. When the case-assignment sand pail sent me open internet cases on three different occasions, my responsibility was to faithfully apply the law, not to promote my own policy preferences. The first case arose because Obama's FCC had done exactly what I'd have done in its shoes: It prohibited internet providers from discriminating among different streams of web traffic. The problem was that the source of congressional authority on which the FCC had relied didn't extend to regulation of the internet. So I wrote an opinion that ruled for Comcast and struck down the FCC's net neutrality rule. That was strike one. Undeterred, the agency adopted a new net neutrality regulation, this time relying on a different source of congressional authority. Again, however, there was a problem: Congress had given the FCC authority to regulate the internet, but only if it first classified the internet as a public utility. Since the FCC hadn't done that, I wrote an opinion ruling for Verizon and again vacating the FCC's new net neutrality rule. Strike two.

The FCC made it to first base on its third swing. It classified the internet as a public utility, so we upheld its authority to require open internet access. Unfortunately, however, net neutrality never actually crossed home plate. Before the regulation could round second, Donald Trump was elected, and his FCC repealed Obama's net neutrality regulations. Biden's FCC is now taking another swing at the issue and working to institute a new set of net neutrality rules. It remains to be seen whether the political winds will shift again before those new rules actually take effect. Did I say this was a politically controversial issue?

Striking down regulations I believed were crucial to a healthy democracy wasn't easy. I never set out to be the judge who blocked the open internet. But in doing so I was certain that I'd done my job and lived up to my oath.

Judge Thomas Griffith, who is, by his own account, a political conservative through and through, was once asked by one of his clerks who he thought was a "model" of "judicial conservatism." Tom didn't mention any so-called conservative justice of the Supreme Court, or even one of the conservative icons on my court. He told his clerk to look at me. As Tom tells the story, "My praise for Judge Tatel confirmed the clerk's suspicion that I'd lost my way." But at the end of that term, the clerk told Tom he'd kept an eye on me — my opinions, the questions I asked at argument, what he heard from my clerks. "You were right," the clerk told Tom. "Judge Tatel's a political progressive, but he's a judicial conservative." The story meant a lot to me. So does the fact that Tom keeps telling it. He and I have different lists of our favorite Acts of Congress. We usually prefer different presidential candidates (though we both share an admiration for the 1960s RFK). But on the bench, despite how we occasionally disagreed about what the law required, we were of one mind on how to be a judge.

———

Appellate judging is a team sport, not a solo endeavor. That's a great strength of our judicial system. Three-judge panels reduce the effects of personal ideology, and working together improves the quality of decision-making. I thoroughly enjoyed discussing cases with my colleagues and trying to reach consensus — or, if we couldn't, to disagree in principled ways. When we do it well, the atmosphere that supports that process is called judicial collegiality. Judicial collegiality has nothing to do with singing holiday songs, having lunch, or attending basketball games together. It has everything to do with respecting each other, listening to each other, and sometimes even changing our minds.

That's easier said than done, particularly in cases that provoke strong feelings. But when the process works, it's impressive. Let me tell you a few short stories about judicial collegiality at its best. It's no coincidence that each example involves judges appointed by presidents of different political parties, for it's in such cases where judicial collegiality is most challenging and most important.

Story #1 is *United States v. Microsoft*, the first major case applying antitrust law to the personal computer. It was such an important case that my court agreed to hear the appeal en banc, which meant every active judge would participate. Shortly after we decided to proceed that way, Judge Stephen Williams, appointed by President Reagan, dropped by my chambers with a novel suggestion: "Let's prepare for oral argument together." We divided up the issues and each set of chambers took the lead on a few topics. I shared my bench memos with him, he shared his with me, and we met together with our law clerks to discuss the case. Antitrust was one of Steve's special areas of interest, and I learned an enormous amount from working through the case with him. Not until years later, however, did Steve reveal exactly why he had suggested that we prepare together. In such an important case, he explained during lunch at The Capital Grille, the nation would be best served if the court spoke with one voice. He believed we'd be more likely to achieve unanimity if a conservative (his word) and a liberal (also his word) could agree. That's exactly how it played out.

Story #2 is also about Steve Williams, but this time the appeal was so minor that no one other than the parties cared much about the outcome. We worked as hard to achieve consensus on the little cases as we did on the big ones. This time, though, Steve and I couldn't reach agreement. I wound up writing the majority opinion (because the third judge agreed with me), and Steve wrote a dissent. As we wrote, we exchanged sixteen drafts, far more than in many higher-profile cases. Each time I read his dissent, I better understood his point of view and revised my majority opinion for the better. He did the same thing with his dissent. By our sixteenth go-round, we had narrowed our differences dramatically but still couldn't agree on the bottom line. Our law clerks were sure we finally stopped out of mercy to them. Steve and I were proud of our opinions, but even prouder of the memos we'd exchanged throughout the drafting process. We wished we could publish them so the public could see how serious judging gets done.

Story #3 features a fascinating case where the police — without a valid search warrant — attached a GPS tracking device onto a suspected drug dealer's car. Judge Griffith and Judge Douglas Ginsburg (both appointed by Republican presidents) were also on the panel. The press assumed, as it often does, that it could predict how we'd rule based on the identity of the president who'd appointed us. In fact, after several weeks of back-and-forth memos, we reached a unanimous decision holding that the use of the GPS tracker was unconstitutional. The press was flabbergasted by the outcome. As Tom remarked, the press would also "have been flabbergasted by the discussion that unfolded at conference." "Doug Ginsburg thought this?" he marveled. "David Tatel considered that?" Despite our differences, Tom explained, we were all "judges wrestling with what the Fourth Amendment meant in an entirely new context. There was no agenda other than to figure out what the law required."

Story #4 is about another Reagan-appointed colleague, Judge David Sentelle. Dave's political views could hardly have been more different from mine. But because Dave, like Tom and like me, believed in judicial restraint, we often found ourselves in agreement, even in cases involving hot-button issues. One such case was about whether the federal law that limits demonstrations near abortion clinics violates the demonstrators' First Amendment rights. Dave and I never discussed our personal views about abortion. I suspect they're quite different. Nevertheless, we agreed that the law restricting demonstrations was constitutional. I was assigned the opinion and had no trouble with the legal analysis. The subject matter was sensitive, though, so before circulating my draft I stopped by Dave's chambers to run it by him. He appreciated the gesture and took the opinion home to think it over. The next day he dropped by with several suggestions. He thought, for example, that repeatedly describing the right-to-life protestors as "anti-abortion," and obtaining an abortion as "receiving care," might unnecessarily alienate people who shared his values. Although I believed both of those terms were accurate, I made the changes he requested. We write opinions not for ourselves, but for our court. Also, I wanted to persuade — not alienate — members of the public with strong feelings about abortion. I'm only sorry that there was no Dave Sentelle at the Supreme Court to convince Justice Alito as he wrote his opinion overturning *Roe v. Wade* that loaded phrases like "abortionist" and "fetal life" have no place in a judicial opinion.

As those stories reveal, judicial collegiality didn't mean that we always reached agreement. I listened to my colleagues and learned from their views, but in the end my vote was mine alone. Most of the time judicial restraint carried the day, but sometimes mine was the dissenting view. How often was sometimes? Pat Wald once told me that the longer she was on the bench the humbler she felt. My dissent rate over time tells the same story. During my first decade on the bench, I dissented thirty-eight times. During my third decade, I dissented only twelve times. During several years, including my last, I didn't dissent once. Why such a dramatic decline in my dissent rate? One reason was that I came to realize that I should reserve dissents for occasions when it really mattered. If you cry wolf too often, the Supreme Court won't take you seriously when, as you'll hear about in *Massachusetts v. EPA,* the wolf actually arrives. Another reason was the confidence I gained in my colleagues. If two of them believed an agency's decision was supported by sufficient evidence, I'd look again. Maybe they were right. Even if they weren't, not all disagreements merit dissents. Just as Pat had predicted, the longer I served, the more I valued conferencing with my fellow judges and listening to their perspectives. And just maybe, the longer I served the more faith my colleagues had in me as well.

⸺ ⊰•⊱ ⸺

For most of us, and certainly for me, being a federal appeals court judge was the job of a lifetime. But for some, the Supreme Court was the dream. For D.C. Circuit judges, that dream isn't as crazy as it sounds. The D.C. Circuit is one of the first places most presidents go looking for new Supreme Court justices. Justice Ginsburg, as you've already heard, started out on our court. So did four of the nine sitting justices: Chief Justice Roberts and Justices Thomas, Kavanaugh, and Jackson.

I never campaigned for the Supreme Court. I loved being a judge and believed I'd make a good justice. But I was happy where I was. There were times, though, when it seemed like a promotion might be in the offing. Late in the Clinton administration, when we all thought Al Gore was on his way to becoming president, the press had me down as a front-runner for any further Clinton administration vacancies, or any that might arise during Gore's presidency. The press coverage produced days of phone calls, notes from old acquaintances suddenly interested in catching up, and some teasing from my kids. It also made my mother proud. But Clinton got no more nominations, and a Gore presidency wasn't to be—thanks in large part to the Supreme Court's deeply problematic ruling in *Bush v. Gore*. (If you're looking for an example of a decision that doesn't reflect judicial restraint, I recommend that one.) Tatel talk picked up again when John Kerry ran for president. But I was getting older. And when Kerry lost to George W. Bush, I knew that a seat on the Supreme Court wouldn't be in the cards. Right place, wrong time. The day after the election, Dave Sentelle leaned over and whispered to me on the bench, "Well, David, looks like you'll be with us for the rest of your life."

Even though I never made it to the Supreme Court, I got to sit with quite a few justices, including Ginsburg, Breyer, and Alito, at the Shakespeare Theatre Company's mock trials. We tried Goneril for treason (*King Lear*), the three witches for aiding and abetting King Duncan's murder (*Macbeth*), and—my favorite—Henry V for war crimes at the Battle of Agincourt. Shortly after RBG and I agreed to try Henry V, a newspaper described the event as a fundraiser. Judges aren't supposed to participate in such things. Ruth called me, wondering what we should do. My suggestion? Ask the theater to put on a lavish reception to eat up all of the profits. That satisfied Ruth, and that's exactly what they did. The canapes were excellent.

I always enjoy participating in these mock trials. As in real cases, I work as well with like-minded judges as I do with, shall we say, less like-minded ones. For example, then–Judge Amy Coney Barrett and I conducted the trial of Peter Pan for kidnapping the Darling children. We both voted to let Peter off the hook. Vixen, who appeared as Nana, stole the show.

Mock trials also let me bring the judicial system to school kids. For years, Edie and I invited around two hundred middle and high school D.C. students into the ceremonial courtroom and told them they'd been selected for jury duty. Then we put on a "trial," with my law clerks, in costume, acting as witnesses. Like any good jury, the students would discuss the case and deliver their verdict. Sometimes we used real cases, choosing issues we thought the students would care about. Student free speech was a popular topic. Once, we reenacted the famous school speech case of *Tinker v. Des Moines* with Mary Beth Tinker—the real-life student plaintiff who, at the age of thirteen, was suspended for wearing a black armband to school in protest of the Vietnam War—in attendance. She showed the students the actual armband that sparked the dispute. Other times, the cases were not so real. A favorite scenario was the Big Bad Wolf and the Three Little Pigs. The kids acquitted the wolf every time.

Those mock trials were as educational as they were fun. The students took their job very seriously. Even twelve-year-olds understand the constitutional requirement that the government must prove guilt beyond a reasonable doubt. "Look around you carefully," I'd tell the students. "This is a very special place. You've read about equal justice. This is where it happens. In America, everyone is treated the same way under the law. It makes no difference if you are Black or white, old or young, rich or poor. Or a wolf."

Our grandchildren loved to hear about my court. They'd ask, "Poppa, can we help you with a real case?" I'd choose one I was working on and tell them all about it. Then we'd have a debate where they'd try to pick out all the different arguments a good lawyer might make on both sides. Over the years, my grandchildren have invited me to speak in their schools. Olin's sixth-grade class in Charlottesville wanted to discuss the Supreme Court case about whether a school principal could search a student's backpack without permission. In Rae and Cameron's fifth-grade classes in Denver I talked about the century-long struggle that gave women the right to vote. In Olivia's sixth-grade class in Vermont I told the students about one of the cases we were hearing at that time — the one about whether the police could attach a GPS tracking device to a suspect's car. The kids were fascinated, and got it just right: The police had acted unlawfully. I know that because we reached the same result a few months later, and a year after that we were affirmed by the Supreme Court 9–zip. More recently, Reuben invited me to his middle-school class in Berkeley to judge a mock trial of a student charged with stealing from a bake sale fund. Reuben was a key witness for the defense. The jury, composed entirely of his classmates, acquitted the defendant. I detected jury nullification.

I've also practiced the art of judging on the stage, if you can believe it. How did a sitting judge end up playing one? It all began in the hills of Virginia, where Edie, Vixen, and I now live nearly full-time. There's a charming 1877 country store down the road and around a few bends from our house. For years, Edie and I walked there every Sunday morning to buy the papers and spend hours sipping coffee and chatting with our neighbors. It was a different milieu from our regular D.C. life, where many of our friends are lawyers and judges, and most vote the same way we do. On the country store's front porch gathered a wonderful mix of interesting people: farmers, artists, musicians, filmmakers, plumbers, truck drivers, journalists, and writers. The group even included a former senator, an ambassador, a CIA director—and, yes, a few lawyers. There were liberals and conservatives, Democrats and Republicans, and a few Libertarians. We openly debated political and cultural issues of the day, and though the conversation could get feisty, we always treated each other with respect. Two members of the front-porch crew weren't American, and when they got their citizenship, I swore them in right there on the front porch. We sang "America the Beautiful." Edie made a sheet cake frosted in red, white, and blue.

One front-porcher had been busy quarrying stone from his property when he noticed his excavations were starting to form an amphitheater. He kept on digging until he created a dramatic theater that could seat an audience of hundreds. An amphitheater like that deserved a performance. Luckily, the author James Reston Jr. was part of our crew and agreed to stage his play *Galileo's Torch* in the new amphitheater. The play was about the seventeenth-century trial of Galileo, whose offense was suggesting that the Earth revolved around the Sun. Pure heresy, according to the Church. I played the Grand Inquisitor, one of history's most notorious judges. Edie played his scribe. Confined in my day job by principles of judicial restraint (not to mention the separation of church and state), it was truly liberating to sentence Galileo: "We pronounce final judgment upon you, Galileo Galilei, and condemn you to formal imprisonment at the pleasure of this holy office." We were a big hit, according to the *Washington Post*. We even reprised our performance at the Italian embassy as part of its celebration of Galileo's 450th birthday, and then again at the Castleton Festival, just two miles from our country home. John Lescault, one of Washington's finest professional actors and the voice you're hearing right now if you're listening to this as an audiobook, played Galileo.

Alas, Broadway never called. But I did act in two more Reston plays with the front-porchers. In the first I was Edwin Stanton, President Lincoln's Secretary of War, as he presided at the military trial of General William Tecumseh Sherman for disobeying the president after Appomattox. Unlike the military judges you will read about in the next chapter, Stanton never applied for a job with the government while presiding over the military commission, nor did he proclaim in speeches that Sherman was guilty as charged. My final role was also my first as someone other than a judge. In *Luther's Trumpet*, I played the Devil—yes, the Devil—who tempted and tortured Martin Luther after he posted his ninety-five theses. All the other actors were professionals, so union rules applied, meaning that I got official coffee breaks and earned $500 (which I dutifully listed on my annual financial disclosure form).

All three plays were technically readings, which meant no one had to memorize their lines. But I had a trick up my sleeve—and I mean that literally. I hid my Victor Reader inside my costume and ran the cord for my headphones up my sleeve. With an earbud in one ear, I could hear my lines just by pressing a button. It worked like a charm, and the audience thought I was the only one who'd done my homework. Who knows, maybe you'll see me back on the stage now that I have a bit more free time. I'm told I make quite a good bad guy.

CHAPTER 16

Stories From the Courtroom

T HEY SAY THERE ARE TWO SIDES TO EVERY STORY. THAT'S certainly true of every lawsuit. Each case arises from a real human conflict, and each case ends with a winner and a loser. My court's docket was filled with interpersonal, corporate, and regulatory drama, and every draw from the assignment-lottery sand pail brought something new to my desk. On Monday I'd hear arguments in a case about electricity markets, on Tuesday I'd read a brief about the mechanics of airport runway lights, and by Wednesday I'd be working on an opinion about Nazi art heists. Some cases were flashier than others, of course. But I can honestly say that I found something interesting in nearly every one of the thousands of cases I heard in my three decades on the court. Many involved events, laws, or agencies that even after years on the court I knew little about. Cracking open each new case file felt like starting a new book.

But a complete catalog of a judge's "Greatest Judicial Hits" would sink any memoir, so I'll resist the temptation to relive all my cases here. Only in a memoir of infinite length would I go into more depth about questions such as: Can the FAA require airlines to allow passengers to cancel their tickets within twenty-four hours of purchase? (Yes); Can copyright owners of porn films obtain the identities of all of the thousands of internet users who illegally downloaded them? (No); Can the House of Representatives prohibit an atheist from delivering the morning prayer? (Yes); Can Congress ban a Russian cybersecurity company from doing business with US government agencies? (Yes). Instead, I'll tell you a few stories about particularly memorable cases that not only are interesting in their own right but also shed some light on bigger questions about judging and the rule of law. Then I'll tell you about one case where I recused myself because of my blindness—and two others where I didn't but, in retrospect, think I should have.

The Gitmo Trilogy

Some of the most difficult and important cases to come before my court during my tenure arose from the government's detention of accused Al Qaeda fighters at the US naval base in Guantanamo Bay, Cuba. The federal government has long sought to hold Al Qaeda responsible for the tragedy of 9/11, and beginning in 2002 it moved individuals it believed had helped Al Qaeda to Guantanamo Bay because it didn't want the small matter of constitutional rights getting in the way of questioning and indefinitely detaining them. This was a moment of constitutional crisis, and lawyers rose to the occasion. Civilian and military lawyers expended tremendous amounts of energy, time, and money representing the detainees, traveling to Washington to review classified documents and argue their cases, to Guantanamo to interview their clients, and abroad to collect evidence. Like the hundreds of lawyers who traveled to Mississippi and Alabama in the 1960s, they were performing in the finest tradition of the American legal profession, ensuring that even the most vilified of suspects has access to our legal system.

At first, our Supreme Court lived up to the moment, too. In a decision called *Boumediene v. Bush,* the Court ruled that the Constitution extended to Guantanamo and that Gitmo detainees were entitled to a "meaningful opportunity" to challenge their imprisonment. *Boumediene* is an example of the Court at its very best, right up there with *Brown* and *Gideon.*

All the many Gitmo appeals filed in *Boumediene's* wake came through the D.C. Circuit, and several of those appeals landed on my desk. Nearly every case involved classified information, which meant I had to spend hours reviewing documents in the courthouse SCIF ("Secure Compartmented Information Facility"), where judges can review top secret materials. The problem for me was that, for security reasons, no one is allowed to take a personal computer into or out of the SCIF—and security officers said that included my Braille computers. Did they worry that our enemies had blind spies who could hack into my Braille computer? I kind of liked the idea of blind spies, and I certainly wasn't going to be the one to say that blind people couldn't do the job. We worked out a solution where one of my two Braille computers—the one I used while reading classified documents—was locked up in the SCIF until we finished the case. It was liberated only after the case was over and I'd erased its memory.

Two of my Gitmo cases were brought by detainees who claimed that the military judges hearing their cases were biased, thus denying them a "meaningful opportunity" to challenge their detention. One involved Khalid Sheikh Mohammed, a Pakistani militant known as "KSM," who was the alleged mastermind of the 9/11 attacks. The other was Abd al-Rahim al-Nashiri, a Saudi militant accused of plotting the 2000 bombing of the American destroyer *USS Cole*. Both KSM and al-Nashiri had endured waterboarding at a CIA black site. Both faced the death penalty. With their lives on the line, both had good reason to worry that the military judges assigned to their cases wouldn't give them a fair shake. The judge presiding over KSM's case had publicly referred to him as one of the "major conspirators in the 9/11 attacks." So much for innocent until proven guilty. The judge presiding over al-Nashiri's case was simultaneously applying for a job with the very government that was prosecuting him. You can imagine his incentive to favor the government. I wrote opinions that brought a halt to those unethical proceedings. "Criminal justice is a shared responsibility," I wrote in my *al-Nashiri* opinion. Although "we do not take lightly" the crimes Gitmo detainees stand accused of committing, "the seriousness of those alleged offenses and the gravity of the penalty they may carry make the need for an unimpeachable adjudicator all the more important."

The third case was the most disturbing. The detainee, Adnan Farhan Abdul Latif, had been held in Gitmo for ten years but never charged with a crime. The government nevertheless continued to detain him and appealed a district court decision ordering his release. I thought the case was easy because the district court had carefully scrutinized the record and concluded that the government's evidence against Latif wasn't reliable enough to justify his continued detention. So I was quite surprised when, at conference, the other two judges decided to reverse the district court's ruling and uphold Latif's continued detention at Guantanamo. Instead of scrutinizing the government's evidence, as the law required, their opinion *assumed* the validity of that evidence and shifted to Latif the burden of discrediting it. Instead of following *Boumediene*'s command that detainees be given a "meaningful opportunity" to challenge their imprisonment, their opinion complained that *Boumediene*'s "airy suppositions have caused great difficulty for the Executive and the courts." "Airy supposition"? *Boumediene*, a decision of the Supreme Court, is binding on all lower federal courts. Perhaps someday the Supreme Court will decide that its "meaningful opportunity" requirement is causing "great difficulty for the Executive and the courts" and clarify or revise that standard. But until it does, my court was required to follow it.

I expected the Supreme Court to intervene. My court had openly defied its authority, and Latif's appeal was supported by persuasive amicus briefs and scholarly commentary. But the same Supreme Court that had recognized a fundamental right in *Boumediene* looked the other way when my court eviscerated that right. *New York Times* columnist Linda Greenhouse was spot-on when she wrote that the Supreme Court had abdicated its constitutional responsibility and, by refusing to take Latif's case and other post-*Boumediene* appeals, it effectively "outsourced" the "Guantanamo issue" to the D.C. Circuit.

The case had a tragic ending. Latif, who had exhibited mental health problems throughout his decade-long confinement, told his guards that "to die is better than to live" in detention. He apparently meant it. The next day, he committed suicide. *Boumediene*'s promise of meaningful review died with him.

Dead Men Tell No Tales

Early in my judicial career, I was assigned a pair of cases that sprang from the political intrigue surrounding the Clinton White House. The first involved a close Arkansas friend of the president and First Lady, Vince Foster, who served as deputy White House counsel during the early years of Clinton's presidency. Hating the rough-and-tumble of D.C., Foster yearned to return to Arkansas. But the rough-and-tumble caught up with him in early 1993 after the administration fired seven employees of the White House Travel Office. Foster was already dealing with clinical depression and was tormented over his role in the firings. He committed suicide nine days after seeking private legal advice, which led to never-ending conspiracy theories about who or what really killed him. Among the evidence Independent Counsel Kenneth Starr sought for his investigation into Foster's suicide were several pages of notes about a conversation Foster had with his personal attorney.

The intriguing question before my court was whether attorney-client communications remain confidential—and subject to what's called the attorney-client privilege—after the client dies. There are carefully defined exceptions to the attorney-client privilege, including an important one called the crime-fraud exception. But where no exception applies, the default rule is that the privilege shields attorney-client communications from disclosure. The other two judges on the panel ruled that the privilege did not apply in Foster's case because the grand jury's need for the notes outweighed any limited posthumous reputational interest Foster might have had. I dissented. "From Andrew Carnegie's libraries to Henry Ford's foundation," I wrote, "one need only count the schools and universities, academic chairs and scholarships...bearing the names of their founders...to understand that human beings care deeply about how posterity will view them." Fewer clients will "confide candidly and fully," I warned, if clients believe a lawyer's vow of confidentiality comes with a "caveat" that sounds like this: "I will hold all our conversations in the strictest of confidence. But when you die, I could be forced to testify—against your interests—in a criminal investigation or trial, even of your friends or family, if the court decides that what you tell me is important to the prosecution. Now, please tell me the whole story."

The judges in the majority were Steve Williams and Pat Wald, both fine judges and great colleagues. We just didn't see it the same way, maybe because as a practicing lawyer I'd represented actual clients whose communications were protected by the privilege. The Supreme Court, in a 6–3 ruling, sided with me and protected the notes of Foster's confidential conversation from disclosure to the grand jury. Attorney-client privilege, the Court held, did extend beyond the grave. Two minutes after the Court issued its opinion, Pat burst into my office and gave me a big hug.

One year later, the Supreme Court refused to hear a different case about Starr's overreach. His passionate quest to pin something on Bill Clinton had reached the President's relationship with the most famous intern in history. Starr sought grand jury testimony about Monica Lewinsky from Bruce Lindsey, a key Clinton adviser who also was deputy White House counsel. Lindsey asserted attorney-client privilege, and again my court ruled in favor of Starr, holding that presidents enjoy no attorney-client privilege in their communications with the White House counsel. I again dissented: "Presidents need their official attorney-client privilege to permit frank discussion not only of innocuous, routine issues, but also sensitive, embarrassing, or even potentially criminal topics." That's especially true, I pointed out, in the treacherous waters of post-Watergate government, where "the nation has compelling reasons to ensure that Presidents are well defended against false or frivolous accusations that could interfere with their duties." (For the record: I would have dissented from my court's abrogation of the privilege regardless of the politics of the president who invoked it.) This time the Supreme Court refused to intervene—though two justices would have—leaving intact my court's holding that the president of the United States enjoys no attorney-client privilege with the White House counsel.

I regard my dissents in both cases as ringing defenses of the need to protect attorney-client communications. The long-standing exceptions to the privilege are more than adequate to ensure that the privilege isn't abused. And while the privilege sometimes means that fact-finding bodies like grand juries are denied important information, I think that's a fair price to pay to make sure everyone gets the legal advice they need—whether it's to defend against an accusation or to ensure compliance with the law. That has been my view ever since my years with the Lawyers' Committee and the Legal Services Corporation.

Around the same time as the Lindsey case in 1998, my court unanimously decided to void the privilege in another, more famous case. We ruled that Monica Lewinsky's lawyer had to testify before Starr's grand jury about what he knew of her plans to lie under oath about her relationship with the president. Why? Because of the "crime-fraud" exception to the attorney-client privilege. Under that exception, the privilege doesn't apply when clients seek advice about how to commit a future crime, like perjury or obstruction of justice. The lasting memory I have of the Lewinsky case, though, isn't about the legal issue, which was straightforward. It was listening to hours and hours of "Linda Tripp tapes," surreptitious recordings made by Lewinsky's "friend" in which they discussed Lewinsky's liaisons with the president. Tripp had given the thirty-seven cassettes to Starr, and long before the public had ever heard of Linda Tripp, I had listened to her recordings in private in order to determine if they contained evidence of Lewinsky's potentially criminal intentions. It was as surreal as it sounds. I spent days hearing about the president of the United States' sexual activities, and I couldn't say a word about it to anyone—not even Edie.

A Reporter behind Bars

The Clinton cases weren't the only times I found myself in the political crosshairs on a grand jury issue and a question of privilege. Perhaps the most important First Amendment case I ever heard concerned Judith Miller, then a *New York Times* investigative reporter on matters of national security. It started when Joseph Wilson, a former American diplomat, wrote a *Times* op-ed questioning President George W. Bush's assertion, made during his 2003 State of the Union address, that Saddam Hussein had sought uranium from Niger to build nuclear weapons. Wilson claimed not only that the assertion was false, but also that the president *knew* it was false. According to Wilson, he had been selected to travel to Africa to investigate reports of uranium buying, discovered that those reports were false, and informed the State Department of his findings. A week after the op-ed, however, newspapers published stories revealing that two top White House officials had tried to discredit Wilson by disclosing that he had been selected to go to Africa only because his wife, Valerie Plame, was a CIA "operative on weapons of mass destruction."

It was good political intrigue, the sort of stuff that sells papers. But there was a serious problem: Revealing a covert agent's identity is a federal crime. A special counsel was appointed and a grand jury convened to investigate. Miller, one of the reporters who had received the tip from White House officials, refused to testify, claiming that the First Amendment's guarantee of a free press meant she couldn't be compelled to disclose the names of her confidential sources. According to Miller, even if it was criminal for government officials to tell her about Plame, she couldn't be compelled to name them. Unpersuaded, the district court held her in contempt of court. She appealed, and I was assigned to the case. Because cases about the press always seem to draw press attention, we anticipated a crowd and heard the appeal in our large ceremonial courtroom. It was standing room only. The oral argument went on for two intense hours as my two colleagues and I probed each side's positions. Two months later we issued our decision unanimously rejecting Miller's First Amendment argument. Although I sympathized with Miller, a 1972 Supreme Court decision called *Branzburg v. Hayes* squarely held that the First Amendment doesn't allow reporters to refuse to disclose their sources to a grand jury. The Miller case was virtually identical to *Branzburg*, and lower federal courts must follow Supreme Court precedent. The district court then sent Miller to jail, where she stayed for eighty-five days until her confidential source released her from her pledge of confidentiality.

Although the First Amendment afforded Miller no protection, I wrote a separate concurring opinion arguing that federal courts should recognize a "reporter's privilege" anchored in the common law, which developed from ancient legal principles we inherited from Britain. You know at least one privilege already: Attorney-client communications, as you read about in the Clinton cases, are privileged if they relate to legitimate legal advice, but not if they involve plotting a crime. I concluded that history and similar logic supported recognizing a common law privilege for reporter-source communications. But history also showed that the reporter's privilege doesn't apply if the government has no other way to obtain crucial information about a leak that did more harm than good. That was exactly the case with Judith Miller. Congress criminalized exposure of covert agents for a good reason: outing spies might deprive the United States of key intelligence sources and even cost lives. Moreover, this was not a whistleblower revealing important information about government malfeasance. To the contrary, the leakers had exploited the press for partisan gain.

I was pleased when Anthony Lewis, the Pulitzer Prize–winning journalist whom I'd admired since college, wrote that my opinion was "thoughtful and persuasive." Although the *New York Times* did its usual superb job of reporting on the case, its editorial page raged about the jailing of Judith Miller and its "chilling" effect on journalism and free speech. It accused us of "palpable hostility" to journalists and declared that "no other newspaper reporter has ever been jailed this long for standing on her constitutional rights." Nowhere, however, did the editorial writers mention *Branzburg* or its holding that reporters have no such constitutional right. Instead, they quoted Justice William O. Douglas for the proposition that "the press has a preferred position in our constitutional scheme," failing to mention that those words come from a dissenting opinion—in fact, Douglas's dissent in *Branzburg*. And of course, dissents are not law. The editorial writers were free to argue that *Branzburg* was wrongly decided, but surely they had an obligation to tell readers about *Branzburg* and what it held. To paraphrase Senator Daniel Patrick Moynihan, editorial writers, like judges, are entitled to their own opinions—but not their own facts.

My problem with the *Times* editorial page wasn't that it disagreed with us. We judges have lifetime appointments and thick skins, and it's entirely appropriate that our decisions come in for public criticism. My concern was that by failing to acknowledge *Branzburg*, the *Times* editorial page skewed public debate on an issue of critical importance: how to balance safeguarding a free press against the need to vigorously investigate national security crimes. The editorial writers seemed not to understand that the Miller case presented a clash between *two* truth-seeking and constitutionally protected institutions—the press and the grand jury.

All the President's Returns

You could hardly be a federal judge in Washington during the Trump administration and escape becoming ensnared in Trump litigation. I heard several such cases. Perhaps the most important was *Trump v. Mazars*, which involved the President's financial records. After discovering that Trump's financial disclosure forms failed to include a $130,000 payment that his lawyer, Michael Cohen, had made to Stormy Daniels, a porn actress, a congressional committee issued a subpoena to Trump's accounting firm, Mazars. The committee wanted several years of Trump's financial information so it could understand the Stormy Daniels payment, investigate other potential inaccuracies, and consider reforms to government ethics codes.

As in the Miller case, we heard oral argument in our ceremonial courtroom. It was packed with reporters, members of Congress, and the public. There was tension in the air, not just because *Mazars* was so politically sensitive, but also because the very next case we were hearing that day involved grand jury subpoenas seeking information from Chinese banks as part of a government investigation into how North Korea was financing its own nuclear weapons program. Because that case involved classified information, we had announced that we'd be hearing it in private, and the fact that we'd soon be turning to nuclear secrets made the President's potential malfeasance seem all the more fraught.

If you can believe it, some cases are so secret that no one even knows we are hearing them. One such case involved a subpoena issued to a foreign corporation (I can't name), owned by a foreign country (I can't identify), seeking information about (I can't tell you that, either). We heard that case in a small room that had been swept for eavesdropping bugs and whose glass doors and windows had been covered with gold foil to thwart any electronic snooping.

But back to *Mazars*. My opinion for the court upheld the subpoena because the committee was seeking information "important to determining the fitness of legislation to address potential problems within the Executive Branch." The Supreme Court reversed. In a 7–2 opinion by Chief Justice Roberts, the Court ruled that we had given insufficient weight to the President's constitutional prerogative and that we failed to adequately consider whether the subpoena had a legitimate legislative purpose; whether it was no broader than necessary to serve that purpose, and whether the subpoena would unreasonably burden the presidency. Excellent questions—though our opinion had already answered every one of them. Nevertheless, the Supreme Court sent the case back to us for further consideration. My court looked at all of those arguments again (I wasn't on that panel, due to random assignment) and reached virtually the same result we had the first time. Mazars finally turned over Trump's financial records.

I can quibble with the Court's rejection of our initial decision, as we'd already addressed every issue the Court ordered us to look at again. My pure speculation is that the justices in the majority asked for a do-over in part because they hoped that, in the meantime, the White House and Congress would work out a compromise, as they had in past subpoena disputes. If that's what was going on, *Trump v. Mazars* was my favorite reversal. The Chief's opinion—which looks very much like mine—carefully balances the interests of Congress and the president. This is important, because as I pointed out in my opinion, "disputes between Congress and the president are a recurring plot in our national story." The decision provides a roadmap for resolving those disputes in the future. I have a pretty good feeling courts are going to need that map more and more as time goes on.

The Children

In my decades on the D.C. Circuit, I heard many cases involving people with disabilities. One especially important case, *D.L. v.*

District of Columbia, arose under the Individuals with Disabilities Education Act—a law that overlaps with Section 504, the very statute I enforced while at the Office for Civil Rights. IDEA, as the statute is often called, offers states a deal: If they agree to ensure that all children with disabilities get an appropriate education, the federal government will pay for the additional services necessary to support those children.

D.L. was a class action on behalf of hundreds of children who claimed that D.C.'s school system had reneged on the deal, taking millions of federal dollars while failing to provide badly needed educational services to disabled students. D.L., anonymous to protect his privacy, was an actual child who spoke not just for himself but for an entire class of students with disabilities who had been denied required services. D.L.'s own story was heartbreaking. His family was homeless, and he had suffered severe social and emotional problems even before he was four years old. Because he bit others, fought with teachers and children, and kept punching himself in the face, he could attend preschool only with extra support. Another plaintiff, O.U.L., weighed two pounds at birth, leaving him with profound physical and mental disabilities. He had difficulty standing and walking, and his asthma was so acute that he'd been hospitalized ten times by age three. Still another child, A.T., was only two when he saw a neighbor die of gunshot wounds. A.T. developed such bad nightmares that he banged his head while sleeping, and his "intermittent explosive disorder" led him at age four to stab a cat.

D.C. schools had failed every one of these children. The school system provided no services to help D.L., sent O.U.L. to a preschool accessible only by staircase even though he used a walker, and failed to evaluate A.T. for years. The trial court ruled for the children. Because D.C. had taken the government's money, it had to provide the services required by IDEA. My court unanimously upheld the trial court's ruling, and I wrote the opinion, explaining that the District of Columbia failed to provide educational services to some of their neediest students in the most formative years of their lives.

While my court was protecting the statutory rights of people with disabilities, the Supreme Court of the United States would soon begin to eviscerate those rights. In 2016, a Texas woman, Jane Cummings, sought treatment for chronic back pain at a rehab center in the Dallas–Fort Worth area. Deaf and legally blind, she asked the center to provide an American Sign Language interpreter during her treatment sessions. Because the center was reimbursed by Medicare and Medicaid for some of its services, it was subject to the nondiscrimination provisions of the Rehabilitation Act—again, the very statute I had enforced at OCR. The center rejected Cummings's request, telling her that she should communicate with her physical therapist through gestures, lip reading, or written notes. Cummings faced a Hobson's choice: skip the physical therapy she needed or debase herself to get it.

Cummings sued. Her claim that the center had violated the Rehabilitation Act was an obvious winner. The center had blatantly violated the Act by refusing her an interpreter. Nevertheless, an ideologically divided Supreme Court ruled 6–3 against her, concluding that Cummings could not receive compensation for her injury because the only harm she had suffered was emotional distress. According to Chief Justice Roberts's majority opinion, ruling for Cummings would be unfair to the rehab center because it hadn't expected to be held responsible under the Rehabilitation Act for emotional harm. But he pointed to nothing in that Act that bars such recovery. Moreover, as Justice Breyer explained in dissent, our long tradition of compensating people for emotional harm that is unlawfully inflicted should have put the rehab center on notice that it could be liable. And what about fairness to Cummings? Or respect for Congress, which passed the Rehabilitation Act to protect people with disabilities from the indignities of discrimination?

Blindness and Judging

So, did my blindness affect my decision in *D.L.* or my view that the Supreme Court got it wrong in *Cummings*? As you by now understand, blindness certainly affected how I functioned as a judge—how I reviewed the parties' submissions, how I interacted with their lawyers at argument, and how I wrote my opinions. But I hope it didn't affect my judicial decision-making. A judge's job is to apply the law to the facts of a case. There's no room in that process for opinions or feelings. We want compassion and empathy in the legislative process, but it would be no more appropriate for me to allow my personal feelings about disability to influence my vote in a disability case than it would be for judges to allow personal or religious views to influence their votes in abortion cases.

I ruled for D.L. because I believed that IDEA, as applied to the facts the children had presented, compelled that result. D.C. schools had taken federal money but failed to provide the educational services they'd agreed to deliver in exchange. My ruling felt as inevitable as 1+2=3. The statute in *Cummings* was equally clear. It protected Cummings from discrimination and contained no limitations on the harms for which she could be compensated. A faithful application of that statute should have compelled a ruling in her favor.

I acknowledge that in both cases I sympathized with the plaintiffs. Although I personally was never denied special services like D.L. was, I understand what it means to need those services. How would I have done my job at HEW, the law firm, or the court—particularly in the pre-computer years—without the readers they provided? And like Cummings, I've experienced humiliation because of my blindness. Remember the waiters and ticket agents who talked to Edie instead of to me? Remember the Lyft driver who ejected Vixen and me from his car? Such indignities hardly rise to the level of what Cummings experienced, but I know what it feels like to be helpless in those ways, and I know that what the Supreme Court shrugged off as "humiliation" and "frustration" are actually very real harms. Nevertheless, that's not how I decide cases. The question was never whether I personally believed that D.L. should get help in school or that Cummings should be compensated for the harm she suffered. The only question was: Did the statutes Congress wrote require those things? If the answer to that question had been no, I'd have ruled against D.L. and Cummings regardless of my compassion for their plights. Indeed, I've ruled against people with disabilities in other cases when the law required it.

Still, there's no way I can be 100 percent sure that my blindness never affected my judging, that there's no case I would have seen differently if I could have, well, seen. All I can say is that I always did my best to ensure that my blindness—like my race, religion, and political views—didn't affect my judging. There's no instruction manual for doing that. I simply tried, in each case, to follow the principles of judicial restraint, which meant respecting text, following precedent, and deciding cases narrowly. That's what those principles are for. They help judges act like judges and, as much as is humanly possible, to eliminate their personal biases from the equation. In cases where that's just not possible—where their biases are too strong to overcome, or at least when they might seem so to the public—judges have an obligation to recuse themselves.

Only once in thirty years did I recuse myself because of my blindness. The case was about money—literally, the ones, tens, and twenties we used to carry around in our pockets. The legal question in the case was how quickly the Treasury Department had to abide by a federal law that, as interpreted by my court, required paper bills to be different sizes or have tactile features so visually impaired people could differentiate them. I had real personal experience with this one. When I travel to Mexico, I can count my cash without help because the bills grow in size as the denominations grow in value. The 500-peso note is bigger than the 100-, the 100- is bigger than the 20-, and so on. At home, however, I can't tell a five- from a twenty-dollar bill without help. "When we were little," Rebecca remembers, "we liked to help Dad organize his bills in his wallet. 'What's this? What's this? What's this?' he'd ask us. Once we told him, he had a folding system for keeping track of which bills were which." Now that we're empty-nesters, that's Edie's job. But if (when) my bills get mixed up, and I pay cash to a cabdriver, I need to ask, "Is this a ten?" As far as I know, every driver has been honest. But why does my government put me in such a dependent position? So, as you can see, although I didn't yet know anything about the legal question, I certainly had strong views about the policy. I very much wanted accessible currency. While I believed I could put that view aside and decide the case fairly, I worried about what the public might think. If I ruled that the Treasury had to move more quickly toward accessibility, would people say I'd done that because I was blind—no matter how clear the law might be?

I asked the other two judges assigned to the panel for advice, and both urged me to remain on the case. Although I appreciated their faith in my neutrality, I still decided to recuse. I worried about public perception and about whether it would be good for my court or for the country to have commentators grumbling that some blind judge forced the government to make costly changes to the nation's paper currency for his own benefit. Because I had to think about it for more than a few minutes (my usual standard for recusal), I decided to err on the side of caution and stay on the sidelines. I've never regretted my decision to recuse.

In two other cases where keen eyesight might have seemed essential, I decided not to recuse. One was another case about money. This time, it was a First Amendment claim brought by a self-described "visual and performance" artist who created exceedingly accurate reproductions of US currency. After telling shopkeepers about his art, he'd spend his fake bills, believing that disseminating them would allow art "to reach people who cannot be coaxed into galleries and museums." The Secret Service was not amused. When it threatened to prosecute him, the artist claimed that his art was protected speech. Thanks to my daughter Stephanie, who spent several hours describing each bill to me, I felt comfortable hearing the case. Suffice it to say that the artist did not prevail. He wasn't happy about it and even complained to a reporter about my involvement. "Swear to God," he said, one of the judges was "stone blind!"

In the second case, an architect claimed that another architect had copied her design for the United Arab Emirates' embassy in Washington. A key question in the case was whether the two designs were "substantially similar." I couldn't see the designs, of course, but I believed I could understand the relevant details anyway. My law clerk carefully described how each architect portrayed parapets, domes, and arches, even tracing them with my finger. The parties' briefs explained the ways in which the two designs were both similar and different. Because the question was too close to call, we sent the case back to the district court for a jury to decide. I wrote the opinion, and unlike in the performance artist case, no one complained about my blindness.

Looking back, I now believe I should have recused myself in both cases. I had no personal stake in the outcomes, and I don't think anyone would have said that my blindness biased me in favor of one side or the other. It made no difference to me whether the performance artist continued performing or which architect deserved credit for the embassy's design. But even though Stephanie had carefully described the counterfeit bills, could I really determine from her description whether they were so similar to real money that the artist was violating the law? (Given the artist's reaction to my blindness, you probably won't be surprised to hear that his bills didn't include features for the visually impaired.) And even though my law clerk had carefully described the two architectural designs, could I really determine whether they were "substantially similar"? Did I miss a critical nuance in either case? Even more troubling, did Stephanie's and my law clerk's descriptions subtly reflect their own views of the legal issues? That would be a serious problem. Like all judges, I relied on law clerks and others to help me do my job. At the end of the day, however, I was the judge. I took the oath, and I was responsible for making the decisions.

For most of my life, I've done everything I could to downplay the significance of my blindness. In doing that, did I become willfully blind to what I could not see? If I had those cases to do over, I'd recuse myself. The performance artist's crack was insulting, but he had a point. He deserved a judge who could see his art before judging it. More importantly, the public deserves not to have to wonder whether a sighted judge would have made a different decision.

Downplaying my blindness affected my ability to acknowledge not only my limitations as a judge but also my strengths. I'd been so busy deleting references to blindness from my Wikipedia page that I'm not sure I ever even thought about *why* Lady Justice wears a blindfold. Thinking about it now, I believe the answer is obvious: A judge who can't see can't be influenced by the physical appearance of the parties before him. The clothes they wear, the gestures they make, the color of their skin—none of that matters to Lady Justice. She rules based on the law alone. That is exactly the judge I strove to be. And perhaps, without my realizing it, my blindness helped me be more objective. At oral argument I could tell a lot about the advocates by how their voices' sounded—whether their tone was respectful or dismissive, whether their speech patterns were effective or distracting. Lawyers' names and tones of voice often (though not always) revealed their genders. But I rarely knew the color of anyone's skin. I couldn't tell if they were short or tall, gaunt or overweight, gray-haired or young. I couldn't see markers of wealth and class, like expensive suits, fancy watches, and manicured fingernails. And I couldn't tell whether one side brought along a dozen well-heeled corporate lawyers to face off against a single pro bono advocate. I hope those sorts of optics didn't affect my colleagues, but implicit biases can be hard to overcome. So maybe I was a tiny bit lucky to resemble Lady Justice in at least this respect: I wasn't influenced, even subconsciously, by how the advocates appeared.

What did influence my judging, however, was my belief—shaped by the sixties, the Kennedy administration, the Civil Rights Movement, and my years at the University of Chicago—that federal courts have a profound responsibility to protect individuals, especially vulnerable ones. That, not my blindness, was the lens through which I saw all my cases. But make no mistake: I never approached a case with the view that individuals should win and corporations and governments should lose. My experiences invariably shaped my understanding of the cases before me, and of the world more broadly. But I always tried to decide those cases using the traditional tools of judicial restraint. Do other judges do the same? You now know enough about judging to answer that question for yourself. Read a few of their opinions and then ask: Is this judge enforcing statutes as written by Congress? Is this judge respecting precedent? Is this judge holding back from deciding unnecessary questions? Is this judge respecting the factual judgments of Congress, district courts, agencies, and subject-matter experts? If they're not doing those things, you can be fairly sure that something other than judging is going on.

CHAPTER 17

The Future of the Planet

B ECAUSE CASES ARE RANDOMLY ASSIGNED, APPELLATE JUDGES
don't get to choose their legacies. Indeed, judging sometimes
felt to me like what reading Chapter 16 may have felt like to you:
I worked hard, I learned a lot, and I had some fun—but I didn't
see any pattern. Some issues arose more frequently than others, of
course. Areas of law once unknown to me became familiar, and
in time I began to master the art of judging. At first, my most
interesting and important cases didn't seem to have much to do
with each other. Each one involved a new set of facts and each
one implicated a new legal question.

Only slowly did the story of my judicial career begin to reveal
itself. In hindsight, I see that story as centered around two issues that have defined our times and will define our future: the
environment and the right to vote. Those issues are fundamental to the continued flourishing of our planet and our democracy.

Unfortunately, it is on those issues where the differences between my approach to judging and the current Supreme Court's are most profound. This chapter tells the first half of that story. It's about two of my most important environmental cases, the legal principles on which they hinged, and what two recent Supreme Court rulings portend for the future of our planet.

It all starts with the Clean Air Act, a landmark federal law that has saved millions of lives in the half century since its enactment. In designing the statute, Congress recognized that air pollution is a dynamic problem: New harmful pollutants will continue to be identified, the science of pollution mitigation will continue to improve, and industry will continue to find new ways around whatever rules Congress puts in place. So Congress crafted a dynamic solution: It set out the basic legal framework for controlling air pollution, but left the details to a specialized federal agency. You'll have heard of this one, the Environmental Protection Agency, otherwise known as EPA.

There are good reasons why Congress wanted EPA to fine-tune and continually update the air pollution regulations. Like other federal agencies, EPA is part of the executive branch. Led by the president, the executive branch is quicker and more flexible than Congress. Whereas members of Congress (like judges) are generalists, each federal agency is staffed with subject-matter experts who know virtually everything there is to know about the area they regulate. Even the most scientifically minded senator will know next to nothing about how quickly heavy-duty trucks emit nitrogen oxides and other pollutants, the health risks those emissions pose to humans, and how those emissions can be curbed through cost-effective measures. An EPA scientist, by contrast, can devote her entire career to the study of nitrogen oxides. Down the hall, a different EPA scientist can work to identify new pollutants. His neighbor can stay abreast of the latest pollution-mitigation technologies in the trucking industry. And across the way a medical expert can study the health effects of various pollutants, including on sensitive groups like people with asthma. Working together and with input from the public, these experts devise and continually update regulatory standards that keep our air clean and our bodies healthy. That's the Clean Air Act at work—exactly as Congress intended.

In reviewing EPA's emissions standards, the role of the courts is limited. Judges, unlike agency officials, are not scientists or subject-matter experts. So when courts decide a Clean Air Act case (or any case involving an agency, for that matter) their job is not to decide whether the rule the agency picked was the one they'd have chosen themselves. Instead, a statute called the Administrative Procedure Act requires courts to respect an agency's scientific judgments unless it acts "arbitrarily and capriciously"—administrative-law speak for "totally irrationally." And under a doctrine called *Chevron* (named for a Supreme Court decision), judges must also respect an agency's reasonable interpretations of the statutes it administers. For example, if Congress tells the EPA to regulate areas "seriously affected by oil spills," courts must defer *both* to EPA's scientific judgment about which areas have been affected (unless that judgment is "arbitrary and capricious") *and* to its interpretive judgment about what "seriously affected" actually means (unless that interpretation is unreasonable). "Arbitrary and capricious" review and *Chevron* deference are important principles of judicial restraint that keep unelected judges from second-guessing agency decision-making. Consistent with those principles, so long as an agency considers the relevant factors, reaches a rational conclusion, and interprets the governing law reasonably, the agency's decision—not a court's—must carry the day. By deferring to agencies, judges respect Congress's choice to delegate and avoid imposing their personal policy preferences.

Congress made another important choice in the Clean Air Act: to centralize disputes about pollution standards in a single court, the D.C. Circuit. It did that because air moves, and it doesn't care much about borders, which means that air pollution is a national problem, not a local one. By choosing the D.C. Circuit as the clearinghouse for national disputes about the Clean Air Act, Congress ensured that different judges across the country can't enter conflicting orders about how much nitrogen oxide power plants can emit or which technologies they must use to mitigate those emissions. It also put D.C. Circuit judges at the center of national debates about the environment.

My first major environmental case, *American Trucking v. EPA*, came five years into my tenure. At first, *American Trucking* looked like the sort of case we saw every day. EPA had set a new emission standard, someone wasn't happy about it, and we had to decide whether the standard the agency had chosen was "arbitrary and capricious." The emission standard at issue was for a pollutant called PM2.5. If you've never heard of "PM" before (and frankly aren't sure whether you're up to, or even interested in, finding out), then you'll understand how I first felt when I opened the case file. But bear with me: It's both less complicated and more interesting than it sounds. PM stands for "particulate matter," which refers not to one specific chemical, but to *any* fine particles or "liquid droplets" of a certain size. Over time, EPA has made its PM regulations both more specific and more stringent, reflecting the agency's evolving understanding of how these tiny particles work and the dangers they pose. EPA has regulated PM10 (particulate matter smaller than 10 microns in diameter) for decades. This time, EPA singled out PM2.5 (particulate matter smaller than 2.5 microns in diameter) for especially strict regulation. A human hair is approximately 70 microns wide, so 2.5 microns is very, very small. And as EPA's scientists recognized, the smaller the particle the bigger the problem. Unlike larger particulate matter, PM2.5 can travel deep into the respiratory tract and even into the bloodstream, causing serious and lasting harm. Ever wonder why health officials suggest staying inside when there's wildfire smoke in your area? Now you know: Wildfire smoke contains PM2.5.

Industry was none too pleased about EPA's new PM2.5 standard. Smoke containing PM2.5 is a by-product of many industrial processes, including the combustion of diesel fuel, and cutting back those emissions can be difficult and expensive. So industry groups joined forces to challenge EPA's new regulation. The American Trucking Association led the charge, with support from other well-funded groups who make it their business to oppose regulations that chip away at corporate profits (think the Chamber of Commerce and the National Coalition of Petroleum Retailers). The challengers argued that EPA was required to treat PM2.5 as a brand-new pollutant even though it had long been covered by EPA's regulation of PM10. (Any particle less than 2.5 microns in diameter is of course also less than 10 microns in diameter.) More broadly, the industry challengers claimed EPA had acted "arbitrarily and capriciously" in setting the new standards.

The science may have been complex, but the "arbitrary and capricious" standard made my job simple. All PM2.5 is bad PM2.5, and there is no level at which PM2.5 emissions are totally safe. EPA had undertaken a rigorous study of PM2.5's effects, made a reasonable scientific judgment that a heightened emissions standard would protect the public health, and exercised its discretion to set the standard accordingly. Whether *I* thought the PM2.5 emissions standard should have been a bit higher or a bit lower was beside the point. As a judge, the only question I had to answer was whether EPA had acted "arbitrarily and capriciously" in setting the standard where it did. Agree or disagree with EPA's ultimate conclusion on PM2.5, I saw nothing "arbitrary and capricious" about how it got there. The agency had considered all relevant evidence and reached a logical conclusion. Case closed—at least to me.

Not so to my two colleagues on the panel. Instead of just applying the "arbitrary and capricious" standard, they latched on to a throwaway argument, made in just one of the many briefs filed in the case, that threatened to unravel the entire modern regulatory state. That argument was about an idea called the nondelegation doctrine. You won't see those words anywhere in the Constitution. But alarmed at the pace of progressive New Deal legislation, the 1935 Supreme Court contrived the doctrine in order to overturn regulations it felt interfered too much with the free market. The basic idea was that the Constitution implicitly prohibits Congress from "abdicating" its "essential legislative functions"—its power to make governing law—by delegating those functions to executive branch agencies. Any statute that does delegate legislative functions, the Court declared, is unconstitutional, and all regulations promulgated pursuant to that statute are void. In theory, the nondelegation doctrine is about preserving Congress's power to legislate—and making sure executive branch agencies don't take that power for themselves. In practice, though, nondelegation is all about the Supreme Court's own power, because by invoking the doctrine, the Court disregards Congress's legislative choices in favor of its own.

Thankfully, it didn't take long for the Court to see the problems with its made-up doctrine, which in its initial form seemed to preclude meaningful agency involvement in federal policymaking. In later cases, the Supreme Court clarified that Congress may delegate decision-making authority to federal agencies so long as it sets out some "intelligible principle" to guide them. Since then, the Court has consistently upheld statutes delegating substantial authority to agencies. An "intelligible principle" isn't a very high bar, and it's one Congress can easily satisfy while still leaving agencies meaningful discretion to exercise their expert judgment.

My colleagues, however, zeroed in on the discredited New Deal cases and all but ignored those that followed. They also ignored that Congress, when designing the Clean Air Act, gave EPA a clear mandate: to set emissions standards at the level "requisite to protect the public health" with "an adequate margin of safety." In implementing that mandate, reasonable regulators might disagree about which measures are "requisite" to protect public health and what an "adequate" margin of safety looks like. But the principle the Clean Air Act articulated was certainly "intelligible," the only requirement under the post–New Deal case law. For that reason, I didn't see any nondelegation problem with the statute. But I couldn't convince my colleagues to see it that way. They thought Congress had given EPA too much power and ruled that EPA's exercise of that power in adopting the PM2.5 emissions standard was unlawful under the nondelegation doctrine. I had no choice but to dissent.

My dissenting opinion (finalized after thirty drafts) was an SOS to the Supreme Court. Congress's delegation of authority in the Clean Air Act, I pointed out, was both narrower and more principled than others the Supreme Court had previously upheld. Adherence to binding Supreme Court precedent, a key principle of judicial restraint, thus required us to uphold it. Far from exercising judicial restraint, the majority had made a power grab, discarding Congress's choice in favor of its own. The implications of the majority's logic were staggering. Its vision of the nondelegation doctrine called into question not only EPA's authority to regulate air pollution but also the authority of many other agencies whose work is crucial to keeping people safe and society functioning—like OSHA's responsibility for overseeing work-place safety, the FDA's for ensuring that drugs are safe and effective, and the FAA's for certifying aircraft safety. At the end of the day, I didn't see how Congress could have spoken more clearly while still giving EPA the flexibility necessary to tailor emission standards to pollutant-specific risks and pollutant-specific technologies. Did my colleagues really think Congress should be in the business of evaluating changing scientific evidence and revising emission standards?

I doubt that's the result they wanted. Industry groups and the lawyers who serve them are well aware that Congress lacks the technical skill—and, frankly, the attention span—to regulate in complex spaces, the environment chief among them. They also understand that hyper-gerrymandering, the filibuster, and money, have made Congress largely ineffective or, worse, more responsive to special interests than to the public interest. So as a practical matter, if Congress can't delegate the regulatory details to expert agencies, it won't be able to regulate in those spaces at all. That's why shrewd legal conservatives serving corporate interests have long recognized that resurrecting the New Deal–era nondelegation doctrine might be the key to a radical shift in American government as we know it. President Trump's White House counsel once told the Federalist Society that "the greatest threat to the rule of law...is the ever-expanding regulatory state." His proposed response? "A strong judiciary," by which he meant judges unchecked by principles of judicial restraint and armed with words like "nondelegation" that threaten to strip agencies of their authority. The Federalist Society endorsed Judge Neil Gorsuch's nomination to the Supreme Court in part because he embraced that idea.

Fortunately, the Supreme Court—in this case, at least—was applying the law, not making policy. It unanimously reversed the mischief-making of my colleagues. Justice Antonin Scalia wrote for the Court, liberally adopting the reasoning of my dissent. "We have almost never felt qualified to second-guess Congress regarding the permissible degree of policy judgment that can be left to those executing or applying the law," he explained. And the Clean Air Act's delegation to EPA, he concluded, fell "well within the outer limits" of the Court's nondelegation precedents. Justice Scalia and I didn't agree often. But he did believe in judicial restraint—most of the time.

———————

Four years later, in 2005, the panel assignment lottery landed me my next big Clean Air Act case. This one was called *Massachusetts v. EPA*. The question was whether the Clean Air Act gave EPA authority to regulate "greenhouse gases," chemicals like carbon dioxide that collect in the atmosphere, trap heat, and change the Earth's climate. It might seem obvious that greenhouse gases are "air pollutants" that EPA should be regulating under the Clean Air Act. At the time, however, it was anything but. George W. Bush was president, and his EPA insisted that it was powerless to regulate greenhouse gases because they aren't "air pollutants" at all. Congress had smog, not climate change, in mind when it passed the Clean Air Act, EPA reasoned. It couldn't have intended the phrase "air pollutants" to encompass greenhouse gases. Plus, because cars are the number-one emitters of greenhouse gases, EPA thought the Department of Transportation should sort it out.

This time, it wasn't industry participants who filed suit since they were pleased with EPA's decision. Instead, the challenge came from Massachusetts and eleven other states. Because climate is global, there was only so much that the states could do on their own to protect their citizens and their coastlines from the devastation of climate change. They wanted EPA's help, and they argued that EPA was obligated to at least seriously consider the threat to public health posed by greenhouse gases. After all, the Clean Air Act *requires* EPA to regulate "air pollutants" that "may reasonably be anticipated to endanger public health or welfare."

The novelist and lawyer Scott Turow called *Mass v. EPA* "the most important environmental law case ever." With the future of the planet on the line, my court again dropped the ball. As in *American Trucking*, my colleagues and I disagreed, and I was forced to dissent. When I say "forced," I mean it. Despite what the last few pages might imply (and unlike my "notorious" friend Ruth), I was no great dissenter. Indeed, in the roughly six years between *American Trucking* and *Mass v. EPA*, I'd dissented only four times. I could usually reach consensus with at least one of the other judges on a panel. I also tried to choose my dissents carefully, saving my capital and credibility for times when it really mattered. If there ever was such a time, *Mass v. EPA* was it. One of my colleagues rejected the states' argument because, in his view, the science of climate change was not 100 percent certain. The other didn't even get that far. He thought the states had no right to challenge EPA's decision at all because climate change affects everyone equally and the states had suffered no special harm. The irony of that logic shouldn't escape you: Where harm is so profound it implicates everyone on the planet, apparently no one can go to court.

My contrary view had nothing to do with the politics of climate change. It had everything to do with the law Congress wrote, the harms the states had alleged, and the proper role of the courts. On the law, Congress had spoken clearly. It defined "air pollutant" to mean *any* "substance or matter" emitted into the air. Greenhouse gases easily checked that box. The conclusion followed directly: EPA had to decide whether greenhouse gas emissions "may reasonably be anticipated to endanger public health or welfare"; if so, it had to regulate them. It made no difference that Congress probably wasn't thinking about climate change when it passed the Clean Air Act. (Few people in 1970 were.) It made no difference that scientists weren't yet 100 percent certain about how much greenhouse gas emissions would affect the climate. (100 percent certainty is too much to ask even today.) And it certainly made no difference, as EPA had suggested, that the Department of Transportation can regulate cars, too. The statute was clear. And as for the states' harm, the question was just as simple. Even putting to one side the obvious risks climate change poses to Massachusetts citizens, the state had alleged its own unique injury: loss of coastline from rising sea levels.

In drafting my dissent—another thinly veiled plea for the Supreme Court to step in—I drew on my own scientific background. Some judges seem intimidated by science. And in fairness, it's not our job in EPA cases to independently weigh the scientific evidence and make our own scientific judgments. But in this one, EPA was hiding behind science in an attempt to obscure what the law required. For example, in refusing to regulate greenhouse gases, EPA relied heavily on a study by the National Academy of Sciences. A close look at that study, however, underscored that greenhouse gases are air pollutants that could "reasonably be anticipated" to endanger public health. EPA's excuses for declining to regulate, my dissent explained, had nothing to do with the scientific question Congress had directed it to answer. I think my grounding in science helped me to see that and gave me the confidence to say it. I wanted my dissent to help the justices see it, too.

Although I hoped the Supreme Court would intervene, this time I wasn't expecting it to. The Court usually takes EPA cases only at the agency's request, and EPA—which had just been handed a victory—surely wouldn't be asking. *Mass v. EPA* also seemed like the kind of political hot potato at least some justices might prefer to avoid. But the Court looks for issues of exceptional importance. And as I wrote, "If global warming is not a matter of exceptional importance, then those words have no meaning." The Court decided to take the case. Maybe my dissent made a difference in its calculus. Maybe it made a difference that almost a third of the justices' clerks had previously clerked on the D.C. Circuit, including two for me. Those clerks would have appreciated how seldom I dissented and understood what it meant in this case that I did. Maybe, too, it mattered that the *Washington Post* had published an editorial, "Warming at the Court," urging the justices to take the case. While I'm very careful about talking to the press, I trusted the editorial's author, Ben Wittes, and spent some time on the phone helping him understand the legal details.

Once the Supreme Court decided to take the case, the stakes ratcheted even higher. When it comes to preventing climate catastrophe, time is of the essence. And it was easy to see how the Supreme Court could make my court's bad ruling even worse. Whereas my colleagues held only that EPA was not *required* to regulate greenhouse gases, many feared the Supreme Court would go further and hold that EPA was *powerless* to regulate greenhouse gases in the future. If it had done that, would we still be debating today whether greenhouse gas emissions should even be regulated at all? That's exactly the sort of politicized debate Congress meant to avoid when it directed EPA to regulate new air pollutants based on science, rather than politics.

Fortunately, I don't know how it would have played out because the Supreme Court reversed my court's ruling and vindicated my dissenting view. This time, though, the vote was much closer than it was in *American Trucking*. Justice Stevens wrote for a narrow, five-justice majority. His opinion (not so coincidentally, it turned out) looked very much like mine. "Any air pollutant," he reasoned, means any air pollutant. Greenhouse gases clearly qualify. As with other pollutants, EPA can exercise its judgment in setting an appropriate emissions standard for greenhouse gases. What it can't do is ignore Congress's mandate for reasons unrelated to whether greenhouse gases could "reasonably be anticipated" to affect the public welfare. Justice Stevens also roundly rejected the argument that the states had no standing to sue, pointing, as I had, to Massachusetts's coastline. I was pleased that he quoted my dissent throughout his opinion. Indeed, he called me to thank me for writing it. I'd given him a "roadmap," he told me, for deciding the case and retaining his fragile majority. Although Justice Stevens and I were not especially close, we always enjoyed talking about our common Chicago roots, and I deeply respected his work as a judge. Late in his life, I interviewed him at the independent D.C. bookshop Politics & Prose about his memoir, *Five Chiefs*. Since he had difficulty hearing, we divvied up responsibility: He'd call on audience members to ask questions, and I'd repeat (and sometimes rephrase) the questions to him. "You're a great team," Edie joked. "He can't hear and you can't see."

As an aside, Justice Stevens wasn't the only justice who reached out over the years when an opinion of mine helped them through a difficult issue. Justice Ginsburg—my closest friend on the Court—used to do that, too. One particularly memorable case involved an energy task force headed by Vice President Dick Cheney. The details of the case aren't important here, except that I wrote an opinion that the Supreme Court reversed 7–2. (It would have been 6–2, but Justice Scalia had refused to recuse himself notwithstanding his recent duck-hunting trip with Vice President Cheney.) Just minutes after the Court announced its decision, my chambers' fax machine sputtered to life with a message from Justice Ginsburg. "Dear David: This is the dissenting statement I just read from the bench. Every best wish, Ruth." Justices rarely read dissents from the bench, doing so only when they feel especially strongly about a case. As you'll see in the next chapter, this wasn't the last time she would read a dissent from the bench in one of my cases.

——•••——

In *American Trucking* and *Mass v. EPA*, the Supreme Court modeled judicial restraint. It respected Congress's judgment, applied statutory text as written, and ultimately let EPA experts make the necessary scientific judgments. Today's Supreme Court, however, is increasingly unrestrained, preferring to make its own calls on difficult policy questions involving environmental issues and beyond. That's not how courts are supposed to operate.

An egregious example is a case called *West Virginia v. EPA*, which involved a regulation known as the Clean Power Plan. Adopted in 2015, the Clean Power Plan was the Obama administration's major effort to fight climate change. It was designed to reduce emissions of carbon dioxide—a greenhouse gas that accumulates in the atmosphere and affects climate—by shifting the nation's power grid away from carbon dioxide–emitting power sources like coal and toward natural gas and renewable energy sources like wind and solar. Yes, the shift would be costly. But the Clean Air Act directs EPA to reduce carbon dioxide emissions to safe levels, including by requiring power plants to use the best "systems of emission reduction." And after much consideration, EPA's scientists had determined that shifting to new power sources was the best "system" for achieving that goal.

The Clean Power Plan was challenged almost immediately, and my court decided to hear the case en banc in the first instance—again, a process the court reserves for only the most important cases. Before the regulation took effect, however, the political winds shifted. Donald Trump was elected, and his EPA repealed the Clean Power Plan. According to Trump's EPA, Obama's EPA had exceeded its authority by issuing the Clean Power Plan because questions about whether and how the nation should move toward greener energy sources are too big—too "major"—for a mere agency to answer. In place of the Clean Power Plan, Trump's EPA issued a scaled-back regulation, branding its version the Affordable Clean Energy Rule. Affordable it was, clean it wasn't. Trump's rule required coal-fired plants to make modest improvements, but gone was any requirement that they shift toward renewable energy sources.

EPA's change of course led my court to dismiss the case without issuing an opinion. The Clean Power Plan had been repealed, so there was nothing left for us to decide. Or so we thought. As it turned out, the saga was far from over. States and public health organizations who believed that shifting to greener energy sources was in fact the best "system of emission reduction" filed a new lawsuit challenging the Clean Power Plan's repeal. This time, we didn't take the case en banc, and I didn't win the assignment lottery. I watched from the sidelines as my court concluded that Trump's EPA had misinterpreted the Clean Air Act when it repealed the Clean Power Plan. "Systems of emission reduction," my colleagues explained, can reasonably be interpreted to encompass changes in fuel source. True, the transition costs for coal-powered plants might be significant. But Trump's EPA had been wrong to conclude that the agency lacked authority to issue the Clean Power Plan. To the contrary, the panel explained, the Clean Power Plan was exactly the sort of novel regulation Congress had designed the Clean Air Act to encourage, and it fit squarely within EPA's mandate to protect public health by reducing air pollution.

Reasonable judges might take issue with their first point. "Systems of emission reduction" is not as clear as the "any air pollutant" language from *Mass v. EPA*. Still, "systems of emission reduction" is an ambiguous term that EPA could reasonably have interpreted to encompass shifts from coal to wind and solar power. Thus, I agreed with my colleagues that, under the *Chevron* doctrine, the EPA's interpretation warranted deference. The question, however, was a close one, because a rigorous textual analysis might also support the conclusion that a different energy source cannot reasonably be construed as a "system" of anything. I would therefore have respected my colleagues if they had reached the contrary result in that principled way—as I would have respected the Supreme Court if it had reversed them on that ground. I would have respected the Supreme Court even more if it had refrained from deciding that question at all. Biden's EPA was already working on a new regulation and the old one had never taken effect, so there was little left to fight over. A restrained Court—one that, in Chief Justice Roberts's words, abided by the principle that "if it is not necessary to decide more to dispose of a case, then it is necessary *not* to decide more"—would have let sleeping dogs lie.

That isn't what happened. The Supreme Court took the case. Writing for a six-justice majority, the Chief Justice ruled that Obama's EPA had lacked authority to adopt the Clean Power Plan, and Trump's EPA was right to repeal it, because questions about fuel sources are too "major" for a mere agency to answer without express authorization from Congress. If that reasoning sounds familiar, it should, because the "major questions" doctrine is a close cousin of the nondelegation doctrine Justice Scalia shot down in *American Trucking*. Both doctrines reflect a fundamental distrust of federal agencies. Both doctrines have no basis in constitutional text. Both doctrines purport to prioritize Congress's authority while ultimately empowering the courts, which can use the two doctrines to override any congressional delegations they don't like. And both doctrines have long been darlings of Federalist Society lawyers intent on stripping back federal regulations. Nondelegation is the bigger fish, as it would prevent Congress from delegating important decisions to agencies no matter how clearly it speaks. Major questions, though, is a good consolation prize, as it allows for such delegations only if Congress speaks with unmistakable clarity.

The deregulatory agenda reflected in the nondelegation and major questions doctrines has implications for everything from broadband internet to health care to workplace safety. It's particularly troubling when it comes to the environment. Environmental issues almost always implicate big, technical problems that demand big, technical solutions. As Congress recognized when it passed the Clean Air Act, expert agencies are best situated to craft those solutions. Also, I have no idea how courts are supposed to decide in a principled fashion whether a particular issue is too "major" for an agency to take up. I suppose they'll just have to guess whether five justices would object to the agency's rule. What I do know is that, by affording itself a roving mandate to disrupt any regulatory regime that strikes five justices as too "major," the Court strengthened its own hand at Congress's expense. Doing so in the name of "separation of powers"—and supposedly out of concern for *Congress's* constitutional prerogative—makes that move all the more worrisome. And here's the kicker: Under the "major questions" doctrine, the more important the regulatory question, the likelier that generalist judges, rather than scientific experts, will make the final call. Doesn't that sound exactly backward to you? Just days earlier, the Chief Justice had cautioned against decisions that "jolt" the legal system. This one was an earthquake, and only time will tell where it falls on the Richter scale.

Justice Kagan's blistering dissent hit the right marks. "The current Court is textualist only when being so suits it," she wrote. "When that method would frustrate broader goals," like protecting industry from environmental regulations, "special canons like the 'major questions doctrine' magically appear as get-out-of-text-free cards." So, too, with historical analysis. The Court's "conservative" majority usually cares about historical evidence and original intent. But as Justice Kagan pointed out, Congress has always delegated important issues—which at the time of the Founding included such things as Indian affairs, territorial administration, and the national debt—to experts in the executive branch. The Founders didn't see those delegations as a threat. Quite the opposite: Delegation was then, as it is now, the most sensible way for Congress to legislate on complex topics that require ongoing expert analysis. By ruling that agencies are powerless to answer any questions the Court deems "major," "[t]he Court appoint[ed] itself—instead of Congress or the expert agency—the decision-maker on climate policy." Justice Kagan wrote that she could not "think of many things more frightening." Neither can I.

I'd like to end this discussion on a hopeful note, though I'm not sure I have much to say that's hopeful about the environment and this Supreme Court. "Major questions" is now the law of the land, leaving agencies without authority to answer any questions five justices consider important. Even more troubling, as I write this chapter *Chevron*—the basic notion of interpretive deference to agencies—is now on the chopping block. And worst of all, a majority of the sitting justices (I'll let you guess which ones) have expressed interest in resuscitating the New Deal–era nondelegation doctrine that Justice Scalia rejected in *American Trucking*. The justices' fear, apparently, is that without these new mechanisms for judicial intervention, agencies will run amok.

That fear is ill-founded. Agencies like EPA need accountability, of course. But for decades the constraints baked into the Constitution, the Administrative Procedure Act, and other congressional statutes have effectively constrained them. Agency heads are appointed by the president and confirmed by the Senate, and the president can fire most of them at any time for any reason. Meanwhile, Congress decides how much authority to delegate to federal agencies in the first place, oversees their work, can repeal any regulations with which it disagrees, and can even withdraw delegations of power or disband agencies entirely. The courts, for their part, hear challenges not only to agencies' actions but also to their failures to act. When a regulation or failure to regulate runs afoul of the Constitution or a statute, or is otherwise "arbitrary and capricious," courts vacate the agency's decision and send it back for a do-over, just like the Supreme Court did in *Mass v. EPA* and my court did in the net neutrality cases. But stripping Congress of its power to delegate to agencies in the first place—or stripping agencies of their power to answer "major" questions and interpret ambiguous statutes—is something else entirely. Our system of government cannot function without agencies and the scientists and civil servants who staff them. As the world keeps getting more complex, we need expert agencies more than ever. Anyone concerned with the environment—or with safe medicines, unadulterated food, or cars that drive safely—has very good reason to worry about where this Supreme Court is headed.

As we learned in June of 2023, anyone with a student loan also has good reason to worry. A statute known as the "HEROES Act" authorizes the Department of Education to "waive or modify any provision" of its student loan programs in the event of a national emergency. In the wake of a global pandemic that left countless

Americans out of work and struggling to get by, the Department of Education did exactly that: It modified the repayment obligations of income-qualified borrowers to ensure that those borrowers were no worse off as a result of the COVID emergency. When that loan forgiveness program was challenged in court by Republican-controlled states, the path of judicial restraint was clear as day. At the first fork, the restrained choice would have been to refrain from opining on the legality of the program at all. No one was actually injured by the loan forgiveness program, so the Court should simply have dismissed the case for lack of standing. Instead, it took the path that seems ever more frequently traveled, wading into a partisan policy dispute without any legal justification for doing so. At the second fork, the restrained choice would have been to determine whether the Department of Education had reasonably interpreted the HEROES Act to authorize its loan forgiveness program. Again, however, the Court chose the other path, applying the "major questions" doctrine and concluding that loan forgiveness was too "major" an issue for the Department of Education to resolve. And just like that, the unelected, life-tenured justices of the Supreme Court — not Congress, and not the expert agency to which Congress had delegated authority — made the final call on a policy question that affects millions of Americans.

Supporters of the "major questions" doctrine might respond by saying, well, all Congress has to do to empower agencies to answer major questions is to say so clearly. That, after all, is the theoretical difference between nondelegation and major questions: Nondelegation prohibits Congress from empowering agencies; major questions requires only that Congress make a clear statement to that effect. But it's really not that simple. As "major questions" supporters well know, Congress often struggles to pass any legislation at all. And when it does pass an important substantive law, it often chooses to delegate to agencies the power to solve complex, evolving problems (like emissions control at power plants or student loan modifications in emergency circumstances) precisely because it doesn't yet know what shape the solutions might take. Congress didn't tell the EPA to use the best "systems of emission reduction *including shifts to new power sources*" because it wasn't yet clear that a power-source shift might prove the best way to reduce emissions. And Congress didn't tell the Department of Education that it could "waive or modify" loan provisions *"including by forgiving loans in the event of a COVID pandemic"* because it didn't yet know that COVID would sweep the nation and justify a large-scale forgiveness program. Congress wanted the experts at EPA and the Department of Education to make those calls, including, in the case of the HEROES Act, on an emergency basis. Moreover, even if Congress had somehow foreseen those "major questions" coming down the pike and spoken clearly enough to satisfy the Court, nondelegation is still lurking in the wings, a tool for empowering the Court to strike down significant regulations no matter how clearly Congress speaks. With this Court, I fear it's only a matter of time before it breaks the glass and grabs that tool.

One final note: Environmental cases always make me think of my father and our last expedition together, and not just for the obvious reason that environmental cases usually involve science. I was never lucky enough to draw a case about the tendency of llamas to disrupt seismograph readings. But I've always believed that the process my father and his colleagues used in Peru is the same one that's required to decide an environmental appeal. High in the Andes we worked with seismological data and principles of physics. On the bench, it's the facts of the case and the relevant legal principles. In both contexts, the principles themselves never change, and good judges, like good scientists, must follow wherever those principles lead. My father taught me to think that way. The justices in *American Trucking* and *Mass v. EPA* thought that way, too. I hope this Supreme Court returns to those principles someday. The future of the planet may depend on it.

CHAPTER 18

The Future of Democracy

COMPARED TO THE FUTURE OF OUR PLANET, THE FUTURE OF democracy may sound like small potatoes. But our great American experiment in democracy is the best chance we have to protect our planet. It's also our best tool for preserving the individual rights we hold dear. Each of those rights—to speak freely, to worship if and as we choose, to keep the things we own, to forfeit our liberty only after a fair process, and so on—is important. But one right undergirds all the others: the right to vote. Voting is how we control our government. By voting for our representatives, we decide who speaks for us on just about every important issue our society faces.

I know a thing or two about voting. I've already told you about my own struggle as a blind citizen to vote independently, a privilege I don't take for granted. This chapter is about the part I played in two of the most important voting rights cases of all time. The story doesn't end happily: In both cases, the Supreme Court reversed my rulings in ways that make me fear for the future of our democracy. It begins with the Fifteenth Amendment.

If you're like most people, you have some idea of what the First Amendment is about. Speech, religion, the press—there's lots of good stuff in that one. If you're a particularly engaged citizen, you might also know something about the Fourth, Fifth, and Fourteenth Amendments. That's where you'll find protection from unreasonable searches, the right to remain silent, and the guarantee of equal protection. If the Fifteenth Amendment isn't ringing any bells, I'm hardly surprised. Its branding department could probably learn a thing or two from the Second Amendment's people. But trust me: This is one you should know. The Fifteenth Amendment is part of a trio of constitutional amendments ratified in the aftermath of the bloody Civil War fought over slavery and states' rights. The purpose of those three amendments? To bring the country back together, overrule the Supreme Court's ignominious ruling in *Dred Scott v. Sandford* that Black Americans are not citizens, eradicate slavery and racial discrimination, and protect all citizens from rogue state governments. Although all three of the Reconstruction amendments (the Thirteenth, Fourteenth, and Fifteenth) are important, the Fifteenth stands out.

The core of the Fifteenth Amendment is a simple promise: that *all* men shall have the right to vote, regardless of the color of their skin. (Women, I'm sorry to say, didn't get the same right until fifty years and four amendments later.) The framers of the Fifteenth Amendment recognized that it's one thing for the Constitution to prohibit racial discrimination in voting but quite another to make sure that states actually let people of color into the voting booth. So the Fifteenth Amendment also provided that "Congress shall have the power to enforce this article by appropriate legislation." Those twelve words make up one of the most revolutionary sentences in the Constitution. Our elections are run by the states, not the federal government. But in one fell swoop, the Fifteenth Amendment prohibited racial discrimination in voting and gave Congress new powers to enforce that prohibition *against the states*. It also gave Congress a trump card over the Supreme Court, which in cases like *Dred Scott* had not proven up to the task of protecting *all* Americans.

The Voting Rights Act of 1965 (VRA), one of the most important civil rights laws ever passed, is the embodiment of "appropriate legislation" under the Fifteenth Amendment. By 1965, nearly a century had passed since the Fifteenth Amendment's ratification, and across the country millions of minority voters were exercising their right to vote. Congress recognized, however, that race-based barriers to voting persisted, particularly in the South. The most obvious discriminatory tactic to keep Black people out of the voting booth was the selective use of literacy tests. So the VRA expressly prohibited states from conditioning the right to vote on a literacy test. But it didn't stop there. Just as Congress recognized in passing the Clean Air Act that industry would find ways around any static set of air pollution rules, so, too, did it recognize in passing the VRA that local governments bent on disenfranchising minority voters would get creative. If the VRA merely prohibited literacy tests, states would simply concoct new and even more insidious mechanisms for curbing minority voting. Therefore, in Section 2 of the Act Congress also prohibited states from using any other "qualification or prerequisite to voting" "to deny or abridge the right of any citizen of the United States to vote on account of race or color." That way, states and localities couldn't replace literacy tests with poll taxes, grandfather clauses, or other bogus requirements to achieve the same pernicious goal.

That was a good start. But Congress understood that even such a broad prohibition wouldn't be enough to protect minority

voters living in states and local communities hell-bent on protecting white politicians and preserving discriminatory policies.
Imagine, for example, a county that moves an inner-city polling location far out into the suburbs just six weeks before an
election to discourage minority citizens from voting. That change
violates the VRA because it disproportionately harms minority
voters. But lawsuits take time, and elections can't be undone. In
the six months it might take to develop evidence proving that the
polling location change had a disproportionate effect, Election
Day will have come and gone. A court order reinstating the old
polling location for future elections won't help people who weren't
able to make it to the new one during the last election. Nor will it
stop the same county from implementing a different discriminatory rule — say, a restrictive voter registration policy — before the
next election. The cycle could continue indefinitely. Even if courts
ultimately strike down each and every discriminatory scheme, the
county can always stay one step ahead.

So Congress baked a solution right into the VRA: Section 5,
which required states and localities with a track record of racial
discrimination to seek federal approval — either from the US Attorney General or a federal court in D.C. — *before* changing their
voting rules. If those "covered" jurisdictions could show that their
proposed rule changes wouldn't disproportionately harm minority
voters, they could implement those changes. If not, they had to
stick with their old rules. The result was that in the places Congress deemed likeliest to discriminate, rules would be screened for
VRA compliance *before* they took effect.

Section 5's pre-screening process — called preclearance —
initially applied to six states in their entirety and parts of two
more, all of which had a history of discriminating against Black
voters. At Hogan, I had worked with the Mexican American Legal Defense and Educational Fund to extend the VRA

to Hispanic Americans and other language minorities who also faced discrimination at the voting booth. As a result, three more states and parts of six others earned their spots on Section 5's roster. Congress identified all of those jurisdictions with a formula reverse-engineered to capture places with a history of discrimination against minority voters. Most of the covered jurisdictions were in the South, where, Congress found, the roots of racial discrimination ran deepest. Even there, however, preclearance was not a "life without parole" sentence. Through good behavior, covered jurisdictions could earn their way off the Section 5 list through a process called bailing out. In addition, Congress was optimistic that racial discrimination in voting was on the way out across the nation and that the VRA would put an end to the practice once and for all. (Optimism that racial discrimination is "almost over," it seems, is something of a national pastime.) So the VRA itself was set to expire after a period of years.

Congress was partially right. The VRA did usher in a new era of equality at the voting booth. Minority voters registered and voted at higher rates, minority candidates were elected more frequently, and racial gerrymanders proved more difficult to pull off. But Congress's optimism that racial discrimination would cease entirely — and the VRA become unnecessary — proved unfounded. Discriminatory practices persisted despite the VRA, so Congress extended the statute before it expired. Then, when that extension was almost up, Congress extended the VRA again, and again, and again. Congress ultimately reauthorized the VRA five separate times. On each occasion, it took a close look at racial discrimination in voting — at the progress we've made and the distance we've left to go — and concluded that Section 5 preclearance remained necessary to ensure that all citizens have an equal chance to participate in the political process. On signing the 1982 reauthorization, President Reagan called the right to vote "the crown jewel of American liberties" and promised "we will not see its luster diminished." The 2006 authorization passed the Senate in a vote of 98–0.

While the VRA remained one of the few issues on which our increasingly partisan legislature could agree, the covered jurisdictions required to use Section 5's preclearance process weren't at all happy. They couldn't "bail out" if they wouldn't stop using discriminatory practices. In the meantime, they deeply resented Section 5, seeing it as both a scarlet letter and an excuse for unwelcome federal intrusion into local affairs. As a result, covered jurisdictions repeatedly challenged the VRA's constitutionality under the banner of states' rights. Four separate times, the Supreme Court upheld the law. In the first of those cases, *South Carolina v. Katzenbach*, the Court recognized that Section 5 had "shift[ed] the advantage of time and inertia from the perpetrators of the evil to its victims." That strategy, the Court concluded, is "a valid means for carrying out the commands of the Fifteenth Amendment."

———

The states' rights crowd was undeterred by their string of losses. In 2008, they mounted a fifth challenge to the VRA. There had been no meaningful changes in discriminatory voting practices in the near decade since the last time the Supreme Court had upheld the VRA's extension. But two things had changed: Samuel Alito had joined the Court and John Roberts had become its new chief justice. The challengers suspected those personnel changes might make all the difference. Roberts, in particular, had argued as a young lawyer in the Reagan administration that the VRA was "constitutionally suspect." There was of course nothing wrong with his doing that. We all had careers before we became judges, and we all come to the job with opinions about legal issues. The crucial question is whether we can put those opinions to one side when we don our judicial robes. The VRA's challengers were willing to gamble that Chief Justice Roberts and Justice Alito could not, and believed they might finally have the votes to get rid of Section 5 once and for all. But first the challengers had to come through a special three-judge district court composed of two district judges and one circuit judge. Through random assignment, that circuit judge was me.

The case was called *Northwest Austin v. Holder*, and it concerned a small voting district in south-central Texas. Because Texas had a long history of discriminatory voting practices, particularly against its large Spanish-speaking population, the entire state was covered by Section 5. The district argued, however, that the preclearance process was unconstitutional and that it should be able to make decisions about election procedures without getting a federal permission slip in advance. In the alternative, it asked to bail out, insisting that Section 5 coverage was no longer justified in light of the district's recent history of nondiscriminatory voting practices. We heard argument in the big ceremonial courtroom, which was packed to the gills, including with people who had long fought for voting rights and traveled from Texas to witness the argument.

The case wasn't difficult. The Fifteenth Amendment prohibits states from abridging the right to vote "on account of race," and empowers Congress to enforce that prohibition through "appropriate legislation." The Supreme Court had repeatedly held that the VRA is "appropriate legislation" under the Fifteenth Amendment. In renewing the VRA, Congress had carefully considered whether Section 5 remained "appropriate" to prevent racial discrimination in voting. After hearing testimony from scores of witnesses—and amassing fifteen thousand pages of evidence—Congress had concluded that the preclearance process continued to serve as a bulwark against discrimination on the basis of race in the place most central to our democracy—the voting booth. My opinion could have rejected the constitutional challenge in a single sentence: "As the Supreme Court has repeatedly held, Section 5 of the Voting Rights Act is a constitutional exercise of Congress's authority under the Fifteenth Amendment." It was really as simple as that.

Of course, my colleagues and I saw which way the political winds were blowing—and we could count to five, just as the challengers could. We worried they might be right about what the Supreme Court might do. Even so, lower-court judges are not prophets; it's not their job to predict what the law will be in the future. Instead, they must faithfully apply existing law—including binding precedents the Supreme Court has issued in the past—to the facts of the present. We were thus clearly obligated to uphold Section 5 even if we believed five justices were prepared to upend decades of voting rights law.

We weren't going to make it easy for them, though. I doubted the justices themselves would actually read the fifteen thousand pages of evidence on which Congress had relied. But I'd read them. (Yes, virtually every word.) I structured my opinion around a comprehensive summary of the extensive evidence supporting Congress's findings, everything from voter registration and turnout data to the supposed burdens on states subject to Section 5. I also emphasized Congress's finding that improvements in voting access in covered states were at least partly attributable to Section 5's deterrent effect. Covered jurisdictions, Congress had found, often refrained from making discriminatory rule changes because they knew they couldn't defend those changes during the preclearance process. The evidence that the covered jurisdictions were still discriminating, plus the evidence that they would discriminate much more with Section 5 out of the way, was overwhelming. If the Court was going to reverse us, it would have to face the same devastating record of ongoing discrimination that Congress and our court had already reviewed.

We also determined that Northwest Austin wasn't entitled to a bailout, the district's alternative request. I'd given a lot of thought to that argument. Judicial restraint means that, where possible, courts should issue narrow, case-specific rulings rather than broad, game-changing ones. In *Northwest Austin,* the bailout argument was certainly narrower than the constitutional challenge. If we could conclude that Northwest Austin met the threshold for a bailout, we wouldn't have to decide whether Section 5 was constitutional. That approach would also have the benefit of insulating the constitutional question from Supreme Court review. I'd even tried to write the opinion that way, something I often did when grappling with a difficult argument. Writing through an argument helped me understand its logic and spot its weaknesses. If an argument *wouldn't* "write," then I tended to think it probably *wasn't* "right." That's what happened with bailout. I couldn't write a convincing opinion concluding that Northwest Austin was entitled to a bailout. So I ultimately rejected that argument and wrote an opinion ruling that Section 5 was constitutional.

Northwest Austin then went to the Supreme Court. I wasn't surprised to see that the Chief Justice wrote the opinion reversing my court's ruling. But I was surprised that *all nine* justices voted to reverse, and that they'd dodged the big question: whether Section 5's preclearance process was constitutional. Instead, the Court bit on the district's alternative argument and held that Northwest Austin was eligible to bail out from Section 5's preclearance requirement.

I wasn't any more convinced by the Supreme Court's bailout analysis than I'd been by my own jettisoned draft. But it was a whimper of a ruling, not the bang I'd felt sure the Court had been working up to. So at first I was relieved. Judicial restraint is a virtue, and the Court was right to avoid answering a big constitutional question if it believed it could resolve the parties' dispute on a narrower ground.

In this instance, however, the veneer of restraint was very thin. Having resolved the case on the narrow bailout ground, the Court should have said nothing at all about the big constitutional question it *wasn't* reaching. Instead, the Court went out of its way to assail the VRA. It warned that Section 5 imposed "federalism costs" by intruding into local policymaking and that Section 5's coverage formula was outdated because "things have changed in the South." The Court even criticized the VRA because it "differentiates" among the states. According to the Court, treating states differently with respect to preclearance might run afoul of a doctrine called equal sovereignty, a doctrine that the Court had previously applied only with respect to the terms on which states were admitted to the Union and so seemed to have nothing to do with the VRA's application to Northwest Austin. (Texas joined the Union in 1845, well before the Fifteenth Amendment, much less the VRA.) So despite the narrow bottom line, the Court's opinion was hardly "judicial," much less "restrained." But it did put Congress on notice about what would happen to Section 5 if it failed to amend the VRA.

What I couldn't figure out was why the four liberal justices had joined the Chief's majority opinion. I could see how they might have agreed with Northwest Austin on the narrow bailout question. I'd initially been tempted by that argument, after all. But the unnecessary and irrelevant jabs at Section 5's constitutionality? Why had they gone along with that part of the Chief's opinion? I suspected I knew the answer, and Justice Ginsburg herself later confirmed my suspicions. The justices had initially voted 5–4 to declare Section 5 unconstitutional, but they later worked out a compromise: The majority agreed to sidestep the big question about Section 5's constitutionality, and the would-be dissenters agreed to let Northwest Austin bail out and to sign on to the critique of Section 5. With that compromise, the liberal justices had bought Congress time to salvage the keystone of the Civil Rights Movement.

They sure paid a high price: an unrebutted opinion that criticized the VRA and, worse, endorsed a new "equal sovereignty" doctrine with potentially profound implications. The Court's opinion in *Northwest Austin* thus planted the seeds for Section 5's destruction. Unless Congress took action or the composition of the Supreme Court changed, the question wasn't *whether* the Court would strike down preclearance as unconstitutional, just *when*.

The answer, as it turned out, was almost exactly four years later. In the interim, Congress had done absolutely nothing to update the VRA—legislative malpractice, if you ask me. In 2006, every single senator had voted in favor of extending the VRA, and now no one could be bothered to update the preclearance formula and head off the Supreme Court? The VRA's foes were not so idle. While Congress sat on its hands, the same group that engineered the challenge to preclearance in *Northwest Austin* put together another case that wouldn't be as easy for the Supreme Court to dodge. This time the challenger was Shelby County, a mostly white county in central Alabama with a long history of racial discrimination in voting. Perversely, Shelby County's impressive record of racial discrimination made it the ideal test case for challenging the VRA. Unlike in *Northwest Austin*, a "good behavior" bailout clearly wouldn't be an option.

I couldn't quite believe it when the case-assignment lottery chose me for *Shelby County*. My presence on the panel even caused reporters to question whether the assignment process had truly been random. The court assured them it was. As with the net neutrality cases, the sand pail balls just kept coming up "Tatel." So, for the second time, the fate of the VRA was in my hands. But not in mine alone. Two of my favorite colleagues, Steve Williams and Tom Griffith, both Republican appointees, were with me on the panel. The three of us had very different views on policy. But when it came to judging, we were of one mind. When I saw we'd been assigned to *Shelby County* together, I didn't know whether we'd reach consensus. But I did know we'd try and that all three of us would engage together in the enterprise of judging. Sure enough, Steve sent me an email that very day: "I've read the briefs, and I realize the Supreme Court has hinted where it's headed," he said, "but I remain uncertain. What's your view, David?" Thus began weeks of discussion among the three of us. We talked a lot—through email, on the phone, and in each other's chambers. More importantly, we listened to each other. All three of us had little doubt that Section 5 would meet its demise at the Supreme Court. *Northwest Austin* had made that much clear. With that writing on the wall, however, we disagreed about what the law required us lower-court judges to do.

Steve thought we should meet the Supreme Court where it was headed—to "lead our receiver," so to speak. He couldn't understand why Congress hadn't updated the Section 5 coverage formula, which relied on data from the sixties and seventies and, in his view, was no longer a perfect fit. Some pretty discriminatory places weren't covered, some less discriminatory ones were, and he didn't see bailout as an adequate solution to the mismatch. More fundamentally, he didn't trust Congress's assessment of the evidence. Although I didn't agree with where Steve landed, I respected how he'd gotten there. In particular, I appreciated that Steve never mentioned the "equal sovereignty" doctrine the Court had effectively invented in *Northwest Austin*. Thankfully, though, Steve's opinion was a dissent, because Tom agreed with me that preclearance remained constitutional. No kinder words have been said about me professionally than when Tom described me as a judge who "played it straight...without partisanship or ideology," even when I didn't "favor the outcome." I hope that was true of me. I know it was true of Tom in *Shelby County*. Tom liked to say he "ruined his reputation" with his conservative friends by voting to uphold the VRA. But for me, at least, he cemented it.

Tom and I agreed that it wasn't *our* job to decide which jurisdictions should be covered under Section 5. The Fifteenth Amendment gave *Congress* wide latitude to enact "appropriate legislation" to prevent racial discrimination in voting, and as we emphasized in our majority opinion, we judges "owe much deference to the considered judgment of the People's elected representatives." When Congress reauthorized the VRA in 2006, it found—based on that fifteen-thousand-page record—that jurisdictions that had discriminated before were the likeliest to discriminate again. It also found that preclearance had a powerful deterrent effect. For those reasons, our elected representatives had determined, consistent with their Fifteenth Amendment authority, that the preclearance process remained "appropriate" to prevent discrimination in covered jurisdictions. Plus, those jurisdictions could bail out if they changed their ways, though for Shelby County in particular, Congress's original formula still hit the mark. As recently as 2008, the Justice Department had rejected a redistricting plan that would have eliminated the only majority-Black district in one of the county's largest cities. So we again upheld Section 5, this time by a vote of 2–1.

As we'd all anticipated, the Supreme Court disagreed. This time its opinion was a bang, not a whimper. The Chief Justice wrote for a five-justice majority, completing the job he'd started in *Northwest Austin*. The Court began by emphasizing that the Founders had "intended the States to keep for themselves... the power to regulate elections," neglecting to note that the drafters of the Fifteenth Amendment, which came later, most certainly did not. Next, the Court gestured to the "tradition of equal sovereignty"—the seed it had planted in *Northwest Austin*—privileging the equal treatment of *states* (guaranteed nowhere in the Constitution) over equal treatment of minority *voters* (guaranteed by the Fifteenth Amendment). Finally, the Court declared that Section 5 was no longer necessary in light of the nation's progress with respect to racial discrimination in voting. According to whom, exactly? Certainly not Congress, which had found that preclearance remained necessary when it last reauthorized the VRA. Justice Ginsburg wrote many memorable dissents during her time on the Court, but no line of hers has stuck with me like her response to the Court's view about the continuing necessity of Section 5. "Throwing out preclearance" because "it has worked," she warned, "is like throwing away your umbrella in a rainstorm because you are not getting wet." Exactly so.

The Supreme Court's evisceration of the VRA was a tragedy for civil rights; its reasoning was a tragedy for the rule of law. The Court could have held that Congress hadn't done quite enough to establish that preclearance was "appropriate" with respect to Shelby County specifically. But instead of that scalpel, the Court used a machete. This new principle of "equal sovereignty"—which, unlike the Fifteenth Amendment, has no basis in the Constitution—extends more broadly than voting. If states must be treated as "equal" in all respects, Congress can't make *any* jurisdiction-specific fixes to jurisdiction-specific problems.

Worse, the Court ignored Congress's judgment, based on reams of evidence and months of hearings, that Section 5 warranted reauthorization despite the very improvements on which the Court fixated. The Court also ignored Congress's finding that those very improvements resulted partly from preclearance's deterrent effect. The Court apparently believed it knew better than Congress. Safe under the preclearance umbrella, the Court convinced itself it was no longer raining at all.

The consequences of that ruling were hardly theoretical. Before *Shelby County*, preclearance had prevented covered jurisdictions from purging voter rolls, gerrymandering districts, and adopting new and more restrictive voting procedures with racially disproportionate effects. I'd seen that firsthand, including in a case where I'd written an opinion denying preclearance to a Texas voter-ID law that disproportionately harmed minority voters. I was deeply moved by the compelling testimony in that case about ongoing racial discrimination against Texas voters and the difficulties minority voters still faced in getting to the polls: the ninety-year-old Black women who didn't have driver's licenses, the twenty-year-old Hispanic students turned away with their student IDs, and the single mothers who couldn't get time off to travel to the DMV.

That Texas voter-ID law we'd rejected as discriminatory took effect just two hours after the Supreme Court issued its decision in *Shelby County*, affecting hundreds of thousands of eligible voters. Other states previously subject to preclearance redrew district lines, tightened voter-ID requirements, purged voter rolls, canceled same-day registration, restricted early voting, and closed polling places—all in ways that made voting more difficult for minority voters than for others. We're only just beginning to understand the full consequences of *Shelby County*. But suffice it to say that without preclearance's umbrella, we're all getting wet.

When the Supreme Court struck down Section 5's coverage formula, it reassured us that Section 2 of the VRA—which prohibits discriminatory voting practices nationwide, though without the preclearance safety net—remained alive and well. Section 2, the Court promised, would fill the gap left by Section 5's destruction and provide a mechanism for challenging racial discrimination in voting—albeit after the fact. It's not yet clear if that's true.

On the one hand, things didn't look at all good for Section 2 in 2021 when, in a case called *Brnovich v. Democratic National Committee,* the Supreme Court upheld Arizona voting laws that disproportionately impacted the state's Black, Hispanic, and Native American voters. Instead of applying Section 2's text as written, the Court concocted a list of factors that, in essence, require challengers to show that a law was passed with discriminatory intent in order to invalidate it. Unless a legislator says something very, very stupid aloud (like, "the whole point of this change is to make it harder for Hispanic people to get to the polls"), evidence of discriminatory intent is nearly impossible to find. So it seemed like Section 2 might be following Section 5 toward the nearest exit.

On the other hand, we saw a glimmer of hope in 2023 when, in a case called *Allen v. Milligan,* the Court voted 5–4 to allow a Section 2 challenge to proceed against Alabama's new congressional map, which diluted the voting power of Black citizens by "packing" most of them into a single district and distributing the rest across several others. It was a good decision, especially because it held in no uncertain terms that "discriminatory intent" is not a "requirement for liability" under Section 2. I was relieved that Section 2 had survived, at least in some form. But *Milligan* was a very easy case, and its effect will be limited to jurisdictions where voting is racially polarized. It's too early to tell how many teeth Section 2 truly has left and whether they'll survive for long.

Moreover, civil rights advocates' win in *Milligan* underscores what was lost in *Shelby County*. The Alabama map at issue in *Milligan* was challenged in court almost immediately after it was adopted. As Congress recognized in crafting Section 5, however, litigation takes time. And while the challenge to Alabama's new map was pending, the state was able to use that map during the 2022 election. The result was predictable: Republicans went on to win six of the state's seven House seats. If Section 5 had still lived, Alabama would never have been allowed to implement its unlawful map in the first place. Now that it's dead, there's nothing to stop Alabama from adopting a different unlawful map. In fact, Alabama legislators rose to that challenge just a few weeks after *Milligan,* passing a new map that again left the state with only one majority-Black district, in open defiance of the Supreme Court. Another lawsuit quickly followed, with no end to the back-and-forth in sight. Even if the courts keep doing their job and promptly invalidating unlawful maps and voting rules, there's no guarantee of a resolution in time for the next election. That's the gap Section 2 can never fill.

As Justice Kagan remarked in *Brnovich,* "If a single statute represents the best of America, it is the Voting Rights Act," which "marries two great ideals" of "democracy and racial equality." But if "a single statute reminds us of the worst of America," she continued, it's also the Voting Rights Act, because its antidiscrimination mandate is *still* "so necessary." We've been living in a world without Section 5 for more than a decade, and the consequences for our democracy have already been profound. How many Black and Hispanic voters have been disenfranchised by Texas's voter-ID law over the last ten years? How many minority voters have had their registrations rejected as a result of a North Carolina bill passed just two months after *Shelby*? How many voters have had their votes diluted by their relegation to racially gerrymandered districts? True, millions of minority voters are making it to the polls despite these obstacles. Minority candidates are still being elected, too. But the costs of these discriminatory measures—both for the affected voters and for our ever-less-perfect union—are enormous. I fear for the future of our democracy, and not just because of what *Shelby County* and *Brnovich* have done to the promise of equal justice under the law.

———•◦•———

The Supreme Court itself—and its apparent disregard for the principles of judicial restraint that are supposed to curb its power—is perhaps even more frightening than the voting rights decisions it has issued. As I write this memoir, poll numbers about public trust in the Supreme Court are plummeting to all-time lows. Toxic judicial confirmations, which these days look more like partisan punching matches than tests of legal acumen and personal integrity, have contributed to that loss of trust. So have the ideological vote counts in many contentious cases. The public apparently believes that Supreme Court justices vote with the political party of the president who appointed them rather than from neutral legal principles. Ignoring statutory text and inventing new doctrines now seem to be the Supreme Court's M.O. And every time it strikes down or reinterprets the laws that Congress passes or the regulations that agencies adopt, the Court effectively accumulates more power for itself. If you asked a few astute ninth graders which government officials have the power to answer the most contentious questions of our day—questions about race, abortion, guns, and the environment—would they say the elected officials in Congress and our state governments? Or would they point to Supreme Court justices?

Reasonable people can disagree about whether the public is right about the Supreme Court. There are certainly more cases in which the Court breaks on nonideological lines than some critical commentators acknowledge. But the loss of public trust is undeniable, and that itself is cause for serious concern. The Supreme Court has no army. Members of the public and government officials obey the Court because they *believe* in its authority. As Tinkerbell could tell you, belief is a delicate thing. Neutral judging fosters public trust in the rule of law, and that trust, in turn, gives courts their power to protect individual rights. The converse is also true: Judging that appears based on a preordained agenda, not on text or precedent or deference, depletes the reservoir of public confidence. Over the last two decades, the Supreme Court has been draining that reservoir, 5–4 decision by 5–4 decision.

You've already heard about what those 5–4 (and now sometimes 6–3) rulings have done to environmental law and voting rights. You've heard about the Court's disregard for statutory text in cases like *West Virginia* (the Clean Power Plan case) and *Cummings* (the case involving the woman who needed an ASL interpreter) and about its disrespect for Congress in cases like *Shelby County* (where the Court eviscerated Section 5) and *Brnovich* (where it mangled Section 2). Those cases are just the tip of the iceberg. In a series of rulings along partisan lines, the Roberts Court has eaten away at the separation between church and state, an idea so important to the Founders of our nation that they put it in the very first sentence of the Bill of Rights. In two blockbuster gun cases, the Court limited the power of state and local governments to enact sensible gun regulations. In cases brought by a group called Students for Fair Admissions, the Court took from colleges and universities the ability to consider race in their efforts to achieve racially diverse learning environments. The very next day, the Court issued an opinion allowing a website designer to discriminate against gay couples—the first time in American history that the Supreme Court has allowed a business open to the public to refuse to serve a disfavored group. And in another first, the Court in *Dobbs v. Jackson Women's Health Organization* revoked a previously protected constitutional right: the right to reproductive autonomy recognized in *Roe v. Wade*. Agree or disagree with the results in each of those cases, everyone should be concerned about how the Court reached them.

Many of these controversial and partisan decisions share an especially troubling feature: disrespect for *stare decisis*. As you might remember, *stare decisis* is the principle that the Court must follow its own prior rulings. Of all the principles of judicial restraint, *stare decisis* is perhaps the most important. That is because our Constitution is not a lengthy document, and it is very, very hard to amend. The Constitution sets out guiding principles (for example, by prohibiting "unreasonable searches"), but the Supreme Court must fill in the details (for example, by deciding what kinds of searches qualify as "reasonable"). As a result, constitutional law consists primarily of centuries of Supreme Court rulings, each building on the last, that every judge in the country is bound to follow. The Supreme Court alone has the power to deviate from *stare decisis* and overrule its precedents, but it should do so only in the rarest and most carefully defined circumstances. There's a very good reason for this, because each decision the Court issues depends on earlier ones, *stare decisis* is the foundation stone of the entire constitutional structure. Pull the wrong block, and the whole tower might crumble. Pull that foundation stone, and it most certainly will.

As a result, the most important question in the *Students for Fair Admissions* cases wasn't whether affirmative action is constitutional. Nor was the most important question in *Dobbs* whether the Constitution protects reproductive autonomy. The Supreme Court had already answered those questions decades earlier. Instead, the most important question in both cases was whether the Court should adhere to its precedents or overrule them. And in both cases, the Roberts Court kicked precedent to the curb. To be sure, *stare decisis* is not ironclad, and the Court has properly overruled precedents on rare occasions in the past. In *Students for Fair Admissions* and *Dobbs*, the justices who voted to overrule the Court's affirmative action and abortion precedents may have had good reasons for doing so. No such reasons, however, are apparent from their opinions.

In *Students for Fair Admissions*, the Court didn't even acknowledge that it was overruling precedent. *Stare decisis*, in the majority's view, merited hardly a mention. Nor, apparently, did the public deserve an explanation for the Court's change of heart. In *Dobbs*, the majority tried to save face by suggesting that overruling *Roe v. Wade* was just like overruling *Plessy v. Ferguson*, the famously disgraceful decision upholding the constitutionality of "separate but equal." In overruling *Plessy* in *Brown v. Board*, however, the Court voted unanimously to expand civil rights based on changed attitudes toward race and new evidence that *Plessy* had been wrong about segregation's harms. By contrast, in overruling *Roe*, a bare partisan majority took away a constitutional right even though public attitudes toward abortion remained almost exactly the same and there was no new evidence that *Roe* had been wrong. The two decisions, in other words, had nothing in common. Overruling *Plessy* looked like judges doing judging. Overruling *Roe* looked like judges doing politics, or even worse, like judges fulfilling their appointing presidents' campaign promises.

Don't "conservative" values mean honoring the decisions of the past, not rejecting them? Don't they mean respecting Congress's authority, not taking power for oneself? Each time the Supreme Court disregards precedent and the other principles of judicial restraint, its power grows but its institutional capital dwindles.

As Justice Potter Stewart once said, a "change in the law upon a ground no firmer than a change in our membership invites the popular misconception that this institution is little different from the two political branches of the Government." "No misconception," he declared, "could do more lasting injury to this Court and to the system of law which it is our abiding mission to serve."

In the case of *Dobbs*, at least, it's hard to call that a "misconception." Indeed, it's clear as day that *Dobbs* never would have happened if Justice Ginsburg had lived, or if she had retired during Obama's presidency and been replaced by a like-minded justice. The timing of her retirement was a subject she and I discussed many times. During one dinner at our house, she took me aside to express her annoyance at commentators who were calling for her retirement. "The timing of a resignation is up to each justice," she told me. "John Stevens didn't step down until he was ninety!" I sometimes wonder if the public pressure to retire made Ruth even more stubborn. She was never one to succumb to pressure. She also believed in the American people, and that Hillary Clinton, not Donald Trump, would succeed President Obama. Ruth had, quite deservedly, become a living legend, and I understood how she thought her story would end: The first female president would get to appoint her replacement. Even when Trump was elected, I know Ruth still believed she could see his term through. She'd survived so much that I believed it, too.

I remember the last time I spoke to Ruth. In the late summer of 2020, I'd read Sonia Purnell's *A Woman of No Importance*, the story of an American woman who became a leader of the French Resistance during World War II. It reminded me of Ruth, so I sent a copy to her apartment at the Watergate. She called to say thank you, and we discussed the book for a few minutes. At the end of our conversation, I asked how she was doing. "OK" was all she said. I knew better than to press further. She died a month later.

I know that Justice Ginsburg will forever be remembered for her enduring contributions to the law, and particularly her hard-fought wins for gender equality. But I'm sorry that she will also be remembered for her decision not to retire before the 2016 election, and the consequences for the Court and the country that followed. Ruth deeply believed in the right to reproductive freedom, a right she thought flowed as much from principles of gender equality as from the due process doctrine on which *Roe* relied. But there's no denying that her death in office ultimately contributed to *Roe*'s downfall. In *Dobbs* the Court overruled *Roe* by a vote of 5–4, with the Chief Justice this time choosing the narrower path of restraint. Without the vote of Ruth's successor, Justice Amy Coney Barrett, *Roe* would still live, and women across the country would still have the right to control their own reproductive destinies.

I announced my own intent to retire from the bench in 2021. I could still do the job, I still loved the job, and I wasn't ready to leave the law altogether. But I didn't want to take the chance that my seat might be filled by a president who'd campaigned on picking judges who would fulfill his campaign promises. Frankly, I was also tired of having my work reviewed by a Supreme Court that seemed to hold in such low regard the principles to which I've dedicated my life. Even more important, my obligation as an appeals court judge to faithfully apply Supreme Court precedent started to feel like a burden I wasn't sure I could continue to carry. It was one thing to follow rulings I believed were wrong when they resulted from a judicial process I respected. It was quite another to be bound by the decisions of an institution I barely recognized, particularly when applying those decisions would mean eviscerating voting rights and eroding the capacity of the federal government to protect the health and safety of the American people. To make matters worse, many of the judges with whom I'd worked so well over the years—all dedicated to the common enterprise of judging, despite our differing political views—had retired or passed away. It was time for me to go.

Despite my misgivings about this Supreme Court, I haven't lost faith in the judiciary altogether. To the contrary, I'm proud of what the Supreme Court and our lower courts have accomplished over the years. The courts ended racial segregation in schools. They guaranteed legal representation for anyone charged with a serious crime. They recognized constitutional rights to interracial and gay marriage. And they continue to vindicate the rights of even our most unpopular speakers. By championing the rights of those for whom the system provides no champion, the judicial branch has long served as a counterweight to majority oppression. When legislation is antithetical to constitutional principles, it is the judge's job to stand up and say so. Over the centuries, American judges—like the Southern judges I'd so respected for defending civil rights in the face of violent racism—have consistently done exactly that, even at great personal cost. That's why I believe in courts.

But I worry that this Supreme Court has strayed far from that ideal. The Court's legitimacy flows from its ability to balance competing imperatives, to respect popular will and elected officials most of the time, but to resist majority rule when the Constitution demands. When it loses that balance, as this Supreme Court has, the public is right to worry. The good news, though, is that it takes only one or two justices for the Court to recover its balance. Time and experience have a way of making us all wiser, and Supreme Court justices are no exception. Throughout history, a few have grown more reckless during their years on the bench, but a greater number have trended the other way, showing more restraint in their later years than in their rookie seasons. True, the Trump-appointed justices were selected because the Federalist Society considered them true believers who wouldn't lose their nerve over time. But I know some of them personally, and I believe they care deeply about the institution on which they are privileged to serve. In time, some of them may yet prove that they are judges first.

Even so, the justices' life tenure means that change on the Court won't come quickly. It's taken me years to come around to the notion that there should be term limits for Supreme Court justices. The idea of staggered eighteen-year terms has been in circulation since at least 2004, and it was among the least intrusive reform proposals considered by a commission President Biden appointed shortly after he took office. Eighteen years on our highest court is long enough. If justices want to keep working, they can serve on a court of appeals, as some retired justices have done. In addition, a predictable appointment schedule under which presidents would appoint new justices in the first and third years of their term would ensure that the Court reflects the views of the people. It would also end gamesmanship (of which I confess I, too, was a little guilty) in the timing of judicial retirements. And it would encourage presidents to choose more experienced and wiser lawyers to serve. I recognize that term limits aren't costless, but the benefits seem to far outweigh the drawbacks.

Still, I know it's unlikely. I'm not a politician, but even I can understand that no party wants to give up a perceived advantage on the courts. That means Congress is unlikely to ever pass such a reform. Moreover, even if the political stars aligned and Congress managed to get it done, the Supreme Court itself might stand in the way. The Constitution says federal judges serve "during good behaviour," which I don't take to mean they must serve on one specific court until they keel over. You can imagine, though, that sitting Supreme Court justices might be motivated to read it that way. A constitutional amendment, of course, would do the trick. Even the Supreme Court can't overrule that. If we can't pass one for gender equality, however, a Supreme Court term-limits amendment might be a difficult sell.

So what else can we do? The only place I know to look for an answer is in the Constitution itself. Until we can amend it, we should use it. *Northwest Austin* and *Shelby County* were the most important cases I ever worked on because the right to vote is our most fundamental right, the one we can use to protect all of the others. In many places voting is harder in this post-*Shelby* world. Many forces are working to stop citizens from voting. Don't let them win. If you're a lawyer, remember President Kennedy's message so many years ago that lawyers have a special obligation to use their legal skills on behalf of those whose constitutional rights are threatened. And no matter who you are, make sure your voice is heard. First and most important: Get your ID, make sure you're registered, find your polling place, and jump through whatever silly hoops might be thrown your way. Even better, help others do the same. Get your family and friends registered. Volunteer to work at the polls. Help people find their polling place and volunteer to drive them there. Yes, all of that applies even to your aunt and uncle hooked on conspiracy theories. Talk to them, see if you can change their minds. But no matter what or whom they choose to vote for, help them exercise their right to do it.

All that might seem like just a drop in the bucket. But elections often come down to razor-thin margins, and yours might just be the drop that counts. As President Obama once said, "If you give up on the idea that your voice can make a difference, then other voices will fill the void."

When you get to the polls, use your precious vote carefully. If what you've heard about the courts in these last few chapters has worried you as much as it worries me, vote like you're worried. Vote for presidents and legislators who respect the courts as an institution, and who will appoint and confirm justices and judges who share that view. If a politician is selling you on a promise that *their* judges will vote for this or that outcome, that's not whom you should vote for, because those aren't the kind of judges you really want. You want judges who have principles, not agendas, and who are beholden to the Constitution, not the political party that appointed them.

That's not all you can do with your vote. Congress has the power to correct most of the Supreme Court's errors, so you should vote for legislators who will do that difficult work. Congress can amend the Rehabilitation Act to overrule *Cummings* by clarifying that people with disabilities can recover damages for emotional distress. It can amend the Clean Air Act to overrule *West Virginia* by saying clearly that EPA can require power plants to use greener energy sources. And it can amend the Voting Rights Act to overrule *Shelby County* and *Brnovich* by updating the preclearance formula and making crystal clear that Section 2 means what it says. Congress shouldn't have to do those things. In each of those cases, it had already spoken clearly enough. But it has corrected the Supreme Court's mistakes before, and it can do it again. So, vote for legislators who are paying attention and who will make the changes necessary to restore Congress's original vision for protecting disabled people, the environment, and voting rights.

What if Congress speaks more clearly and the Supreme Court *still* doesn't listen, you might wonder? I don't think we're there yet. But we may be closer to that scenario than I'd like, and it's exactly why the rise of doctrines like "nondelegation," "major questions," and "equal sovereignty" scares me so deeply. Those doctrines are nowhere in the Constitution; they were invented, recently, not for principled reasons, but to produce the Court's preferred outcomes. All of them are ways for the Court to take away Congress's power, and with it, your own. When the Court relies on those doctrines to strike down a statute, it doesn't vindicate individual rights or states' rights, and it certainly doesn't vindicate Congress. It serves only itself. The popular press might not be paying much attention to these doctrines. But please keep your eye on those balls—and call 'em like you see 'em. The future of democracy may depend on it.

CHAPTER 19

The Dog Who
Changed My Life

Y OU HAVEN'T HEARD MUCH ABOUT BLINDNESS IN RECENT
pages. That's intentional. My blindness wasn't central to
my judging. But blindness is part of who I am, and that part of
my life changed forever—and for the better—in the summer
of 2019, when I met my amazing German shepherd guide dog,
Vixen. If talking too much about my dog is a crime, I plead guilty.
I just love to talk about Vixen. There's a sign on my desk that Edie
bought me. It says, ASK ME ABOUT MY DOG. I'll assume
that by picking up this book you've asked.

My life with Vixen started with a visit from our then-eleven-
year-old grandson, Reuben, who lives in Berkeley and has a black
Labrador named Pete that he absolutely adores. Reuben had just
finished listening to a "Stuff You Should Know" podcast about

guide dogs, and a light went off in his head. "Poppa," he said, "I want you to listen to it with me." I always grant motions from my grandchildren, so Reuben and I settled onto a couch and began listening.

By that point, I'd been using my white cane for more than forty years. I'd traveled all around the country navigating airports, hotels, and restaurants. If I was so good with a cane, why would I want a dog? Lots of blind people use a cane with great skill, but for me at least, the cane had challenges. For example, it can be difficult to cross an open plaza or other big space that has no curbs or walls to tap on or echo sound off of. Loud trucks and outdoor construction can make it difficult to hear the traffic and other sounds that help me navigate. Street signs can be a real hazard, because if my cane misses the support post, my head bonks into the sign. In midtown Manhattan, a taxi once ran right over the end of my cane and sped off, with the cabbie shouting back at me, "Hey, fella, look out!" And a cane is no good on the dirt roads where we live in rural Virginia.

Even so, I'd never thought too seriously about getting a guide dog. For starters, I was under the impression that in order to get one I'd have to live at the training program's facility for at least a month to learn how to use the dog. Given my day job, there was no way that was going to happen. I couldn't take weeks off to live in a dorm with a pack of puppies. Besides, I had never been much of a dog person. When our four children were young, we had two collies, Mack and Huck. While Edie and the kids loved them, to me they were obstacles to trip over. When our kids were little, when I put my hand on their elbow or shoulder, they loved to pretend they were guide dogs. That was cute, but the game never lasted long—and, unlike a dog, they could just use words to tell me which way to go.

I also worried that learning how to use a guide dog would be too labor-intensive, and I think it's fair to say that my frustration threshold can be relatively low. I was already what Edie described as "a high-maintenance husband," and she quite fairly assumed that caring for a dog would fall on her. We both also worried that a guide dog would come between us. Would we no longer hold hands as much? What would happen to our long walks together?

It had been years since we'd given the idea of a guide dog more than a few minutes' thought. But Reuben's podcast intrigued me in a few ways. First, I was amazed by what guide dogs could do. Also, after describing the comfortable dorms where people stay while learning to use a guide dog, the trainers said that if you're too busy to come for a month, they'd bring the dog to you. I was tempted, so asked Edie to have a listen. To our mutual surprise, she was amenable. In his typical analytical way, Reuben asked: "On a scale of one to ten, Poppa, with one being not very sure, and ten very sure, how do you feel right now about getting a guide dog?" I was a warm 4. Edie was a tepid 3. We still thought a guide dog wouldn't be right for us, but I agreed with Reuben that our combined average of 3.5 was enough to warrant a few investigatory calls.

First I called our friend Karen Petrou, who founded and manages an international financial analytics company. Karen had Zuni, her third dog, and knew all there was to know about guide dogs. Karen introduced us to Robert Heidenberg, president and CEO of a major real estate development firm, who'd gotten his first guide dog, Zoe, just two years earlier. We met Karen, Robert, their spouses, and their dogs outside a fancy downtown restaurant where Karen was a frequent guest. After we were seated, Zuni and Zoe went "under and down," the command for a guide dog to go underneath a table, lie down, and wait quietly.

Our conversation was eye-opening. The first thing we learned was that it takes at least a year to become proficient with a guide dog. The learning curve, Karen and Robert both stressed, was a steep one. Robert's wife, Susan, added another valuable insight: Having a guide dog in the house, she warned, would be a major change. If we got one, Edie would no longer be the top dog in my life, so to speak. On a third point, the group was also unanimous: If we decided to get a guide dog, they urged us to look into Fidelco Guide Dog Foundation in Connecticut where Zuni and Zoe had come from. Fidelco breeds and trains only German shepherds, and it does it so methodically that their strong, intelligent animals are sometimes known as a breed within a breed. It takes two years and thousands of dollars to train each dog, which Fidelco does at no cost to the blind person. Most important to me, they believe in bringing the dog to the user, so you can train together where you live and work. Since its founding in 1960, Fidelco has successfully placed more than fifteen hundred dogs across the United States and Canada.

After that lunch, Edie and I checked with each other using Reuben's scale. I'd bumped up to a 7, and Edie rounded herself up to a 5. So we kept thinking about it. We made more phone calls and read as much as we could. All the while, Reuben kept checking in with us. "Okay, Poppa, last time you were an eight and Mamie was a six. Where are you now?" As the months passed, we both got closer and closer to 10. The timing couldn't have been better. Even at age seventy-six, I yearned for more independence. So we began the long process of getting a dog.

It turns out that applying for a guide dog is like applying to college. I had to fill out forms confirming that I was mobile enough to merit the assistance of a guide dog, that I was healthy enough to use the dog for at least a decade, and that I could afford dog food and vet bills. I needed three references and a medical clearance from my doctor. When we got through all that paperwork,

Fidelco scheduled a home visit and took me out for a test-drive. I held on to a leather dog harness while the evaluator, steering from the front end, walked briskly ahead, imitating how a dog would lead me. They call this a "Juno Walk." The evaluator was assessing how fast I walked, whether I would be capable of relying on the harness, and whether I knew where I was and where I wanted to go. Good news, I passed the test.

There was just one problem: I'd never had any formal "mobility training" and wasn't "cane-certified" by any official training program. Before giving me a dog, Fidelco wanted me to brush up on my navigational skills. So, when my law clerks met me at the Metro each morning, I no longer took their arm. Instead, the clerks began acting like my ski guide (but silently, and without the neon orange bibs). They walked behind me to make sure I didn't get run over as I tapped my way to the courthouse or the pool. It was up to me to cross the streets by listening to traffic and deciding when it was safe to go. The hardest part was getting into the courthouse during a high-profile political trial when scrums of reporters and TV cameras clustered on the sidewalk outside the entrance. A neon vest might have come in handy.

After a month, I contacted the Columbia Lighthouse for the Blind, which sent a mobility trainer to assess my cane skills. I had to get on and off the Metro, walk up to Capitol Hill and over to Pennsylvania Avenue, and maneuver through intersections and whizzing traffic. I even had to find my way to The Capital Grille. When I crossed C Street because I didn't hear any cars—ignoring the fact that the safe-to-cross signal wasn't beeping—I thought I'd flunked. But the evaluator gave me a second chance. After forty years of using my white cane, I finally became "cane certified." And with that, Fidelco approved my application.

Then, the big wait began. Fidelco knows their animals well, and carefully matches each one with the right user. The dogs spend their first year and a half with puppy-raiser families who socialize the puppies and do basic training under Fidelco's direction. The dogs then spend six months at Fidelco's kennel with a trainer who teaches them to be guide dogs. The program is so rigorous that only half the dogs graduate. Dogs who chase their own tails or go after squirrels don't make good guide dogs. The flunk-outs—politely called "career changers"—become other kinds of valuable service dogs, like bomb sniffers and rescue dogs. A sweet little film called *Pick of the Litter* documents the whole process.

Seven months later—July 25, 2019—the big day arrived. Fidelco had matched me to a dog they thought could walk at my pace, wouldn't mind snoozing in my office for hours, and could travel on subways, trains, and planes. Her name was Vixen. Filled with anticipation, Edie and I were up at the crack of dawn to meet her. Pete, the trainer, pulled into the parking lot of our apartment building, his van decorated with giant photos of German shepherds. He opened the back door, unlatched a crate, and out leapt my future. Vixen was two years old and sixty pounds of fur. She danced around us with excitement. Her big brown eyes stared deep into ours. Her ears pointed straight up. She leaned against my leg as I patted her head. I felt numb. Edie laughed with joy.

We adored Vixen instantly. She shed so much—a "German shedder"—that Edie ordered a Roomba. Vixen's shedding wasn't Edie's only problem. Vixen was supposed to bond with me, so for the first three long months Edie wasn't allowed to pat her more than once each day. She wasn't even supposed to use Vixen's name because when guide dogs hear their names, they immediately alert for a command. So only I could call her Vixen. I also had to do everything else involved in taking care of her: feed her, groom her, walk her, and pick up her poop. I'd dreaded the poop part in particular, but soon I didn't mind that at all. Taking care of Vixen is my way of giving back to her for all she gives to me.

Although Vixen arrived fully trained, I most certainly was not. So began two and a half weeks of intensive nine-to-five training as I learned to become Vixen's teammate. I'll never forget our first walk. I held the harness and leash while Pete held a second leash. I'd imagined there'd be training wheels, perhaps a walk in a safe grassy space or an empty parking lot where we'd be safe. Nope! From the very start we went into the neighborhood, tackling sidewalk obstacles, steps, and street crossings. Only later did I learn that Edie lurked behind us that first day, nervous about whether she could trust Vixen and Pete to take care of me. After an hour she left, confident that I was in good hands.

On the second day, Pete removed his leash. Vixen and I were on our own. "Vixen, forward," I said. And off we went. Just as she'd been trained to do, she stopped once we reached the curb cut at the end of the block to wait for instructions. It's my job to decide when to cross. I have to listen to the traffic to be sure it's safe, or if there's a beeper, to listen for the safe-to-cross sound. But here's the good news: If I make a mistake and it's not safe, Vixen will refuse to cross. She'll turn and stand in front of my legs to block me. "Vixen, forward," I said again, and she guided me across the street and stopped at the next curb cut.

Over the next few days, Pete taught me other commands. If I want to turn right I say, "Vixen, right," and she turns right and leads me to the next curb cut. Guide dogs actually know left from right. And there are many other commands: "Vixen, over left," for moving farther left. "Vixen, find right," for when I need her to continue until she finds the next right. "Vixen, follow," for when I want Edie (or someone else) to take the lead, and for Vixen to follow Edie's down-stretched palm. "Vixen, halt," to stop her in her tracks.

As I quickly learned, Vixen is a superb problem solver. If we're inside, I'll say, "Vixen, find outside," and she'll lead me to a door.

If there's an obstacle in our way, like a scooter on the sidewalk or a branch across the road, Vixen will stop, signaling to me that there's a problem. I'll then say, "Vixen, find way," and she figures out how to get around the obstacle safely. As I learned when there was construction around the courthouse, Vixen can thread me through barriers and parked cars like a mouse through a maze.

Stairs can be dangerous if you're blind. When we're going up, Vixen puts her two front paws on the first step and waits for a command. "Vixen, hup up," I say, and up we go. Going down, Vixen stops at the top of the staircase and waits until I figure out what's going on. I search with my foot, discover we're at the top of a staircase, say "Vixen, forward," and she carefully guides me down the stairs. In both directions, she controls her momentum perfectly.

Each day we explored more territory, first a few blocks near my home, then the doctor's office, and eventually a ride on the Metro to the courthouse. Vixen had trained with Pete on the Boston T, so she already knew all about escalators, elevators, and subway platforms. At the courthouse we explored the maze of hallways, visited my courtroom (where, after I took off her leash, she explored every nook and cranny), and met Brando, the courthouse's bomb-sniffing dog and a guide-dog-school dropout. (Perhaps Brando had a thing for squirrels.) In anticipation of Vixen's arrival, I had sent a memo to the entire courthouse staff explaining that I would be learning to use a guide dog and that it was important that everyone give us space, always direct comments to me and not to the dog, and wish us luck. We sent the same memo to our neighbors. Everyone was supportive and fascinated to watch us in action.

One thing Pete had to tell me over and over is that I should give each command only one single time. Repetition gives Vixen power to ignore me the first time. (Apparently the same was not true of me, as Pete was happy to repeat his instructions over and over until I finally internalized them.) I never yell at Vixen, but my voice needs to be firm, particularly if her mind seems to wander even for a second. Sniffing while working is particularly discouraged. Every bush and tree offers olfactory delight. But while Vixen might prefer to sniff, sniff, sniff, I prefer to walk, walk, walk.

To keep Vixen on the straight and narrow, praise — not punishment — is the coin of our realm. Praise can be verbal ("Good dog!"). Or it can be physical, like a small pat or a big hug. Treats are reserved for exceptional performances. Vixen especially likes Edie's home-baked specials. At Fidelco, the go-to treat was hot dogs. Vixen gets a treat of some kind every time she leads me to a trash can to dispose of her poop. She also gets treats when she behaves well in new or particularly distracting situations. As you've already heard, guide dogs are trained to be good citizens in restaurants, to go "under and down" and wait quietly for their humans to finish eating. That can earn her a treat, too.

During our training weeks, Vixen remained with us at night while Pete stayed at a hotel. At first, Vixen had to stay attached to a four-foot tether. The idea was to give her a sense of security. And Pete made sure that we didn't spoil her. A friend of ours had given us a fluffy pillow for Vixen, but Pete said that should be a reward to be earned. Pete was tough, but he was tough for a reason. "Safety first — yours and Vixen's," he kept saying. He had lots of other sayings, too. "Commands to the dog must be followed," he'd say. "They aren't optional." Another of my favorites was "Do you want to win this fight? Praise her when she does it right." Above all, Pete insisted that Vixen must respect me. To earn that, I'd have to be "patient but firm." "She won't hate you — she'll respect you. She'll even love you." None of that came easily. "But I'm not a dog trainer," I pleaded. "You are now," Pete shot back.

At the end of the first week, a passing dog lunged at Vixen, surprising and frightening us both. Vixen growled and lunged back. Of course, I couldn't see what was going on, so it felt like chaos. "Great!" said Pete. "A teachable moment!" The trick to encountering other dogs, he taught me, is to pull back on the harness and press on. It can be hard to remember in a panic, but I've gotten a lot better at it. I can usually tell when I'm approaching another person with a dog because of the way Vixen pulls on the harness and huffs with her breath. Message to dog walkers: When you see a blind person with a guide dog coming toward you, please either give them a lot of space or say, "Hello, I have a dog." In time, Vixen learned to ignore most dogs, except the small, yappy variety.

Just as bad as lunging dogs are people who interfere with the owner-dog link, even if unintentionally. Putting a hand on my arm or Vixen's harness while I'm walking with her is like someone else touching the steering wheel when you're driving. Please don't do that. If you want to help, just ask if I need assistance. And remember that while you may be surprised to see guide dogs in a place where dogs aren't typically allowed, the law allows guide dogs to go anywhere.

More than once during those first two weeks I worried I'd fail, which I hadn't done since ninth-grade Spanish. The most serious crisis came when, on our fourth morning, Pete called and said, "OK, you two are on your own. Get Vixen in her harness, leave the house, and walk a few blocks. It's solo time. I'll be watching." And he was, but just far enough away to be out of Vixen's sight or sniffing range. I was overwhelmed, especially since I'd been given no time to prepare. It went just as badly as I'd feared. I couldn't remember how to put on the harness, so we struggled even to get out the door. Despite my familiarity with the neighborhood, I got lost in the first ten minutes. I was in sensory overload, disoriented by passing cars and beeps from reversing trucks. Had we already gone the whole block? Had Vixen turned a corner and I failed to notice? Was it possible I was in the middle of the street? Desperate, I phoned Pete. In the minute it took for him to arrive, I worried that for sure Vixen was going to be reassigned to a better blind partner. I was a flop. I confessed my despair to Pete, who, I gather, had heard such meltdowns before. "David," he said calmly, "if I thought you were going to fail at this, Vixen and I would already be gone."

I was reassured, but only two days later Vixen and I needed another rescue. "Pete," I said, "I just can't do this." This time, he called my bluff. "That's okay," Pete said. "She'll make a great guide dog for someone else." That was all I needed to hear. I was determined that Vixen was going to be *my* guide dog.

As our two weeks continued, I got better and better each day, gaining confidence in my command, and trusting that Vixen would guide me safely, I also sensed Vixen's growing confidence in me. Gradually, through the harness handle, I could feel small differences in her behavior. I could tell when she was sniffing something and when she was looking to the side to signal that we were passing an alley. In addition to using my voice and hand signals, I communicate with Vixen by shaking or pulling on the leash, or by pulling back on the harness. Fidelco guide dogs are trained not to relieve themselves while in harness, so a wet nose on my knee or hand means it's time for a pit stop.

The most intriguing part of Vixen's training is her ability to disobey when it's unsafe to comply. Remember how she won't cross the street if it's not safe? She won't obey other commands when she's worried about safety, either. When we're taking the Metro, for example, Vixen won't let me get too close to the track. She'll stand in front of me blocking me at a ninety-degree angle to stop me from moving forward. She wasn't trained to do that, a visiting trainer once confirmed, she just started doing it. There was also a time in the country when I insisted we keep going, but Vixen refused to budge. I wanted to squash her little revolt, so I repeated my command and jiggled the leash to get her moving forward. Vixen kept refusing. A few seconds later, I understood why: A car came over the hill and passed right by us. Vixen had heard it way before me. Good dog.

Vixen is also responsible, sort of, for getting me to see a psychiatrist. Our dog-owning daughter Emily told Edie and me that "the dog will spawn tension between the two of you. You'll need to talk about it." Emily was right to point out the potential problems, and Edie and I agreed that talking about the dynamics of adding a guide dog into our marriage could be valuable. After two visits, though, we were both done with that highly recommended psychiatrist. He hadn't thought about the issues, he recommended we buy a book he'd written, and he asked three times, "Are either of you still working?" Maybe I should have worn my black robe to the sessions.

During those first few months with Vixen, I devoured books about dogs, their amazing senses, how they think, their enormous intelligence, and the fact that today's dogs are the result of thousands of years of coevolution. One of my favorite books, *Inside of a Dog* by Alexandra Horowitz, describes dogs as anthropologists constantly observing the humans they live with in order to accommodate their moods and schedules. Vixen is definitely an anthropologist. In our D.C. apartment, she doesn't even bother getting up when she sees me in my gym shorts in the morning because she knows I'll return after my workout. If I'm holding a coffee cup when we leave the apartment, she turns right toward the coffee room. If I don't have a cup, she turns left toward the exit. If she sees suitcases around, she blocks the front door to make sure we don't leave without her.

Even after reading all those books, I am constantly amazed by Vixen. How on earth does she know which hotel door to take me to when she was only there once before at check-in? And how, how, how did she know to guide me to our parked car in the airport garage five days after we'd parked? We'd even returned via a different elevator, but she led us straight to our car like a laser beam, walking by eight successive lanes of cars, turning right at the ninth row, then left at the fifth car. Amazing.

Learning to use a guide dog is hard. It's definitely the hardest thing I've ever done. Try shutting your eyes and walking around with an animal leading you. I have to set aside all my normal instincts and habits and rely totally on a dog. It would have been easy if I weren't blind and Vixen weren't a dog.

It was hard on Edie, too. Although seeing your blind spouse go off on his own is exhilarating, it can also be terrifying. On the first day I went to work alone, she was so anxious when Vixen and I left without her that she wept.

The learning never ends. The process of a blind person and a guide dog adjusting to one another, bonding to each other, is a continuous one. It's mutual, it's magic, but it's not equal. Vixen expects me to be in control. And my confidence bolsters hers.

With great brilliance, however, often comes a great propensity for boredom. Or so it is, at least, in Vixen's case. Pete warned me at the start that German shepherds are especially curious animals and can grow bored with routines. "Vary your route to the courthouse," Pete suggested. "Or else she might decide to take a right when you want to take a left." I soon learned that lesson. After a few weeks of walking from the Metro station to the courthouse, Vixen apparently got bored and decided to veer right along a new path instead of going straight. Fortunately, one of the marshals was watching and got us back on course. Lesson learned. I varied my routes, which was good fun for both of us.

Vixen and I have now been a team for more than four years. It's not an understatement to say that she's changed my life—and Edie's, too. Thanks to Vixen, we both have more independence than we've had in decades. Before Vixen, Edie or one of our kids would walk with me to the Metro station every morning because, even with my cane, it was just too dangerous for me to cross the busy streets alone. At the other end, a law clerk would meet me and walk with me to the courthouse. With Vixen, I kiss Edie goodbye in the morning and she's free to go about her own business. Vixen guides me across those busy streets to the top of the first escalator and stops to let me know we've arrived. I drop the harness handle, step on, and Vixen follows. She loves escalators. On the platform, Vixen sits next to me until the train arrives. When the doors open, she leads me on and settles at my feet. At our destination, she hops up and leads me off the train, up the escalator, through the fare machines, and up to the street.

Vixen's as skilled in the country as she is in town. During our two weeks of training, Pete spent a weekend with us in rural Virginia. Guide dogs are trained to lead on dirt roads, which Fidelco calls "country travel." When Vixen guides me to the side of the road for an approaching car, we can be in for a little delay because lots of drivers stop to say hello, admire Vixen, or ask questions about guide dogs. As I said at the very start of this book, dogs bring people together.

Edie and I both love our long country walks. Before Vixen, though, I couldn't do them alone. Now Edie sometimes joins us, but other times she prefers to garden or read or, hard to believe, just have a little time without me. We both agree that time alone is important, and it's because of Vixen that I can again enjoy that simple pleasure. When I walk along our country roads listening to the birds and the ripples in the river, I don't feel like I'm blind. And I have a wonderful friend with me.

Shortly after Pete left us on our own, Reuben sent us a hand-written note: "Dear Mamie and Poppa," he wrote. "Congrats on finally getting Vixen. We listened to the podcast about guide dogs. Now look where you are. To be honest, I had a hunch that this was going to work out. I am very happy for you guys."

———◆◇◆———

When Vixen and I began walking on our own, our kids worried about the sharp curve on our country road. "Dad," they said, "this isn't safe. You're going to be run over. There should be a sign." So I called the state highway department, beginning a two-year effort to get a sign that would alert drivers that Vixen and I might be on the road. The first sign they put up displayed a tubby walker over the word "Disabilities." It was both offensive and inscrutable. Drivers would stop and holler, "Wow, I wasn't looking for some-one with a dog." I contacted more state agencies and our repre-sentative in the state assembly. They were all very nice, but very unhelpful. Not until the *Rappahannock News* was about to pub-lish a front-page story did the state install a new sign: No tubby walker, just big, bold words that warned, "Watch for Blind Pedes-trians." Well, there's only one blind pedestrian, but I'm not quib-bling. Now drivers stop and say, "Great sign."

I'd long been curious about how airlines and guide dogs got along. While we were still considering whether to pursue the guide dog option, I interrogated every flight attendant I met. The results of that unscientific survey were unanimous: Flight atten-dants do *not* like "comfort animals" that pee, bark, and sometimes even bite onboard. They love well-trained service animals.

Fidelco trains their dogs to fly in airplanes. Vixen learned on a test flight to Las Vegas. She's a real pro. At airport security,

Vixen sits, I hold her leash, walk through the magnetometer, turn around, and say, "Vixen, come." She walks through and then gets a security pat-down because her harness and leash hardware set off the machine. She loves those pat-downs. When boarding, Vixen sometimes turns into the first-class rows. "Vixen," I'll tell her, "we're in coach." Reluctantly, she leads me to the back of the plane. Then she lies down at my feet, and usually doesn't move again until we land. Wherever we sit, Vixen is always a first-class dog.

———◦••◦———

How do the puppy raisers and trainers work their magic? We are so incredibly grateful for their skills. I'm the lucky beneficiary of all the hard work and devotion an incredible team of people put in during Vixen's first two years. On Pete's last night with us he called Dakota, Vixen's kennel trainer, who had sent along Vixen's favorite red rubber ball. Dakota was so excited to talk to us, to learn where "her" dog was placed, and to tell us some of her favorite Vixen stories. We got to thank her voice-to-voice for all she'd done to create our dog.

When Vixen isn't in her harness, she's just a happy dog. In the country, she loves to play with her dog buddies and chase sticks, terrorize deer and rabbits (fortunately she's never caught one), and prance in the river. She roughhouses, lolls in the sun, and—bliss!—sniffs every scent that interests her. German shepherds love new adventures and challenges, and Vixen is no exception. She loves new people, new places, and new things. When she got bored with her old tug toy, Edie connected a fifteen-foot rope to a big nylon doggie donut. I hold one end of the rope and then throw the toy. Vixen sinks her teeth into it, wrestles it to the ground, and hangs on the whole time I reel her in. We both have a ball.

Vixen is a member of our family, and we love to watch her have fun on her off time. But we always have to remember that Vixen isn't a pet. She reminds us of that herself. If she's lying around, she'll stay flopped down if Edie or anyone else steps near. But for me, she's up like a flash and makes sure to stay out of my way and be ready if I need her. How great is that? As soon as she dons her harness, she stops goofing around and turns into a working dog. She's a professional, consummately trained to perform a task, and it's a task she loves to do. If she didn't, she never would have made it through her training.

Patience, practice, trust, and the occasional treat have been our recipe for success. Three months after Pete left, he checked in with me. "I think you'd be proud of your student," I told him. Indeed he was. Every now and then I still need some advice, so I call Fidelco and get quick pointers. And a trainer visits every year or so to be sure we haven't become lazy about curb cuts and to give us some tips on any new challenges we're facing. Vixen twirls with joy at the old familiar kennel smell and shows off her skills proudly. It's still mostly me who needs the tune-ups.

I'd hoped that Vixen would help me become more independent, and she certainly has. But I never expected to fall in love with a dog. Vixen ushered me into an emotional relationship that's been a huge surprise. It's actually a surprise that it's a surprise. We'd long marveled at the deep attachment Rebecca always had to her horse and cats and dogs. I sort of gagged when my granddaughter Daria laughed with joy as her dog Sadie kissed her on the lips. Rae and Ozzie let their dogs sleep with them in their beds. I didn't understand why they'd do any of that. But guess what? I finally get it. Vixen and I snuggle together all the time. And when she licks my face, and even my lips, I, too, laugh with pleasure. No dog in our bed, though, not as long as Edie's there.

My connection with Vixen is much deeper than just snuggling and face licking. I love her like a best friend. I talk to her. Sometimes Edie, in another room, wonders who's with me. Well, I'm chatting with Vixen. She listens closely as I tell her about a legal question or ask her opinion about a case. She doesn't care at all that I can't see her. She doesn't mind if I spill my glass of water. In fact, she laps it right up. She doesn't even mind when I step on her foot by mistake, and she never ever holds a grudge. Josh says I don't really behave as if Vixen's a dog. "When the two of you are together, she is certainly not a dog and you are not blind," he says. "Well, you *are* blind, but you are free and you are independent. With her, you have no handicap." Edie, who knows me so well, says that Vixen has changed me in the nicest ways.

Just as I was finishing this book, Edie, Vixen, and I met the President of the United States. The occasion in the East Room of the White House was a reception celebrating the sixtieth anniversary of both the March on Washington and the creation of the Lawyers' Committee. I was deeply moved to hear President Biden commemorate two of the most formative events of my professional life—and in the exact same place where JFK had called for the creation of the Lawyers' Committee. After President Biden delivered a terrific civil rights speech, he made a beeline for Vixen, who was stretched out at my feet. The president, who has two German shepherds himself, eagerly patted Vixen as he chatted with Edie and me. Vixen, true to form, seemed far more interested in the other guide dog at the reception.

EPILOGUE

The Future

As I approached retirement, I had lots of ideas about how I might spend my newfound free time. Writing a memoir was not among them. Even though I've had a long and exciting career, would anyone really want to read a book about a federal judge who never made it to the Supreme Court? With Vixen's help, I'd become more comfortable with my blindness, but I definitely didn't want to write a book about being blind. Also, I felt no need to write a book for my children and grandchildren. They already know me in ways that no number of pages can capture.

Nevertheless, a few people, both family and friends, encouraged me to think seriously about sharing my story. "You're not just a blind person," they said. "And you're not just a federal judge. You're a federal judge who happens to be blind. And you have a beautiful guide dog to boot." They believed that my story might inspire others, and not just people living with disabilities. That made me stop and think. I've spent my entire professional life, from my early days at the Lawyers' Committee to my three decades on the D.C. Circuit, trying to use the law to improve people's lives. If my life story might help other people, why not share it with the world? Maybe my story would challenge preconceived notions about what people with disabilities can accomplish. Maybe it would even inspire people to attend law school and to work for civil rights, either from inside the government or from out. And maybe, just maybe, I could convince a few more people to vote. I decided to give it a shot. I'd written thousands of legal briefs and judicial opinions. How hard could it be?

Hard, it turns out. Writing this memoir has demanded far more than just putting my story on paper. Grappling with the meaning of that story has been something else entirely.

When I began this book, I couldn't have imagined how much I would learn about myself. The process has truly been a revelation. It's forced me to think deeply about my career, what I've accomplished, and what I haven't. It's helped me refine my views about the Supreme Court and the threat it poses to the values and institutions we hold dear. And most difficult of all, it's made me think deeply about my blindness—my decades of denial, how I adapted to life without sight, and the ways my blindness affects Edie and our life together. My younger self—the one who counted rows in the theater, who asked that press releases not mention his blindness, who deleted references to blindness from his Wikipedia entry, and who waited years to get a cane and decades to get a guide dog—couldn't have dreamed of ever sharing all this with the world.

Nor could he have imagined meeting incredible scientists doing cutting-edge research and actually restoring sight to the blind. Sounds like the stuff of science fiction, right? But it's very real, and the details are even more amazing. While finishing up this book I met Dr. Sheila Nirenberg, a Cornell neuroscientist who won a MacArthur "Genius" Grant for cracking the code the retina uses to transmit images to the brain. She's created a device that can speak that neural language. Google Translate for the eyeballs, if you will. The device looks sort of like a pair of ski goggles. As she explained it to Edie and me when we visited her in her lab, when you put on the goggles, they record an image of the world, translate that image into the retinal code she deciphered, and trick the brain into "seeing" what the goggles see. It's a bit more complicated than that, of course—the goggles have to interact with a gene her team injects into the eye—but what matters is that the treatment, a kind of "optogenetics," seems to work. Dr. Nirenberg's RP patients are nearly blind when they come to her but, with the help of her device, they can now see apples, shapes, movement, and even some colors. One woman called her to say: "I just realized my couch is red!" I've never seen our couch, but Edie tells me it's blue.

I also met Dr. Shannon Boye, a University of Florida neuroscientist who is doing equally incredible work. While Dr. Nirenberg's device bypasses the retina, Dr. Boye's gene therapy treatment restores the function of the retina itself by injecting it with a healthy, non-mutated gene—housed, if you can believe it, in the husk of a defunct virus. It's like rebooting a buggy computer with the right software. Her preliminary results, like Dr. Nirenberg's, are promising. One patient saw a star for the first time; another, her first snowflake; and still another found, suddenly, that she could read the wrappers of her children's Halloween candy. I could pass on the Reese's wrapper, but I'd love to see another star, another snowflake.

Those scientists' amazing work is just the tip of the iceberg. Scientists around the world, funded by millions of dollars from the government, private foundations, and pharmaceutical companies, are developing many techniques to prevent inherited retinal diseases from progressing further, and even to restore lost sight. The FDA has already approved a gene therapy treatment called Luxturna for a retinal disease different from mine. It was developed by Dr. Jean Bennett at the University of Pennsylvania, another brilliant scientist devoted to finding a cure for blindness. The first person to receive Luxturna was a boy named Jack, who was not much younger than I was when I received my diagnosis. Only two months after treatment, he said, "I don't have to hold on to my friend's shoulders anymore when I go to a movie theater." I can only imagine his relief.

Each technological advance combines the rigor of science with the magic of possibility. Although we don't yet know which new treatments will succeed, when I listen to these extraordinary scientists, I can't help but share their optimism that someday we will cure blindness. I'd like to tell that to the teenage boy who so desperately wanted to play right field without fear and to see the moons of Jupiter through his father's telescope.

As I finished writing this memoir, I returned to my roots and rejoined Hogan Lovells' pro bono program, the place where I did so much exciting work early in my career. I won't any longer be writing opinions of national significance, but I can continue my lifelong commitment to equal justice, one pro bono case at a time. In the words of Robert Kennedy, maybe I can "change a small portion of events"—and change them for the better.

Edie's also excited about this new chapter in our lives. As she reminds me, "I married you for life, not for lunch." And Vixen? She's already found a cozy spot to snooze in my new, much smaller office.

Acknowledgments

Like most everything else we've done in our long marriage, Edie and I wrote this book together. Day in and day out we sat at our long desk overlooking an immense oak tree and the hills beyond, Edie on the left with her laptop, me on the right with my Braille computer. We wrote, we debated, we argued, we laughed, we deleted words, paragraphs, and pages. We re-wrote, and re-edited. Slowly but surely, this book emerged. Edie has always been my very best editor, but could we collaborate on an entire book? We could. And it became as much an adventure of discovery for Edie as for me. Not until we wrote this memoir did Edie learn about my bloody stumble on 57th Street, my L7 subterfuge, and my following women with high heels, just to name a few revelations. Did that create tension? It sure did. But we pressed on, and we're still happily married.

Our four wonderful children, Rebecca, Stephanie, Joshua, and Emily—and all their children—are the center of our lives. They patiently responded as I probed their childhood memories. Their honest, sensitive, and sometimes hilarious answers to our questionnaire about growing up with a blind dad enriched my story and warmed our hearts.

Several special people encouraged me to write this book. Peter Osnos, founder of PublicAffairs, began lobbying as far back as our running days. Susan Osnos, who spent the summer of 1969 helping me get the Chicago Lawyers' Committee up and running, urged me on. Joe Hassett, my once and current Hogan Lovells colleague, and author of fine books on Irish literature, always insisted my story was worth telling. (Joe argued LSC's recess appointments case.) Paul Taylor, former political reporter for the *Washington Post*, and Stefanie Taylor, regularly blurted out at many of our delightful dinners together, "You should write a memoir." Michael Abramowitz, President of Freedom House (my cousin and one of the few people in this book I've known longer than Edie) and journalist Susan Baer gave me wise advice. I officiated their wedding, though they weren't one of those couples who asked me to share the duties with their rabbi. All redoubled their exhortations after Ann Marimow's July 2021 *Washington Post* article about my retirement — though it was Vixen who captured most readers' attention. In the wake of Ann's article, Bob Barnett, literary agent and fellow University of Chicago graduate, weighed in. Candidly, there were moments over the past three years when I never wanted to see any of these people again, but now that the book is finished, I can't thank them enough.

A special thanks to Bruce Nichols, my gifted editor and then-publisher of Little, Brown. Bruce's very first email during the bidding process — "I want to edit and publish this book!" — gave me confidence that it might actually happen. Apologizing for posing as my therapist, Bruce encouraged me to confront my blindness and the ways it affected my life and work. His sensitive editing and probing questions made this a more honest book. Thanks also to the great team at Little, Brown, including Terry Adams, who steered us to the finish line with great enthusiasm, Executive Director of Publicity Sabrina Callahan, Art Director Mario Pulice, Senior Marketing Director Bryan Christian, Production Editor Linda Arends, Senior Managing Editor Ben Allen, and Editorial Assistant

Annie Martin. Vixen and I love Deborah Feingold's beautiful cover photo and Edie's delightful picture of us on the inside flap.

This book would never have happened without my fierce and dedicated agent, Gail Ross of William Morris Endeavor. Gail guided me through the writing and publishing process and, like Bruce, urged me to address difficult personal issues. Her clarity, focus, and humor helped immeasurably.

Many former law clerks and readers were as important to this book as they were during their year in chambers. I am especially indebted to Amanda Rice, whose perceptive questions, creative ideas, and sparkling writing enriched the book immeasurably. Goodwin Liu offered valuable insights, helping me think though tricky issues. Goodwin, along with Jean Galbraith, Zayn Siddique, Kelsi Corkran, Karen Stevens Pierce, and Cate Stetson (Cate argued the death penalty case in the Prologue) spoke at my portrait hanging ceremony, and many of their delightful recollections found their way into this book. Greg Silbert and Robert Niles-Weed provided wise and patient legal advice. Other former law clerks, too many to list here, filled in details as I wrote about the D.C. Circuit years. Paloma O'Conner, my reader during my last year on the court, found time for thorough research, thoughtful editing, and laser-like fact-checking. Paloma's predecessor, Molly Culhane, contributed valuable research. Amanda Grace, my talented, unflappable judicial assistant, not only helped keep track of the research and writing but offered perceptive edits of her own—all while managing my chambers. Jana Frieslander, my secretary for forty-three years, transcribed interviews and helped retrieve many memories.

Sue Lehmann, Steve Engelberg, Eden Martin, and Steve Pollak's recollections of when they first noticed that there might be something wrong with my vision appear in Chapter 9. Sue and Steve E. were my Michigan classmates, and it was Sue who was with me at the Lincoln Memorial listening to Dr. Martin Luther King Jr.'s "I

Have a Dream" speech. Eden and I, fellow associates at Sidley, wrote the *Tometz* amicus brief together. Steve Pollak, who headed the Civil Rights Division during the Johnson administration, interviewed me for the D. C. Circuit Historical Society Oral History Program, yielding hundreds of transcript pages that have been a critical resource.

Thanks to Edward and Lynn Dolnick for their enthusiastic support and wisdom. When I was uncertain about how to deal with the science of RP—briefly, deeply, or something in between—Ed wrote me a note: "Blindness handed you the case of a lifetime. But it's different from the legal cases you're accustomed to tackling. The facts emerged over decades, not several intense months. The stakes aren't just practical, they're personal." Ben Shaberman, Vice President, Science Communications of the Foundation Fighting Blindness, helped me understand the science of RP, reviewed and sharpened Chapter 2, and introduced me to the amazing neuroscientists in the Epilogue. Marie Schuetzle of Informed DNA patiently explained my own mutation and its implications for my family. Bob Adler (skipper of the sailboat in Chapter 8) and Andy Adler, who go all the way back to our years together in Ann Arbor, reminded us of forgotten details. Karen Lygizos, Edie's special niece, shared her diary entries about her teenage and college years when she joined us on family vacations. Sari Horwitz and Bill Schultz cheered me on and were generous sounding boards. Risa Goluboff shared her views about the law clerk hiring process. Chris Eastwood, one of the dedicated Fidelco trainers so important to Vixen and me, did a close read of Chapter 19.

An unexpected pleasure in writing this memoir was reconnecting with many colleagues I'd worked with during my pre-court years. Hogan partner Pat Brannan offered perceptive comments about Chapter 11. Pat, Alan Snyder, and Elliot Mincberg shared their recollections of our work together in Saint Louis and Milwaukee. Susan Uchitelle, one of the state officials who supported the St. Louis desegregation effort, and her book, *Unending Struggle:*

The Long Road to an Equal Education in St. Louis, were most help-ful. UCLA professor Gary Orfield, co-director of The Civil Rights Project, and his book, *The Walls Around Opportunity,* contributed data about desegregation and its educational consequences. (Gary was the expert who introduced me to the St. Louis superintendent.)

My OCR deputy, Cindy Brown, and John Wodatch, the world's expert on Section 504, improved Chapter 10. Burton Taylor, Fred Cioffi, and Art Besner spent hours on Zoom with me and unearthed long-forgotten OCR documents from their files. Two other extraor-dinary public officials helped fill in the HEW years: Patricia Gra-ham, Director of the National Institute of Education and later Dean of the Harvard Graduate School of Education, joined me at the New York negotiations "in the dark." Dick Beattie, HEW's gifted General Counsel, played a critical role in our desegregation cases, especially North Carolina. Both Pat and Dick attended the famous meeting where baby Emily broke the tension with the women's groups.

For background on the Lawyers' Committee, I turned to Peter Connell, who headed our Southern Africa project; to Armand Der-fner, who headed our voting rights project, and his superb book, *Justice Deferred: Race and the Supreme Court;* to Spencer Gilbert and John Maxie for stories from Mississippi; and to Courtland Milloy, who covered Cairo as a student reporter for his Southern Illinois University newspaper, *The Daily Egyptian.* For insights about legal services, I consulted Ron Flagg, President of The Legal Services Corporation; Mark Freeman, LSC's Senior Assistant Deputy Gen-eral Counsel; and Earl Johnson, author of *To Establish Justice for All,* the definitive history of Legal Services. Georgetown Law professor Peter Edelman, former aide to Robert F. Kennedy, told me about the devoted group of D.C. law firms that he organized and that so generously support legal services for the poor.

My D.C. Circuit colleagues Sri Srinivasan, Harry Edwards, Tom Griffith, and Robert Wilkins all spoke at my portrait ceremony, and their stories contributed details I'd forgotten or suppressed. Mark Langer, Clerk of the Court, answered my many procedural questions, and Pat Michalowskij, the court's librarian, somehow found every obscure report and legislative history I needed. Thanks also to the dedicated Library of Congress archivists who organized and indexed the hundreds of boxes of my papers. What a pleasure to sit in the beautiful Library of Congress reading room and review with ease so much of my past. Shaun Hardy, archivist at the Carnegie Institution for Science, beautifully preserved my dad's papers and answered my historical questions. My new professional home, Hogan Lovells, provided indispensable support—with special thanks to Montana Love, Supreme Court and Appellate Practice Researcher, for her editorial suggestions and meticulous fact-checking.

I couldn't have written this book—and I mean that literally— without the technical assistance of Douglas Walker, an iPhone genius who knows everything about VoiceOver, and Mike Tindell, who helped me transition to the BrailleSense. Thanks to both for so promptly responding to my constant calls for help. Bob Watson and Scott White at the National Federation of the Blind answered all my questions about NewsLine, whose vast collection of newspapers and magazines has been an invaluable resource.

Many others provided helpful advice and information: Ava Abramowitz, Shelly Broderick, Bruce Brown, Warren Chapman, Louis Cohen, Michael Dobbs, Dionne Danns, Adele Fabrikant, Lara Pender, Kaya Henderson, Lee Ingram, Anthony Kheil, Mark Levin, Chris Lee, Dan Marcus, Michael MacCambridge, Ted Miller, Sammy Shotz, David Shipler, Abigail Smith, and Gordan Ziegenhagen.

All these names might seem like my entire Rolodex (for those under forty, a Rolodex is yesteryear's "contact list"). That's because so many people contributed in so many ways to this memoir. Apologies and thanks to anyone I accidentally omitted.

Index

Mathews, David, 144
Maya (granddaughter), 105
McGee, Willie, 76
McKissick, Floyd, 138
Meltzer, Bernard, 40
Mentschikoff, Soia, 39
Michigan Daily, 34
Mikva, Abner, 198
Miller, Judith, 239–41
Millett, Patricia, 7, 8
Milliken v. Bradley, 156–57
Mills, Cheryl, 175
Milwaukee
    school desegregation, 161–64
mobility trainer, 307
mock trials, 225–27
Mohammad, Khalid Sheikh, 233–34
Mohr, Charles, 72
Mohr, Norma, 149
Mondale, Walter, 142
Montgomery Blair High School, 16
Moynihan, Daniel Patrick, 241

NAACP, 75–83, 138, 157–58
NAACP v. Claiborne Hardware, 81–82, 175
National Academy of Sciences' Committee on Science, Technology, and Law, 39
National Federation of the Blind (NFB), 125, 127, 330
National Institutes of Health, 25
National Lawyers' Committee, 58, 70, 73, 97, 103
Newsline, 125

New York Times, 3, 64, 219, 241
NFB app, 125
night blindness, 27
Nirenberg, Sheila, 323
Nixon, Richard, 54, 56, 86, 88–91, 103, 130–32, 134, 144, 146
nondelegation doctrine, 258–60, 268, 270, 301
Northwest Austin v. Holder, 281–85, 287, 300
Nussbaum, Bernard, 175

Obama, Barack, 7, 131, 219, 266, 296, 300
    EPA, 267, 268
Oberdorfer, Louis, 58, 89, 180, 181, 184
O'Connor, Sandra Day, 198
Office for Civil Rights (OCR), 129–52
    Section 504. *See* Section 504
    guidance documents, press releases, public reports, and letters, 148–58
    Title IX. *See* Title IX
Office of Economic Opportunity (OEO), 87–90
Olin (grandson), 227
Olivia (granddaughter), 227
Online System for Clerkship Application and Review (OSCAR), 201
oral arguments
    assignment process, 188
    blindness in courtroom, 193–94